5/20/15
$35.00
B+T

AS-14

6|15

Neil Gaiman in the
21st Century

Withdrawn

Also of Interest

Feminism in the Worlds of Neil Gaiman: Essays on the Comics, Poetry and Prose, edited by Tara Prescott and Aaron Drucker (McFarland, 2012)

Neil Gaiman in the 21st Century

Essays on the Novels, Children's Stories, Online Writings, Comics and Other Works

Edited by
TARA PRESCOTT

McFarland & Company, Inc., Publishers
Jefferson, North Carolina

LIBRARY OF CONGRESS CATALOGUING-IN-PUBLICATION DATA

Neil Gaiman in the 21st century : essays on the novels,
    children's stories, online writings, comics and other works /
    edited by Tara Prescott.
        p.   cm.
        Includes bibliographical references and index.

    ISBN 978-0-7864-9477-4 (softcover : acid free paper) ∞
    ISBN 978-1-4766-1994-1 (ebook)

    1. Gaiman, Neil—Criticism and interpretation.   I. Prescott,
Tara, 1976– editor.

PR6057.A319Z785 2015
823'.914—dc23   2015001172

BRITISH LIBRARY CATALOGUING DATA ARE AVAILABLE

On the cover: Neil Gaiman at the 2007 Scream Awards in
Los Angeles (Photograph by Pinguino Kolb)

Printed in the United States of America

McFarland & Company, Inc., Publishers
    Box 611, Jefferson, North Carolina 28640
        www.mcfarlandpub.com

For Sheila Jayne and Gary Michael,
Fortunately, the Parents

Table of Contents

Acknowledgments

I recently met a struggling artist who was driving for Uber in his spare time to help make ends meet. I asked him if he had ever read Neil Gaiman's "Make Good Art" speech, and when he said he had not, I began to read it aloud to him. "That describes my life," he said simply. For those of us who love Gaiman's work, who feel he describes us, and who struggle to keep up with where he's going and what he's doing next, this book is for you.

I want to thank my contributors, who wrote assiduously through vacations and divorces and moves and graduations and births (congratulations, Tom Zlabinger). "Life is sometimes hard," as Gaiman says in "Make Good Art." "Things go wrong, in life and in love and in business and in friendship and in health and in all the other ways that life can go wrong. And when things get tough, this is what you should do. Make good art." The contributors in this collection each devoted their energies and minds towards a small slice of Gaiman's recent oeuvre, and they all did it as a labor of literary love. They also made good art in the process.

Writing, editing, and making art are all endeavors that I love—but I could not have finished this book without a lot of support as well. I would like to thank Seth Anderson and Aaron Drucker, who both helped me refine ideas and acted as the behind-the-scenes barbers who cut the barber's hair. I would also like to thank Samuel Bird, a Microsoft Word wrangler I met via Task Rabbit (my forays into the newly emerging online sharing economy seem appropriate for writing about an author who so heartily embraces online communities). Special thanks to the photographer Amy Dunton, who spent six hours with me one day on the UCLA campus, lighting my visual work (and my person) to create some of the incredible images you will see here. The incomparable Catharine McGraw and Yulduz Ismatullaeva moved heaven and earth (or at least many, many boxes of books and kitchen supplies) in order to help me settle into my new home during the final stages of editing this collection. I am particularly grateful to Judd Winick, whose *Pedro and Me* I successfully nominated as a Common Book at UCLA, who kindly supplied an essay on the Gaiman art he owns. Thank you, Judd, not only for the essay, but for your continued efforts to raise awareness about living with HIV and AIDS.

And finally, as always, to Neil Gaiman—thank you for stories I just love to read over and over again.

Introduction

"I spent years praying to the spirits of architecture, 'Take my balconies, cellars, and wings, give me hands, and let me open that box!'"—Neil Gaiman, *Wayward Manor*

This collection is not exhaustive. It couldn't be, without being exhausting. To write on Neil Gaiman is to be comfortable with an embarrassment of riches; to know that by the time your essay on one of his works goes to press, he's written six more. In the foreword to *The Art of Neil Gaiman,* Audrey Niffenegger offers this caveat: "Neil's entire body of work thus far. Thus far: because, of course, Neil is still writing" (6). To be a scholar or fan of Neil Gaiman is to become okay with the fact that you cannot cover it all.

In a recent interview with Steve Inskeep for NPR, Gaiman states that writers "get to direct people; we get to give them waking dreams. We get to take them places, do magical things to their heads. And, with any luck, send them back slightly changed and not the person that they were when we got our hands on them." *Neil Gaiman in the 21st Century* offers you several "waking dreams" to choose from, and it is my hope that you will be "slightly changed" by the experience.

Never content to be pigeonholed into one kind of story or one kind of storytelling, Gaiman released his first foray into video games, *Wayward Manor,* in the summer of 2014. Although this point-and-click puzzle platform game was not particularly successful, either with Gaiman fans or gamers, it is nonetheless a great example of why Gaiman continues to inspire new generations of fans. The author could easily have stayed with the tried and true: his blockbuster comics (and novels, stories, poems, children's books, screenplays, reading tours, performances, blogs, tweets, etc.), but instead, he reached out into a new format to plumb its depths and see what happened. Perhaps *Wayward Manor* is one of Gaiman's self-described "fantastic mistakes," but as he says, "if you're making mistakes, it means you're out there doing something" (*Make Good Art*).

1

Wayward Manor is a collaboration—another characteristic that reappears frequently in the author's work. The product of Los Angeles developers the Odd Gentlemen, *Wayward Manor* features an anthropomorphized, sentient house who asks for the player's help in scaring off unwanted inhabitants. It features short narration by Gaiman as the Victorian house, whose whimsical British tenor never fails to delight. It adds a new level of experience to Gaiman's vocal performances, which include radio plays, audio books, spoken word, and even singing. The project was also crowd-funded, another example of Gaiman's thorough embrace of technology and the creative possibilities of social media. It offered Kickstarter-like rewards for early backers (including over 3,000 fans who supported the presale ["Store"]). As a game, *Wayward Manor* is not particularly good. But as a way of examining Gaiman's astonishing flexibility and willingness to transcend genres, it is a fitting object lesson.

In addition to the challenges of keeping up with Gaiman's creative output, his genre-blending work is famously difficult to characterize. The Harper edition of *The Graveyard Book*, for example, simply divides Gaiman's books into "For adults" and "For all ages." In the same way that his work is not always specifically tied to age, it is also difficult to classify in terms of genre. This does not stop devoted fans and scholars from trying, however.

Although there is no shortage of fan sites, interviews, press releases, and short essays on Gaiman and his work, for scholarly readers interested in digging further into his texts, there are few comprehensive sources that offer rich analysis. Some targeted collections, such as *Feminism in the Worlds of Neil Gaiman* and *Neil Gaiman and Philosophy*, look at his work through a specific theme or scholarly field of study. The best general overview of Gaiman's work to date is Hayley Campbell's *The Art of Neil Gaiman*, which among its many attributes contains an incredibly helpful bibliography that lists everything— "art, doodles, and photographs," articles, audio recordings, books, comics, essays, speeches, tributes, films, "introductions, afterwords, and forewords," poems, songs, and short stories (it was published before Campbell could add the new category, "video games"). The book offers full color photographs, handwritten drafts, and a quick overview of nearly everything. Gaiman editors clearly must choose if they will include as many types of works as they can in a short space, or privilege a few representative texts at greater lengths. In many ways, trying to cover the works of Neil Gaiman is like trying to plot out a European vacation: you could try to hit all the major tourist spots in six countries in six days, or you could carefully scrutinize the beautiful lichen on a stone stile in Cornwall. Both are lovely and interesting, but it is nearly impossible to have both experiences on the same journey.

At the rate Gaiman writes, collections of essays on his work become outdated (in the sense of being incomplete) quickly. However, what is particularly intriguing about the current stage of Gaiman's career is not just how prolific he is, but how quickly he has embraced the rapidly changing technologies in the modern world and used them to push storytelling boundaries even further. Gaiman has always been an innovative writer who looks to the past to reinvest myths and stories for the future. But his publications post–2000 in particular show the leaps and bounds of his experimentation—they are the work of a mature, confident, celebrated writer with far more opportunities to try new ideas than in his struggling early days.

Building on the success of McFarland's *Feminism in the Worlds of Neil Gaiman* (2012), *Neil Gaiman in the 21st Century* offers seventeen original scholarly essays, one exclusive interview, and one personal narrative, all focused on individual texts from Gaiman's post–2000 work. Although several of his most recent releases began as ideas far earlier, and several overlap or were delayed, this collection organizes them by date of first publication.

The collection begins with essays focused on the 2001 novel *American Gods*. In "The American Odyssey," Jenn Anya Prosser examines how Gaiman takes Homer's epic and Joseph Campbell's Hero's Journey and transforms them into a mythos for modern America. Next, Michael B. Key uses the Derridean concept of freeplay to examine the shifting of centers in American culture in *American Gods* in his essay, "The Anxiety of Disappearance."

Following the great success of *American Gods,* Gaiman quickly gained prominence as a beloved children's book writer after the 2002 release of *Coraline,* which was later adapted into a popular film and musical.[1] He followed with several books for younger readers, including his first picture books. In fact, over past several years, Gaiman has become celebrated for his children's books, including *M Is for Magic* (2007); *Interworld* (2007), *Crazy Hair* (2009) *The Dangerous Alphabet* (2008), *Instructions* (2010), *Fortunately the Milk* (2013), *Chu's Day* (2013), and *Chu's First Day of School* (2014). Renata Lucena Dalmaso focuses her attention on two of Gaiman's children's books in particular, *The Wolves in the Walls* (2003) and *Blueberry Girl* (2009). In "Towards a Feminist Reading of Gaiman's Picture Books," Dalmaso uses both Sigmund Freud and Charlotte Perkins Gilman to break apart the traditional literary hierarchies that privilege written works for adults over visual works for children, examining the feminist aspects of these two striking stories.

By 2005, Gaiman was ready to return to one of the secondary characters in *American Gods,* exploring Mr. Nancy's relationship with his son Fat Charlie in *Anansi Boys.* In "'The old man was gone': The Problematic Unity of Tricksters, Gods and Fathers in *Anansi Boys* and *American Gods*," Laura-Marie von Czarnowsky tackles the fatherly role of the exuberant Mr. Nancy and his mythical forebear Anansi. Noting *Anansi Boys'* unusual dedication to Zora Neale Hurston, Danielle Russell takes a fresh and unexpected approach, comparing *Anansi Boys* to the 1937 novel, *Their Eyes Were Watching God*. Her essay, "'You heard her, you ain't blind': The 'Haunting' Presence of *Their Eyes Were Watching God*," examines the power of public speech in both texts and their implications in terms of power and race.

After his return to novels with *Anansi Boys*, Gaiman explored shorter forms again. He published the short story collection *Fragile Things* in 2006, then returned to young adult fiction once more in 2008, publishing a delightful reimagining of Rudyard Kipling's *Jungle Books* where the orphaned boy is raised by ghosts instead of jungle beasts.[2] Like *The Wolves in the Walls*, *The Graveyard Book* focuses on creatures existing just beneath the surface of what can be observed. In "The Jungle, the Graveyard and the Feral Child: Imitating and Transforming Kipling Beyond Pastiche," Jennifer McStotts turns her critical eye to the communities living behind the walls in Gaiman's texts, focusing on the wainscot fantasy and its source text. Margaret Seyford Hrezo's essay "Wisdom, Strength and Courtesy: Graveyard-Favor Go with Thee" then takes the *Jungle Book/Graveyard Book* comparison into an ancient Greek context. Hrezo examines how *Graveyard*'s moral reinforces the classic or noetic understanding of reason as a prerequisite for a good life.

In addition to his publications in children's literature and popular fiction, Gaiman expanded his oeuvre by venturing into television, most notably in 2011 with "The Doctor's Wife," his script for the BBC's reimagining of the classic television series *Doctor Who*.[3] On the heels of this much-lauded episode, Gaiman returned in 2013, this time revising and re-horrifying the Cybermen for "Nightmare in Silver." In "'We've upgraded ourselves': Gaiman's Resurrection of the Cybermen" Emily Capettini looks at this new iteration in relation to the 1960s series and its effectiveness as a scary and entertaining installment of a long-beloved series.

Having released new stories in these formats, Gaiman offered a rare glimpse into his own life in 2013 with the release of his semi-autobiographical short novel, *The Ocean at the End of the Lane*. This book, written in response to Amanda Palmer wanting to know more about Gaiman's childhood, beautifully blurs the boundaries between fact and fiction, biography and imagination.[4] It is notable for its scary depictions of parental betrayal and violence as it is for its luscious descriptions of food and friendship. The food descriptions are a reminder that people in fact have many kinds of hungers that demand to be sated, Monica Miller notes in her analysis of *The Ocean at the End of the Lane*. "What Neil Gaiman Teaches Us About Survival: Making Good Art and Diving into the Ocean" looks at acts of domesticity in the novel as one of several ways the narrator recovers from his childhood trauma. In "Remembering the Dead: Narratives of Childhood," Rebecca Long focuses her critical attention on how the narrator's experience underscores the need for myth and memory. Without a remembered past, Long argues, one cannot have an identity or a future.

The problem of memory is not only a central theme of the novel but also a particularly complicated one. In "Augustinian Memory and Place," Andrew Eichel approaches the theme from a different perspective, taking Augustine of Hippo's theories of memory palaces, fractured selves, and the faculty of recall and applying them to *The Ocean at the End of the Lane*. The connections between loss of memory and loss of home is also connected to Freud's concept of the *unheimlich,* Yaeri Kim claims in "Not at Home: Examining the Uncanny." In this way, Gaiman explores how familiar and everyday scenes and behaviors become frightening and foreign. And finally, in "'The essence of grandmotherliness': Ideal Motherhood and Threatening Female Sexuality," Courtney M. Landis examines the novel in terms of its performances of femininity, from the narrator's mostly-absent mother and diabolically sexy Ursula Monkton to the powerful Hempstocks, and in particular, the hero-in-disguise Lettie.

Perhaps the characteristic that most sets Gaiman apart from other contemporary writers is how much he has embraced the unprecedented changes in technology that have accompanied the twenty-first century, particularly in regards to social media and the opportunities to interact and collaborate with fans via the internet. From his early days starting a blog to joining Twitter in 2008 and amassing over 1.5 million followers to date, Gaiman has consistently pushed the boundaries of literature and media. In 2013, he embarked on the type of rare and delightful collaborative project that makes the most of internet culture: crowdsourcing storytelling. Over twenty-four hours, Gaiman posted twelve questions to his Twitter account, each based around a month of the year. Fans posted answers to those questions, and Gaiman then selected one response for each month and used them as the genesis for twelve short stories. He recorded himself reading each story. Fans then completed the story feedback loop by providing illustrations and videos for those stories, and the entire opus including text, images, and media files, was published online as *A Calendar of Tales*, which can be accessed on smartphones, laptops, tablets, and other devices. In "Remixing Time and Space," Merideth Garcia takes a

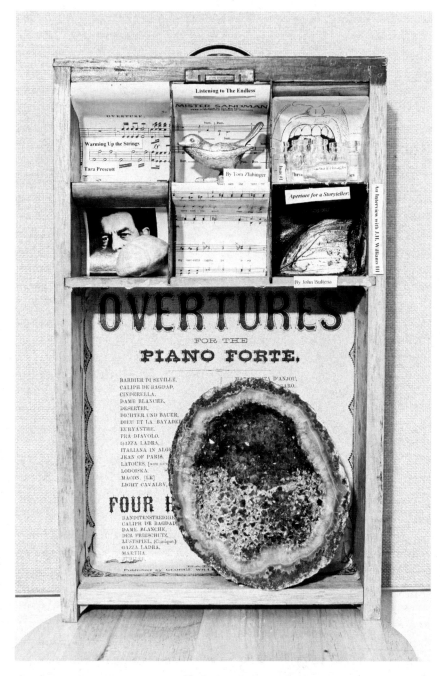

Neil Gaiman in the Twenty-first Century. Mixed media assemblage by Tara Prescott, photograph by Amy Dunton.

rare look at this multi-sensory, multimedia, collaborative online project and what it reveals about the ways that social media sites are shifting experiences of time, reality, and storytelling.

This collection ends with several essays focused on the most exciting Gaiman release so far, the highly-anticipated return to the *Sandman* series, *Sandman: Overture*. After the end of *Sandman* twenty-five years ago, Gaiman stopped working in comics for several years. He returned for *Marvel 1602* (2003), *Sandman: Endless Nights* (2003), and individual issues of different comic series.[5] In celebration of the twenty-fifth anniversary of *Sandman*, Gaiman returned to his most famous creation, pairing with artist JH Williams III. In an exclusive interview, "Aperture for a Storyteller," John Bultena and JH Williams III discuss the artist's experience working with Gaiman on *Overture*, collaborating with Alan Moore and others, the impact of social media on the world of comics, and the "pop and sizzle" of collaborative storytelling.

The release of *Overture* in its serialized format allows new readers to experience the delicious torture of delayed gratification that the original readers of *Sandman* knew well. In "Warming Up the Strings," Tara Prescott performs a close reading of issue #1 with an eye towards the reader's experience of *Overture* in its serialized format and the ways in which Gaiman uses the genre to reinvent his own myth. Fans of *Sandman* often remember their first interaction with the series, but few can remember what it is like to enter Gaiman's world of the Dreaming without knowing who the Endless are or how they function within the greater narrative. Nadia Eshraghi's "Issue #1 Through a New Reader's Eyes" offers a rare glimpse into what the first issue of *Overture* is like for a first time reader.

Tom Zlabinger turns his ear to the musical references and imagery implied in *Overture*'s title and within the larger *Sandman* universe, paying particular attention to the influence of Lou Reed, Elvis Costello, and David Bowie. "Listening to the Endless: Music and Musicians in the Extended *Sandman* Universe" offers a wide introduction through the musical landscape of the series.

And finally, in "Beginnings and Endless-ings," cartoonist and *Real World: San Francisco* cast member Judd Winick offers a short tale about his own discovery of *Sandman* and how the original Michael Zulli artwork from the last issue of "The Wake," which was recently featured in the "Grains of Sand: 25 Years of *The Sandman*" exhibition at the San Francisco Cartoon Art Museum, landed in his possession.

As any scholar focusing on the work of a living author knows, it is hard to gain a full perspective on a body of work that is ongoing. In the case of

Gaiman scholars, this is particularly magnified by the author's astonishing productivity. If only we could bottle him up, genie-like, and carry his creative energy with us like Dream's bag of sand. As of this publication, Gaiman has completed a music-and-readings tour with his wife Amanda Palmer, discussed plans for the film version of *Sandman,* published a groundbreaking reimagined fairy tale which frankly illustrates a queen saving a woman with a kiss (*The Sleeper and the Spindle*), and is finishing *Sandman: Overture.* One might expect after all of this work that Gaiman would take a breather for a while. But as the Victorian in *Wayward Manor* notes, "I've learned from experience, after all. A house like me ... isn't going to stay vacant for long."

Notes

1. In the interests of space, several of Gaiman's post–2000 works that are not included in this volume but are investigated in essays in *Feminism in the Worlds of Neil Gaiman* will be noted here. For an engaging essay on *Coraline,* see Danielle Russell's "Unmasking M(other)hood: Third-Wave Mothering in Gaiman's *Coraline* and *Mirror-Mask*" in *Feminism in the Worlds of Neil Gaiman.*

2. Yaeri Kim's essay in this collection touches on "The Flints of Memory Lane," one of the essays reprinted in *Fragile Things.*

3. See Emily Capettini, "'A boy and his box, off to see the universe': Madness, Power and Sex in 'The Doctor's Wife'" in *Feminism in the Worlds of Neil Gaiman.*

4. For an essay on the collaboration that was pivotal in Gaiman's and Palmer's early courtship, see Monica Miller, "Feminist Fairy Tales in *Who Killed Amanda Palmer*" in *Feminism in the World of Neil Gaiman.*

5. See Renata Dalmaso, "When Superheroes Awaken: The Revisionist Trope in Neil Gaiman's *Marvel 1602*" in *Feminism in the Worlds of Neil Gaiman.*

Works Cited

Campbell, Hayley. *The Art of Neil Gaiman.* New York: HarperCollins, 2014. Print.

Gaiman, Neil. *The Graveyard Book.* New York: Harper, 2008. Print.

_____ (w), and Chip Kidd (a). *Make Good Art.* New York: HarperCollins, 2013. Print.

Hanks, Henry. "Neil Gaiman's Acclaimed Comic Book 'Sandman' Returns After 25 Years." CNN. 25 March 2014. Web. 27 Aug 2014.

Inskeep, Steve, and Neil Gaiman. "Recurring Dream: Morpheus Returns in Gaiman's 'Sandman' Prequel." NPR's Morning Edition. 31 Oct 2013. Podcast.

Niffenegger, Audrey. "Foreword." *The Art of Neil Gaiman.* By Hayley Campbell. New York: HarperCollins, 2014. Print.

The Odd Gentlemen. *Wayward Manor.* Moonshark, 15 July 2014. PC.

Prescott, Tara, and Aaron Drucker, eds. *Feminism in the Worlds of Neil Gaiman: Essays on the Comics, Poetry and Prose.* Jefferson, NC: McFarland, 2012. Print.

"Store." *Wayward Manor*/whohauntsneil.com. Web. 9 Sept 2014.

American Gods (2001)

The American Odyssey

JENN ANYA PROSSER

"For in the beginning of literature is myth, and in
the end as well."—Jorge Luis Borges, *Labyrinths*

Neil Gaiman is a prolific adapter. His novels, short stories, and comics frequently reimagine the stories that are often considered "literary classics." From Ancient Greek and Roman myths to the stories of Sir Arthur Conan Doyle and H.P. Lovecraft, Gaiman has transformed a wealth of familiar tales into a series of modern and compelling fictions. His most epic novel to date, *American Gods*, is a tale about the evolution of myths, stories, and beliefs. Ancient pantheons arrived in North America over the centuries, carried there by their believers. Over time, the explorers and immigrants abandoned their old gods and adjusted to their new lives. The old gods, stuck in the new world, were forced to adapt in order to survive. *American Gods* envisions a world populated with new versions of the ancient mythological gods. By sending the hero, Shadow Moon, on an epic journey guided by a peculiar mentor, Gaiman beautifully weaves the myth of Homer's *Odyssey* into a new American tapestry set in the modern world.

Homer follows Odysseus from his triumph in the Trojan War through a ten-year journey back to his wife and son in Ithaca, encountering mythical creatures and great trials. The Ancient Greek gods both help and hinder him along the way. Comparatively, Shadow goes on a Hero's Journey filled with fantastic and mythical adventures as he assists his father in the battle between the old gods and the new. Both heroes, Shadow and Odysseus, are attempting to return home to reclaim their lives after serving time: Shadow completes his prison sentence and Odysseus finishes fighting in the Trojan War. The female characters of *American Gods* further this comparison; Gaiman's women echo the women of Homer's *Odyssey*. The most significant of these is Laura, Shadow's wife. The reader might expect this character to represent Penelope—the patient, faithful, dutiful wife of Odysseus. In Gaiman's adaptation of the *Odyssey*, Laura is instead a flawed Athena, the cheating wife who serves as Shadow's mentor and guide, assisting the hero through his quests. In order to forge an American version of Homer's epic, it is critical for Gaiman to fuse American culture with the vast library of pantheons inherited from a multiplicity of traditions. All of these elements reveal *American Gods* to be a modern recreation of the *Odyssey*, told from an American perspective, reflective of American culture and history.

Shadow's Odyssey

While *American Gods* is an adventure-laden road trip, it is at its core, like Homer's *Odyssey*, a quest for home. Shadow begins his journey cut off from his life, having served three years in prison. Like Odysseus, he wants nothing more than to return home after his time away. Before he can get there, though, Shadow's concept of home is destroyed: he learns that his wife and his best friend (who is also his employer) have died in a car accident. The enigmatic Mr. Wednesday coerces and manipulates Shadow into becoming his protector and assistant, sending Shadow on his Hero's Journey.

Shadow's adventure adheres to the structure of Joseph Campbell's Hero's Journey: the mythological hero reluctantly sets off after receiving the Call to Adventure. He encounters a supernatural helper and then crosses the threshold into the world of the unknown. The hero endures a series of tests, including facing one or more temptresses. When he arrives at the nadir of his journey, he undergoes a supreme ordeal, reaches apotheosis, and gains his boon. The hero then arrives home, returning to the world of the known and leaving the mystical behind. Rarely does any hero strictly adhere to Campbell's outline of the Hero's Journey, and Shadow and Odysseus are no exception. However, the two heroes follow a similar path which includes the departure from a place of isolation, the fights and challenges brought on by strange and fantastical creatures, and a journey to the underworld (211).

Each story begins *in medias res,* with both heroes starting their journeys after years away. Odysseus's quest starts after the Trojan War, where he emerged as the victorious hero. Shadow's quest begins as he is days away from his prison release, the end of a sentence for "beating the living crap out of" two VCR repair store employees (472). Both narratives establish the heroes as strong, powerful men. Odysseus is revered by the gods for his abilities. Zeus himself states, "How on earth could I forget Odysseus? Great Odysseus who excels all men in wisdom" (79). Similarly, Shadow is introduced with an air of strength and calm: "Shadow had done three years in prison. He was big enough and looked don't-fuck-with-me enough that his biggest problem was killing time" (3). Both ache for the wives they left behind. Odysseus is described as "one man alone ... his heart set on his wife and his return" (78). Athena pleads to her father on his behalf, "But my heart breaks for Odysseus, that seasoned veteran cursed by fate so long—far from his loved ones still, he suffers torments off on a wave-washed island" (79). Shadow's thoughts equally fixate on his spouse: "he kept himself in shape, and taught himself coin tricks, and thought a lot about how much he loved his wife" (3). As Odysseus has moved past the triumph of the Trojan War, living in a desperate state, hoping to die on Calypso's island, Shadow too has "plunged as low as he could plunge ... no longer scared of what tomorrow might bring, because yesterday had brought it" (3). The mighty heroes are detached from civilization; they yearn for home and the comforts of their wives. Homer's patterns ring familiar in the character of Shadow; he becomes an Odyssean hero in the mind of the reader.

Along the journey, Odysseus battles the Cyclops and receives assistance from Circe and Aeolus to aid in his other trials. Shadow encounters equally fanciful characters, such as the new god Technology, and finds help in Mister Ibis and Mister Jacquel. Among his many trials is the confrontation with the temptress Media, who serves as the seductive distraction to lure the hero into abandoning his quest. According to Campbell:

> [The] testings of the hero, which were preliminary to his ultimate experience and deed, were symbolic of those crises of realization by means of which his consciousness came to be amplified and made capable of enduring the full possession of the mother-destroyer, in his inevitable bride. With that he knows that he and the father are one: he is in the father's place [121].

As this passage shows, Odysseus must withstand the temptations of Circe and the Sirens in order to complete his journey. He demonstrates his role as the leader, the ultimate father figure, by showing his strength over these women in front of his crew. He outwits Circe and survives the Sirens' song. He shows his ability to endure the full possession of the mother-destroyer, not by hiding from or evading the temptresses, but by persevering against the women who would take his life, refusing to abandon his quest.

Media is the equivalent temptress in *American Gods*. By resisting her, Shadow proves his strength and fortifies his conviction to stand against the new gods. About a quarter of the way through the book, Shadow settles into a hotel in El Paso, Illinois, to rest before continuing his drive to Cairo. He sets the television on a timer and puts on a *Nick at Nite*-style channel. After a few minutes of watching, "the picture dissolved into phosphor-dot fuzz" and Lucy Ricardo appears on the screen (175). In the form of Lucy, the new god Media tries to seduce Shadow, calling him "sweetheart" and "honey" while attempting to convince him to abandon Wednesday's team and work for the new gods. Her seduction fails; Shadow is unswayed by her advances. The television automatically turns off after she begins her attempts at seducing Shadow. Just as Odysseus is released by his crew and continues his journey once his ship moves past the Sirens, Shadow recommits to his journey once Lucy is silenced. He falls asleep reflecting on why the old gods are more appealing than what is offered by the new gods (176–177).

Yet Media/Lucy's power lingers. While crude, crass, and ineffective, her Siren song sticks with Shadow through the novel. Her disturbing offer, "You want to see Lucy's tits?" becomes a refrain, a nightmarish thought Shadow unwillingly remembers as his journey continues (176). Furthering her parallels to the Sirens, Media reveals her wicked side, the sacrificial element of her existence: "The TV's the altar. I'm what people are sacrificing to." When Shadow asks what is sacrificed to her, Lucy replies, "Their time mostly.... Sometimes each other" (175). The television's central position in most American homes establishes it among the more intimate of modern elements (*American Gods* was first published in 2001, before smartphones and wireless internet became ubiquitous). What makes Media especially insidious is that families gather around the television set under the guise of sharing a meaningful experience together, but then ignore each other in favor of submitting to the TV. The television is the seductive temptation: people are drawn to the Sirens' song and fail to recognize the gut-wrenching sacrifice they are making. Lucy's comments insinuate that people are not sacrificing just anyone for her sake, they are passively sacrificing their own kin. They are giving up all that they love to worship her instead.

Media's dogged pursuit of Shadow pulls the hero further into the mystical world of the gods. Shadow is not even safe in the confines of his hotel room—he is vulnerable at all times. Furthermore, the new gods' dedication to finding Shadow establishes his significance. As Campbell states, the hero is "in the father's place" (121). The new gods are fixated on finding Shadow; their pursuit of him is far greater than their interest in his father Wednesday. Shadow is the critical figure in the story.

Arguably, the greater challenge for the heroes is not the temptress, but the journey to the underworld. Shadow finds himself in the underworld after holding his father's vigil. His experience there echoes Odysseus's time in Hades.

While in the underworld, Odysseus consults with Tiresias, the blind prophet who relates to the hero his remaining trials. Odysseus speaks with his mother, lamenting her death. She tells him how poorly Ithaca has fared without him. Odysseus's remaining time in the kingdom of the dead is spent recognizing the heroes and legends who rest in the underworld. Shadow's introduction to the afterlife, on the other hand, is a reflection of his life, and focuses on two major events: his crime and the death of his mother. Shadow does not interact with his mother like Odysseus does, he only watches as scenes unfold. Still, the moment is highly relevant to the novel's plot: Shadow sees Mr. Wednesday seducing his mother and finally realizes that the Norse god Odin is his father. Shadow then revisits the characters he encountered earlier in the novel: Bast, Mr. Ibis, and Mr. Jacquel. In this scene, Gaiman constructs a familiar underworld, one that would resonate with the reader's memories of Egyptian mythology in the same way that Odysseus's description of the kingdom of the dead would have been familiar to an Ancient Greek audience.

Greater challenges reap greater rewards. At the nadir, both heroes travel to the underworld where they receive the guidance necessary to complete their journeys. Tiresias foretells the remainder of Odysseus's travels, complete with dire warnings and advice. Shadow encounters Whiskey Jack who, like Tiresias the prophet, is more than a man but not a god. "I'm a cultural hero," he states. "We do the same shit gods do, we just screw up more and nobody worships us" (512). It is Whiskey Jack who finally helps Shadow to understand this complicated fantasy world. He reveals what is to come, clarifying, "It's not going to be a war.... It's going to be a bloodbath" (514). Armed with Whiskey Jack's counsel and a better understanding of the complicated world of the gods, Shadow is forced back into the land of the living. Like Odysseus, the knowledge he acquires in the underworld ensures that he is able to survive the final crisis and complete his Hero's Journey.

Laura, a Flawed Athena

While Shadow repeatedly shows his strength and power as the hero, he is not the seasoned warrior that Odysseus was. He unknowingly requires help throughout his Hero's Journey, and he finds this in the animated corpse of his dead wife. While living, she served as his inspiration for good behavior and perseverance. His goal in prison was solely to return home to her. Yet she dies before being introduced in the novel. Her role as the virtuous wife is corrupted by her infidelity (she dies in a car crash while performing oral sex on Shadow's best friend). Reanimated by the coin Shadow won off Mad Sweeney, Laura transcends the role of wife and becomes Shadow's mentor, bringing strength and guidance to his journey. By throwing the magical coin into Laura's grave, Shadow unwittingly gives her the power of the sun and brings her back from the dead. This effectively transforms Laura Moon into Laura Sun and establishes her existence as Shadow's guiding light. Laura becomes a mystical and powerful source for Shadow, both solar and lunar, dead and alive.

Laura exhibits many traits of her Homeric counterpart, Athena. Whereas Athena wears golden armor, Laura wears Mad Sweeney's gold sun coin as a pendant. As Odysseus's patron goddess, Athena guides Odysseus and Telemachus through their respective journeys, frequently aiding them in times of need. Laura's returns to the land of the living and becomes Shadow's protector as well as his guide. She has an element of otherworldly wisdom and a preternatural awareness of impending events, often alluding to or warning Shadow of what is to come.

Yet her role is more complicated than that of her Greek counterpart. While Athena was a beautiful, virginal goddess, Laura is a dead, decaying adulteress. Laura died cheating on her husband. This separates her from the wife of Odysseus, Penelope, who patiently denied suitors for twenty years while waiting for her husband to return. Laura's failure to wait even three years for Shadow's release would seem to make her a bad wife, unworthy of his long months of love and devotion. However, this plot point creates a separation between Shadow and his wife: she will rise above her failures in life, but not as a love interest. Instead, she returns to Shadow as a guide and mentor. She is his Athena.

Laura is also placed into a form of celibacy, supporting her role as the mentor rather than the wife. Her brief kiss with Shadow at the start of the novel serves to distance dead Laura from his promiscuous living wife. The disturbing description of the moment, "[Her tongue] was cold and dry, and it tasted of cigarettes and of bile," illustrates that Shadow no longer considers Laura a romantic figure (64). He withdraws from her, ending any consideration of her as a sexual being: "If Shadow had had any doubts as to whether his wife was dead or not, they ended then. He pulled back" (64). As the novel continues and the hero's strength and power grow, Laura's body corrodes. The hero has less need of her (although her role remains critical to the story until the very end), and she decomposes, gradually leaving Shadow to lead his own life.

Laura is the strongest of the women in *American Gods*. She fights for Shadow and repeatedly rescues him. The first time Shadow is in real peril, he is kidnapped and locked in a train car by Mister Wood and Mister Stone. The two men beat the hero for information before confining him to a cell. Unaware of where he is, Shadow is at a complete loss. Laura comes to save him, violently killing the guards, appearing before him covered in blood. In this scene, Laura reveals her new approach to mortality, which imitates the gods' callous approach to life. After rescuing Shadow for the first time, she explains her willingness to kill: "It's easier to kill people, when you're dead yourself ... I mean, it's not such a big deal. You're not so prejudiced anymore" (151). Laura has a macro view of the world and sees human lives as insignificant and expendable, much in the way that gods view human life. Laura repeatedly rescues Shadow throughout the novel. Near the end of *American Gods*, as Laura is cutting Shadow down from Odin's tree, she comments, "I spend too much time rescuing you" (467).

Athena also repeatedly rescues Odysseus. In the final books of the *Odyssey*, as Telemachus and Odysseus begin to struggle in their battle against the suitors, Athena appears in the form of Mentor, ultimately saving them. When she appears, Odysseus begs for her help, addressing the goddess as Mentor and recalling their long history together. The hero "[k]new in his bones it was Athena, Driver of Armies" (446). She tests Odysseus and his son before engaging in the fight. She then serves as a lookout by redirecting the arrows and objects being hurled at the protagonists and finally ends the battle by intimidating the suitors with her divine powers. Similarly, Laura contributes more to the concluding battle than any other character. By killing Mr. Town, stealing the stick from Odin's tree, and using it to stab Low Key, she enacts more violence and force than any of the other characters. The remaining battle is a cacophony of disorder compared to Laura's swift and purposeful actions, proving she is truly the disciplined warrior of the story.

Laura's decision to be put to rest at the conclusion of the novel is the final testament to her strength. While Shadow's other companions, Mr. Wednesday and Low Key, have revealed their true selfish nature, Laura shows a selfless appreciation of the cycle of life. Shadow has completed his Hero's Journey and is reborn into a full life with enough power to stop the gods. Laura, aware of the drastic thunderbird sacrifice that is necessary to bring her back to life, requests the finality of death. "I think I must have earned it," she says (541). She concludes her role as Shadow's guide and mentor, returning to the underworld with serene confidence in her husband's ability to exist without her. Shadow disappears the tangible coin sun, exits the cavern, and walks into the "fresh and clean and new" night air (542). This brief moment fulfills the role of the hero's crossing of the threshold. Shadow, strong enough to exist without his warrior goddess, exits the womb and enters the stormless world.

An American Pantheon

Recognizing the similarities between Homer's *Odyssey* and Gaiman's *American Gods*, there are still significant differences between the two narratives, primarily the slew of multicultural gods and cultural tones from Gaiman's novel. This deviation is a critical element of Gaiman's adaptation of the great Homeric poem. By drastically altering the story of the *Odyssey*, Gaiman transforms it into a modern American mythos with a complex pantheon that is representative of the country where the novel takes place.

Pantheons are representative of the cultures that created them. The Egyptian pantheon focused on the cycles of death and rebirth, reflecting the cycles of drought and flood that created such turmoil in Ancient Egypt. The Greek pantheon was built on the family structure, a representation of a rich, powerful family that is burdened with the challenges of life, arrogance, and stubbornness that accompany elitism (Leeming 102). David Adams Leeming states, "To 'read' a pantheon is to read a culture's sense of itself and the nature of the cosmos" (95). Gaiman constructs a pantheon that borrows from the variety of immigrant (and native) cultures that populate America, including a new collection of gods that is representative of modern cultural influences.

By creating a modern-day, multicultural pantheon, Gaiman adds *American Gods* to a monomyth that extends across the globe. The term "monomyth," as developed by Campbell, references the similarities between different cultures' mythologies:

> Whether we listen with aloof amusement to the dreamlike mumbo jumbo of some red-eyed witch doctor of the Congo, or read with cultivated rapture thin translations from the sonnets of the mystic Lao-tse ... it will always be the one, shape-shifting yet marvelously constant story that we find, together with a challengingly persistent suggestion of more remaining to be experienced than will ever be known or told [1].

As America is a new country, its myths are young. In *American Gods*, Gaiman has created a Hero's Journey that is worthy of being the American monomyth.

The consistency between iterations of the monomyth—in this case, the similarities between *American Gods* and Homer's *Odyssey* and Campbell's Hero's Journey—create a familiarity in the narrative. There is a comfort in Gaiman's tale, because we, as readers, already know the arc of events. However, it must be adapted to reflect American culture. America is a collection of diasporas, a quasi-melting pot. The country consists of cultures from around the world, cultures that have blended and to some degree, been diluted, as they have helped America develop. In addition, there is a modern element that must be addressed: no longer do we pay tribute to a messenger god or a goddess who brings the spring. Instead our energies are devoted to technology, media, transportation, and other innovations. If the pantheon within *American Gods* is going to accurately represent American culture, there must be gods who reflect our sense of self. We find these in the new gods.

This multicultural, all-encompassing concept of beliefs lays the foundation for the novel. In a dream near the start of *American Gods*, the buffalo man tells Shadow, "If you are to survive, you must believe ... *Everything*" (18). This theme resonates throughout the novel. It is repeated by the buffalo man, and again when Shadow is speaking with Whiskey Jack before being brought back to life, and most extensively by Sam, the college-aged hitchhiker, who assists Shadow on his journey:

> I can believe in things that are true and I can believe in things that aren't true and I can believe things where nobody knows if they're true or not. I can believe in Santa Claus and the Easter Bunny and Marilyn Monroe and the Beatles and Elvis and Mister Ed. I believe that all men are just overgrown boys with deep problems communicating and that the decline in good sex in America is coincident with the decline in drive-in movie theaters from state to state.... I believe in a personal god who cares about me and worries and oversees everything I do. I believe in an impersonal god who set the universe in motion and went off to hang with her girlfriends and doesn't even know that I'm alive.... I believe in a woman's right to choose, a baby's right to live, that while all human life is sacred there's nothing wrong with the death penalty if you trust the legal system implicitly, and that no one but a moron would ever trust the legal system [394–395].

In this extensive speech, Sam's beliefs range from the meditative to the absurd, interspersed with ideas relevant to the storyline that nearly function as metacommentary. Sam's monologue becomes a representation of American culture; it shows a wealth of ideas, traditional and new, political, personal, scientific, and otherwise. She truly believes *everything*, without concern about contradiction or mutually exclusive beliefs, and in this memorable moment, her speech encompasses one of the major themes of the novel: being American means being a part of a collection of ideas and beliefs.

Conclusion: Americanizing the Odyssey

Homer's *Odyssey* is arguably the most famous epic in western culture. For millennia, it has been studied, taught, referenced, and adapted. However, as the world becomes more culturally aware and more globally interconnected, acknowledging the wealth of differences that exist among us, the *Odyssey* resonates less and less with who we are as a people. Gaiman's multicultural representation of this Hero's Journey becomes a truer myth for America. Where Homer's Odysseus is the great Greek hero, Gaiman creates an American-Norwegian Odysseus. Shadow's muddled heritage alone is representative of the culture he is intended to reflect. His journey incorporates the great many pantheons that migrated to America, and he requires the help of a variety of mythological figures in order to succeed.

By modernizing the tale, Gaiman renders the story relevant to a twenty-first-century audience. The introduction of the new gods correlates to both the modern and the ancient pantheons. Americans still worship gods, but the pantheon has changed. We sacrifice our time and attention to elements of technology and modern innovations, rather than personified deities who assist in times of harvest or war. Even Gaiman's allegorical characters, those most reflective of the *Odyssey*, carry within them an element of modernization. Laura is an Athena, but one that is more realistic by today's standards. She is a flawed, unfaithful wife, but proves her loyalty to Shadow by repeatedly saving him and helping him, by being his warrior. Her power and significance within the story become a testament to feminine strength and independence in a story format that is traditionally anthropocentric.

The story of *American Gods* is familiar, not only because of our long association with the Hero's Journey and the parallels between Gaiman's epic and Homer's *Odyssey*, but also because of its relevancy to us: this new mythology brilliantly captures the assorted facets of American life and culture. Gaiman's tribute to the ancient epic also serves as a subtle critique of its place within the literary canon. We need myths and stories that more accurately represent our culture—compelling tales based upon our own pantheon. And Gaiman charmingly crafts it for us in *American Gods*.

Works Cited

Borges, Jorge Luis. *Labyrinths*. Eds. David A. Yates and James E. Irby. New York: New Direction Books, 2007. Print.

Campbell, Joseph. *The Hero with a Thousand Faces*, 3d ed. Novato: New World Library, 2008. Print.

Gaiman, Neil. *American Gods*. New York: Harper Torch, 2001. Print.

Homer. *The Odyssey*. Trans. Robert Fagles. New York: Viking, 1996. Print.

Leeming, David Adams. *The World of Myth*. New York: Oxford University Press, 1990. Print.

The Anxiety of Disappearance

Michael B. Key

> "[A]nxiety is invariably the result of a certain mode of being
> implicated in the game, of being caught by the game, of being
> as it were from the very beginning at stake in the game."
> —Jacques Derrida, *Writing and Difference*

National borders and beliefs are constructed by polarized binaries: good/bad, old/new, them/us. The intersection of these binaries identifies a cultural midpoint—or center. This center often becomes personified as the ideal or purest presence of the nation's identity—most commonly as a pantheon, god, or symbol. The main tension in Neil Gaiman's *American Gods* is a battle between premodern and modern myths. The premodern gods fight to once again become dominant centers in society while the modern gods fight to extinguish any competition for the center they currently hold. Each side of the war is fighting to stop their inevitable extinction. These myths were created because of a society's anxiety about disappearance. But is power even an attainable goal for these gods? Will one side's victory simply end the cycle of replacing old cultures with new paradigms? *American Gods* presents a chilling reality.

The center of any social or cultural structure is held sacred and protected with rigid traditions and rituals (Todorov 21). These safeguards and practices calm a civilization's anxiety about chaos or destruction. Cultures deify these central forces through worship in the hope of a more stable future. These ideal forms are the *presence* or purest concentration of a structure. As Low Key Lyesmith explains to Shadow, "You got to understand the god thing. It's not magic. It's about being you, but the you that people believe in. It's about being the concentrated, magnified, essence of you. It's about becoming thunder, or the power of a running horse, or wisdom. You take all the belief and become bigger, cooler, more than human. You crystallize" (*American Gods*

19

443). The "concentrated, magnified, essence" (*American Gods* 443) of an idea, function, or state becomes immobile and attempts to halt chance or freeplay. However, no matter how many people worship this center, Mr. Nancy warns, "The center is not a stable place for anybody" (*American Gods* 437). Mr. Nancy is right of course.

According to French philosopher Jacques Derrida, centers are illusions since a center must precede its parametrical binaries. The true origin of structures is freeplay (Derrida 352). Derrida defines freeplay as "the disruption of presence" (369). Hence, freeplay is the spontaneous—human—force that creates, interdicts, and destroys constructed centers (Derrida 352). In *American Gods*, Mr. Wednesday and Low Key Lyesmith construct an elaborate con in order to fuel chaos and bloodshed among both the premodern and modern gods to serve as a type of sacrifice to both party leaders so that they can gain ultimate power. Mr. Wednesday orchestrates Laura's death in order to convince Shadow to play his role in the con. Shadow, however, is a repeating element of chance—or freeplay. When he tosses Mad Sweeney's gold coin in Laura's grave, she is reanimated and later saves Shadow multiple times. Laura kills Low Key Lyesmith before he can dedicate the gods' battle to Mr. Wednesday. She dedicates both her suicide and her slaughter of Low Key Lyesmith to Shadow, changing the structural center from Mr. Wednesday to Shadow. Laura's return from the dead disassembles their structure of chaos and war. As a wildcard, Laura is an excellent example of freeplay within the novel.

The freeplay of history, however, demonstrates that cultural centers repeatedly fall into the hands of new societies—new paradigms. Civilizations have been relentless in building structures around countless elemental and functional centers of life and society in an attempt to make sense of a chaotic world. This pattern is also illustrated in *American Gods* when ancient deities remain nostalgic for the premodern societies that created them. These premodern gods anxiously anticipate their disrupted presence in the epoch of the new gods of modernity. Ironically, the modern gods—despite their hubris— also have a growing sense of anxiety toward their own obsolescence and disappearance. If time shifts power from one center to another, is it possible for one true center to exist? As the text asks, "What is the center of a man? What is the center of a dream?" (*American Gods* 426).

In his analysis of mythscapes, Duncan S. A. Bell discusses three typological nationalisms: primordialists, modernists, and perennialists. Primordialists believe in sacred bloodlines or ethnic purity in order to determine the origin of their nation (Bell 67). These are predominantly seen in premodern cultures who attempt to trace their origin to a specific familial god-like figure. Modernist nationalism identifies industry, capitalism, the economy, and politics as the unified centers of society (Bell 68). This is the present American paradigm. Perennialists, however, see the trends and shared genealogy of cultural beliefs and practices. This is more of a postmodern approach to rejecting grand narratives of history (Bell 67). These nationalisms show the particular structures held sacred by premodern, modern, and postmodern societies.

As primordialists, premodern societies believe their origins are physical and exclusive. The prevalence of demi-gods and cultural heroes in ancient societies demonstrates that great feats were attributed to blood ties with the gods. Gilgamesh, Heracles, and Jesus are just three classical examples. These figures give a biological hope for worshippers to believe they have greatness within them since they are descendants of the gods. The premodern gods are products of these primordialist systems. For example, since Mr. Wednesday (Odin) is Shadow's father, Shadow is the modern Baldar and a demigod. Shadow is unaware of his bloodline for most of the novel and he possesses no supernatural qualities, but he does have extraordinary characteristics: primarily his strength and height. Primordialists would attribute Shadow's distinctive features to his bloodline with Mr. Wednesday.

Gaiman inserts cross-cultural narratives in *American Gods* to emphasize the premodern era. The novel's "Coming to America" segments show how these gods were real and demanded libations in order to protect their followers. The earliest narrative mentioned in *American Gods* occurs in 14,000 BC and tells the story of the priestess Atsula and the nomads of the Northern Plains. The tribe's cultural center is the presence of the mammoth god Nunyunnini. Atsula experiences clairvoyant nightmares of "bright lights moving fast, of rock mountains filled with lights spearing upward like icicles" (*American Gods* 413). The strange illumination of cars and skyscrapers that appear in her dreams threaten the tribe's survival. She consults, however, with the tribal elders, using *pungh* mushrooms and urine as "a libation to Nunyunnini," in order to receive guidance from their god (*American Gods* 414). The elders believe that Nunyunnini speaks through them to warn of a coming evil and spiritual famine if they travel into the land that will eventually become America. This omen frightens Atsula and she challenges Nunyunnini's presence. The nomadic tribe of the Northern Plains is then cursed for Atsula's insolence and will only occupy the pre–American territory "for seven generations, and seven sevens" (*American Gods* 415).

Atsula's faithlessness disrupts the tribe's center and social structure and therefore results in their eventual extinction. Nunyunnini no longer speaks to the elders because the god is no longer the truest presence of the tribe. These nomadic tribes of the Northern Plains dispersed and populated the Americas and created new gods and traditions that no longer remembered Nunyunnini. The center is lost and the cultural anxiety about danger, chance, and freeplay are no longer contained. The tribe's generations "spread out across the land, and formed new tribes and chose new totems: ravens and foxes and ground sloths and great cats and buffalo, each a beast that marked a tribe's identity, each beast a god" (*American Gods* 418). These new tribes will become the scraelings encountered by the Northmen who create the buffalo god that appears to Shadow. The skulls of Nunyunnini and Atsula are eventually redis-covered, but since they had been replaced by the gods of the New World, their remains were destroyed and forgotten.

Atsula's freeplay allows her to discover an important secret: "Gods are great.... But the heart is greater. For it is from our hearts they come, and to our hearts they shall return" (*American Gods* 417). She discovers that the gods are human creations, and for that, she dies. Because this realization appears at the earliest point in the chronology of the novel, it is indicative that a main tenet is the understanding that gods are illusions and that there is no constant center. Gaiman states that cultures are always "arguing over things that many people regard as imaginary. Chiefly, gods, religions, and national boundaries, which are absolutely imaginary. They're completely notional. They don't tend to exist" ("An Interview with Neil Gaiman"). Paired with Atsula's revelation, Gaiman's perspective magnifies the significance cultural centers play in the novel.

The new tribes also make an appearance as the scraelings in the next nar-rative of immigration to America. As the Northmen reached the land that their successors would eventually call Vineland, the sailors become fearful and lamented, "Here on the edge of the world we will be forgotten by our gods" (*American Gods* 67). This immediate act of faithlessness foreshadows the raid on their encampment. Since the Northmen forget the reach of their gods, their sacrifice is rejected when they lynch the wandering scraeling to honor the All-Father. The Northmen left their cultural center when they set sail for Vineland. They do not realize that they have immigrated to an already native center. The dominant paradigm in the settlement is that of the three hundred scraelings—not the thirty Northmen. This narrative creates important dis-tinctions among the series of "Coming to America" stories—immigration is the story of having to leave old traditions behind whereas colonization is the story of constructing satellite centers of foreign powers. Gods are only as powerful as the society that creates them. Each migration, war, and invention has an accompanying shift in paradigms.

The next premodern story in *American Gods* is about immigration in 1721, after European colonization has already begun. Essie Tregowan becomes an indentured servant in Virginia who must worship her Cornish gods in order to survive many trials. She is compulsive about leaving milk out at night for the pixies and carrying salt and bread in her pockets so that she will always be protected from harm. Her resilience saves her, several times, from prison, execution, and disease, "Essie gave thanks for her escapes from her vicissitudes to all the creatures that she had been told of as a child ... her friends laughed at her; but she had the last laugh, as her friends got the pox or the clap and Essie remained in the peak of health" (*American Gods* 95). Essie epitomizes superstitious behaviors and in turn worships figures who symbolize the purest presence of those traits. Consequently, everyone who mocks her rituals perishes. Nevertheless, Essie's Cornish gods were not the dominant centers in either England or America during her lifetime. After the colonization of indigenous tribes in America, Judeo-Christian myths became the new center of the colonies. The "American colonies were as much a dumping ground as an escape, a forgetting place" of indigenous and immigrant gods (*American Gods* 92). Likewise, despite the dominance of Judeo-Christian traditions in America, new paradigms will eventually take over. Gaiman states, "Myths are compost. They begin as religions, the most deeply held of beliefs, or as the stories that accrete to religions as they grow" ("Reflections on Myth" 76). Due to America's habit of composting other cultures and religions, national centers come and go often.

The last "Coming to America" installment occurs in 1778 during the Atlantic slave trade. The story of Wututu demonstrates how cultural structures often overlap or intersect: "There was a girl, and her uncle sold her.... That is the tale; the rest is detail.... Put like that it seems so simple" (*American Gods* 322). Wututu's slave narrative demonstrates the unfortunate cyclical nature of human cruelty—her story shares characteristics with the Holocaust and other atrocities. The main difference in stories is perspective. Mr. Ibis remembers a Nazi who writes home to his wife and son, assuring them that he is doing good work, and that his main concern is not the massacre of thousands of camp prisoners and instead is concerned about his son's low marks in school.

Gaiman discusses the similarity of immigrant stories by stating, "The immigrant experience is, I suspect, a universal one" ("How Dare You?" 540). This universal immigrant perspective can better identify hegemonic influences because native citizens know of no other alternative. Gaiman responds to this outsider knowledge by stating, "I don't think *American Gods* could have been written by someone who was American. A lot of that is because, if you're a goldfish in the water, you don't go, 'This water tastes odd.' You go, 'This is what water tastes like'" (Bissette and Gaiman 493). Wututu hears rumors about successful slave rebellions in St. Domingo. She holds on to the hope that the incalculable number of slaves in America will also rebel. However, "It was as if the whole American nation had decided that they could, by an effort of belief, command a good-sized Caribbean island to no longer exist merely by willing it so" (*American Gods* 334). The immigrant experiences in the "Coming to America" installments distinguish between premodern and modern nations but also how the anxiety of disappearance or decentering is common to all cultures.

Similarly, panic and anxiety is almost always centered on extinction or disappearance: the loss of tradition, scarcity of resources, surrendering of power, and death. America's modern anxieties focus on labor, security, and freedom. *American Gods* underlines these anxieties through a particular type of disappearance—obsolescence. Since the Industrial Revolution, manpower has been increasingly devalued in favor of cheaper, faster, and more efficient machines. Likewise, wealth became more centralized toward titans of industry rather than skilled laborers. Czernobog is an excellent example of obsolescence. His services in the slaughterhouse are now done mechanically. Therefore, technology has rendered him obsolete as a laborer just as changing religious beliefs rendered him obsolete as a god.

Despite the fear of being replaced by machines, the Hindu goddess of death, Kali, reminds the premodern gods that machines are also vulnerable to obsolescence. Kali states, "I've watched the new ones rise, and I've watched them fall again.... They worshiped the railroads here, only a blink of an eye ago. And now the iron gods are as forgotten as the emerald hunters" (139). Even some of the new gods Mr. Wednesday warns the council about—"gods of credit card and freeway, of Internet and telephone, of radio and hospital and television, gods of plastic and of beeper and of neon"—have become obsolete since the novel's publication in 2001 (138). In another ten years, even the most high-tech gadgets will be replaced or absorbed by newer technologies. Kali's point is that change is inevitable.

However, the premodern gods make adjustments when new paradigms gain dominance. Bilquis makes the most notable adjustment when she prostitutes herself in order to receive her libations. Bilquis is the Biblical Queen of Sheba and has no history as a goddess, only as a monarch. However, monarchs and deities are similar in that they are both the centers of their societies and desire to be worshiped. Prostitution allows Bilquis to still be worshiped in a democratic society. Other examples of premodern gods adjusting under a new paradigm are the ifrit Salim, who must change his profession from a powerful jinn to a taxi driver; the Celtic deity Gwydion, who pumps gas at a filling station; and the Slavic goddess of the dusk, Zorya Vechernyaya, who must tell fortunes to support her sisters. Conversely, there are only a few deities that seem to retain their central importance. For example, Mr. Ibis and Mr. Jacquel are judges of the dead and death is not a dying business.

This new paradigm is described by Jakub Jerzy Macewicz as postcapitalism, or "the right to own, the free market, the freedom of entrepreneurship. There are places of worship: shopping malls, banks, financial centres, or television programmes devoted only to the economy.... Finally, there is the area of sacrum: the '*Invisible Hand of the Market*'; and virtual money, the 'wealth'" (110). This is the current dominant center in America. The Technical Boy and Media are symbolic of America's fascination with global communication and information. After wondering how Media became a goddess, Shadow asks her, "What do they sacrifice?" and she responds, "Their time, mostly.... Sometimes each other" (*American Gods* 175).

Gaiman takes particular interest in data consumption in modern America, "For all of human history, we have lived in a time of information scarcity.... Information was a valuable thing, and those who had it or could obtain it could charge for that service. In the last few years, we've moved from an information-scarce economy to one driven by an information glut" ("Why Our Future Depends on Libraries, Reading and Daydreaming"). Despite the present desire for unlimited information, it is by no means a new fascination. This is a continuation of the theme that cultural centers continue to shift and dissipate over and over again—"Information and knowledge: two currencies that have never gone out of style" (*American Gods* 24).

American Gods' uses the term "meme" to explore the replaceability of the gods, which is particularly prescient given how pervasive the term has become in American popular culture. When Shadow meets the modern-day Jesus, the god clarifies, "Have you thought about what it means to be a god? ... It means you give up your mortal existence to become a meme.... It means that everyone gets to re-create you in their own minds. You barely have your own identity any more.... Nothing is fixed, nothing is stable" (*American Gods: Author's Preferred Text* 528). This echoes Mr. Nancy's observation about the center. If gods or centers were truly the purest form of a construct, they would therefore be indestructible since they would be irreplaceable. As seen in the "Coming to America" segments, centers are not stable because they are illusions. The Technical Boy explains that religions and rituals do not exist in modern society because he has "reprogrammed reality" and realized "that language is a virus and that religion is an operating system and that prayers are just so much fucking spam" (*American Gods* 53). If reality, religion, and prayers are programmed, they are therefore constructed centers in order for cultures to identify the purest identity and presence.

Cultural tension arises between the premodern and modern gods when they realize that their central foundation is not as immobile as believed. Amongst the tension between the premodern and modern gods, the center of America is, according to Mr. Nancy, neutral ground—"when a place is less sacred than any other place. Of negative sacredness. Places where they can build no temples" (*American Gods* 430). The center, if it exists, has to be as Low Key Lyesmith describes, "It's about being the concentrated, magnified, essence of you.... You crystallize" (*American Gods* 443). Derrida concurs, "At the center, the permutation or the transformation of elements (which may of course be structures enclosed within a structure) is forbidden" (279). Since cultures do disappear and become decentered, this indicates that permutation and mobility exists. There is no center. Why then is it so important for nations, cultures, or people to construct central beliefs? As Bast tells Shadow, "Think of us as symbols—we're the dream that humanity creates to make sense of the shadows on the cave wall. Now go on, keep moving.... The fools are gathering on the mountain" (*American Gods: Author's Preferred Text* 425). Bast calls the gathered gods—both premodern and modern—"fools" because they are oblivious to the fact that gods are just projected images of humans. And since the gods are unaware of this, they still gather for war because there seems to be a latent desire to believe the illusions.

If centers do not exist, what is *American Gods* really about? Based on the continuous tension between the premodern and modern gods and their tug-of-war with Shadow, the novel illustrates that wars are caused by the belief and deification of ideas. Believing in a pure form of reality is a type of utopianism. And the problem with utopias is that no single interpretation of paradise or purity is like another. For example, the symbolic figure of death in India is presented as Kali whereas in Egypt it is an entire chthonic pantheon. This illustrates the postmodern assertion that there is no one truth and instead countless truths. These individual truths are never truly unified to one encompassing center, "Determining the exact center of anything can be problematic at best.... What is the center of a man? What is the center of a dream? ... It's about what people *think* is. It's all imaginary anyway. That's why it's important. People only fight over imaginary things" (*American Gods* 426–7). Despite the lack of truths or tangible centers, wars exist because people feel the need to believe in something that explains the world in which they live.

After realizing that there are no truths or centers, Shadow better understands something Sam told him earlier in the novel:

> I can believe things that are true and I can believe things that aren't true and I can believe things where nobody knows if they're true or not.... I believe in a personal god who cares about me and worries and oversees everything I do. I believe in an impersonal god who set the universe in motion and went off to hang with her girlfriends and doesn't even know that I'm alive. I believe in an empty and godless universe of causal chaos, background noise, and sheer blind luck.... I believe that life is a game, that life is a cruel joke, and that life is what happens when you're alive and that you might as well lie back and enjoy it [*American Gods* 393–5].

Sam's soliloquy states one essential tenet of postmodernism—there is no one truth. If nothing is true, then what should be believed? Shadow asks himself and the buffalo man this same question: "What should I believe? ... and the voice came back to him from somewhere deep beneath the world, in a bass rumble: Believe everything" (*American Gods* 133). Sam's words illustrate the simple purpose of life is to live it.

Only one reoccurring figure remains constant after all this decentering: people. This is explained by Shadow, "I think I would rather be a man than a god. We don't need anyone to believe in us. We just keep going anyhow. It's what we do" (*American Gods* 539). People are the freeplay that creates, defends, and destroys centers. The purpose for the construction of centers is to create a sense of continuity from one era to another. This creation calms cultural anxieties by having something to believe in or work toward in the future. This practice repeats in every culture—not necessarily in the form of religion but instead by created cultural identity. Derrida echoes this: "the transformations, and the permutations are always *taken* from a history of meaning *[sens]*-that is, a history, period-whose origin may always be revealed or whose end may always be anticipated in the form of presence" (Derrida 279–80). *American Gods* chronicles the endless exchange between paradigms as human constructs. Gaiman begins with a "Caveat, and Warning for Travelers" that concedes that the novel is a work of fiction, that "[o]nly the gods are real." This essay could position itself against Gaiman's caveat, however, if gods are projections of cultural centers throughout history, then the gods are indeed the only real things in *American Gods*.

Works Cited

Bissette, Stephen, and Neil Gaiman. "The Interview." *Prince of Stories: The Many Worlds of Neil Gaiman*. Ed. Hank Wagner, Christopher Golden, and Stephen Bissette. New York: St. Martin's, 2008. 447–505. Print.

Derrida, Jacques. "Structure, Sign, and Play in the Discourse of the Human Sciences." *Writing and Difference*. Trans. Alan Bass. London: Routledge, 2001. 351–70. Print.

Gaiman, Neil. *American Gods*. New York: Harper Perennial, 2003. Print.

_____. *American Gods: Author's Preferred Text*, 10th Anniversary Reprint ed. New York: William Morrow Paperbacks, 2011. Print.

_____. "How Dare You?" *American Gods*. New York: William Morrow, 2011. 539–41. Print.

_____. "An Interview with Neil Gaiman." Interview by Jessa Crispin. *Bookslut*. N.p., Oct. 2006. Web. 28 Jul. 2014.

_____. "Reflections on Myth." *Columbia: A Journal of Literature and Art* 31 (1999): 75–84. *JSTOR*. Web. 28 Jul. 2014.

_____. "Why Our Future Depends on Libraries, Reading and Daydreaming." The Reading Agency. The Barbican Centre, London. 14 Oct. 2013. *The Reading Agency*. Web. 30 Jul. 2014.

Institute for Communications Technology Management. *How Much Media? 2013 Report on American Consumers*. Los Angeles: University of Southern California, 2013. Print.

Macewicz, Jakub Jerzy. "The Air We Breathe: Capitalism and Mythology." *Subtle as Serpents, Gentle as Doves: Equality and Independence*. Praha: BGÖI & WSCF-CESR, 2005. 105–155. Print.

Todorov, Tzetan. "The Uses and Abuses of Memory." Trans. Lucy Golsan. *What Happens to History: The Renewal of Ethics in Contemporary Thought*. Ed. Howard Marchitello. London: Routledge, 2001. 11–40. Print.

The Wolves in the Walls (2003) and Blueberry Girl (2009)

Towards a Feminist Reading of Gaiman's Picture Books

Renata Lucena Dalmaso

Neil Gaiman's picture books *The Wolves in the Walls* (2003), illustrated by Dave McKean, and *The Blueberry Girl* (2009), illustrated by Charles Vess, are overflowing with the potential for feminist readings. Just as the cross-discursive nature of comics is central to their narratives, illustrated children's books construct multiple narratives through the continuous interplay of written and visual text.

As Charles Hatfield points out, up until recently, children's literature scholars have shown little interest in comics as a field of study, and the same could be said for comics scholars in relation to children's literature (361). The picture book is an ideal place to start bridging the theoretical gap, as it combines elements of both genres in its narrative.

As with many other art forms, the definition of the picture book has changed over time in response to social, cultural, and technological factors (Kiefer 19). Some authors, like Uri Shulevitz, choose to distinguish between "picture books" and "books with pictures." Shulevitz, for example, defines the "story book" as a work in which the story is told mainly through writing, with the aid of pictures (15). The illustrations, in this sense, work primarily as auxiliaries to the written narrative.

In contrast, a picture book, according to Shulevitz, tells a story through both text and images: although both are "read," the visual narrative takes precedence (15–16). Other scholars, such as Barbara Bader, focus on the interdependence of both types of narrative, rather than assigning a primary role to written or visual discourse (qtd. in Kiefer 9). Michèle Anstey and Geoff Bull also rely on the connectedness between written and visual texts that "work interdependently to produce meaning" in the picture book (329).

In sum, picture books can be defined as works in which the visual and

29

the written narratives contribute different layers of meaning to the story, without the implication of a hierarchy between the two.

Despite his contribution to the study of picture books, Shulevitz is an example of a generation of critics that understands them basically as works to be read to young children. Pre-literate children follow the narrative through its illustrations. However, many scholars have recently challenged this fairly common assumption about children's literature and the picture book. That assumption of intended audience appears to disregard the meanings produced by adult readers also engaged with the reading of the story. An adult's understanding of metanarrative techniques and intertextual references produces different meanings, which in turn affect the experience of the child listener. In addition, as critics such as David Rudd and Peter Hollindale point out, children often experience children's literature through multiple readings at different times in their lives, so there is truly no singular or fixed experience of a story (qtd. in Anstey and Bull 329). Thus, if a reading can be revisited, as Rudd and Hollindale argue, the experience of creating the meaning of a particular book can also be revisited several times during a person's life (qtd. in Anstey and Bull 329). Scholars such as Michele Anstey and Geoff Bull conclude that the issue of intended audience of such works has "become largely irrelevant, as childhood and reading are socially determined" (329). They cite the "blurring of boundaries between picture books and other genres, and between adult and children's literature" as a basis for disputing the notion that picture books are meant for younger readers only (328). Neil Gaiman's works are a good example of the blurring of such boundaries, as he produces works for all ages, with evident overlaps between expected readership.

Both written and visual language work simultaneously to produce the rich possibilities in meaning in picture books (329). By taking different reading experiences into account, as critics like Rudd and Hollindale suggest, a reader can relate to the different types of discourse each time in a unique way. Christina M. Desai notes that "whether the plot of the story could be understood without the illustrations is [ultimately] an irrelevant question, since the illustrations do have an impact in either case" (409). She adds that, despite this known cross-discursive characteristic of the picture book, the written narrative ends up receiving far more attention both in critical literature and in the classroom (409). Focusing on the interplay between images and the texts in *The Wolves in the Walls* and *Blueberry Girl* reveals the appropriation and subversion of traditional narratives, one that forces the reader to coauthor the texts as she navigates the different layers of meaning.

The Parallels in the Walls

Neil Gaiman and Dave McKean's *The Wolves in the Walls* is a rather dark tale of a family forced out of their house by wolves that were living in the walls. The young protagonist Lucy is the first person in the household to notice the lupine squatters. Her family ignores all of her warnings, so eventually she is the one that takes charge to reclaim the house from the wolves. McKean's complex artistic style is characterized by a juxtaposition of collages, photographs, digital images, drawings, and paintings that results in a unique, postmodern, quasi–Gothic style. These stylistic elements can appear together in a single frame, in a purposefully chaotic composition, almost competing with one another. Or they can alternate between different pages, shifting from more traditional pen and ink drawings to Photoshopped collages, depending on the tone McKean wants to give to that particular part of the narrative at that particular time. The unity in McKean's illustration is often its consistent disunity and surprise.

One example of McKean's contrasting styles in *The Wolves in the Walls* is the depiction of the wolves versus the depictions of the family members. The wolves are all hand drawn, in black ink, mostly colorless except for their vivid yellow eyes. Their crude two-dimensional figures reflect the typical depictions of wolves from fairy tales, whereas the rest of the scenery is composed of Photoshopped collages of photographs and three-dimensional digital compositions of the characters. In the scene where "The biggest, fattest wolf of all was playing an old wolf melody on Lucy's father's second best tuba," the reader sees a monochromatic, hand-drawn two-dimensional wolf playing a colorful, three-dimensional, digitally composed instrument. This image represents two different worlds interacting: the real and the imaginary, the old and the new. Throughout the narrative the wolves are consistently portrayed through these simplistic drawings against the backdrop of the realistic objects of the house. The ambiguous nature of the wolves is, thus, conveyed through the graphic component in the narrative.

An initial reading of this difference in artistic style could point towards the imaginary status of the creatures. But whether or not the wolves are imaginary, their effects on Lucy's family are verifiably real. Despite all of Lucy's warnings being dismissed as part of "an overactive imagination," the house does get taken over by wolves and the family is left homeless. The imaginary status of the wolves is never settled, as the cross-discursive narrative does not provide closure to the reader. McKean states, "as a general rule I don't really like illustrations that just literally show a selection of scenes from the story …

the imagery has its own job to do, then that is the ideal" (qtd. in French). Instead of merely illustrating action, the images in *The Wolves in the Walls* add a different layer of fantasy to the narrative. The contrast of artistic genres in the narrative, from the fantastic to the realistic, encourage the reader to question what exactly is real in the story—the same problem that haunts Lucy from the start.

The recurring question of veracity in Lucy's story is reminiscent of one of Aesop's fables: "The Boy Who Cried Wolf." The boy repeatedly tricks villagers into thinking that there is an imminent threat of attack by wolves, and, when they are fooled, laughs at them. They warn him against creating false rumors and when the wolves finally do attack his flock, no one believes him (Aesop). In Gaiman and McKean's story, Lucy is the girl who cries wolf, but instead of raising false alarm, like the anonymous boy in Aesop's fables, she is sincere. Nevertheless, she suffers the same fate and no one believes her. Whereas the boy in the fable has credibility from the start, only to lose it later on; Lucy's claim is only taken seriously when the wolves actually materialize, proving her right. This allusion to a known fable could be seen, then, as a particular feminist revision when one sees how, in a similar situation, a female protagonist must strive to provide proof of her account whereas a male protagonist is automatically considered credible.

Besides the obvious reference to Aesop's fable, the narrative of *The Wolves in the Walls* evokes other instances of intertextuality, such as Sigmund Freud's "The Uncanny" and Charlotte Perkins Gilman's "The Yellow Wallpaper." Freud defines the "uncanny" as "that class of the frightening which leads back to what is known of old and long familiar" (620). In his 1919 essay, the psychoanalyst describes at length the eerie feeling that is a mix of familiarity and strangeness, a feeling he names as "*das unheimlich*," or "uncanny" (620). Among the phenomena that can cause the uncanny feeling, Freud cites the "double," in which one is left to wonder about the true nature of identity and the self, such as when "the subject identifies himself with someone else, so [...] there is a doubling, dividing and interchanging of the self" (629–30). Once the wolf family expels Lucy's family and moves in, they become doubles of the original inhabitants of the house. The image of the wolves, wearing the family members' clothes, using their utensils, eating their food, and basically living *their* lives in *their* house is quite disturbing, particularly because they appear to be impersonating the previous homeowners. The wolves are doubles, or animal versions, of the family. By scaring off the invaders, the family exorcizes their wild selves.

Bringing Freud's concept of the uncanny to Gaiman's story sparks additional questions as to the nature of the wolves. Looking through this lens, *The Wolves in the Walls* is mostly about facing up to one's doubles or demons. As the wolves represent the family members' unrestrained selves come to life, the narrative is structured in a way in which the climax happens precisely when they are able to stand up against the invading animals and reclaim their territory. In this scenario, one can think of the animals as both real and unreal: they are a physical manifestation of the family's unconscious wild impulses. It makes sense, thus, that the mother, father, and brother keep repeating the cautionary saying about wolves to Lucy: "You know what they say about wolves, if the wolves come out of the walls, it's all over." And for them it is indeed, at least for a while, as they contemplate the idea of moving someplace else entirely and leaving the wolf-occupied house behind. Lucy changes their minds and refuses to give in to the wolves' occupation of their home and their lives. She is a strong female character that refuses to be passive in the face of difficulty or others' incredulity, a characteristic that sets her apart from a tradition of submissive feminine characters in children's narratives and fairy tales.

The trope of the distressed heroine seeking help is pervasive in literature and is one that Gaiman often appropriates and subverts in his works. As a female character whose story is widely discredited, Lucy has a lot in common with the female protagonist of Charlotte Perkins Gilman's "The Yellow Wallpaper." Gilman's 1892 short story famously expresses female anxieties in a paternalistic and oppressive environment through the first-person narration of a woman slowly going insane. Jane, the protagonist in "The Yellow Wallpaper," senses something in the house to which the others are oblivious. Jane feels something "queer" about the house, and in particular the wallpaper in the master bedroom, but despite relentless pleading with her husband she cannot convince him of the validity of her concerns (403). In both "The Yellow Wallpaper" and *Wolves*, the female protagonist cannot convince the family members of a dangerous situation, and is dismissed as having too much imagination. Lucy's father in *Wolves* tells her that she has an "overactive imagination" and the overbearing husband in "The Yellow Wallpaper" patronizes the protagonist by telling her that "nothing was worse for a nervous patient than to give way to such fancies" (Gilman 406). Both unlucky protagonists sense an evil presence in or on the walls of their homes—and like the Greek Cassandra, will not be believed. What sets both narratives apart is their outcome: Lucy's tale and leadership reclaim the house from the wolves whereas Jane enters the world inside her wall to her demise. In that sense, Lucy's story works as a feminist appropriation of all those narratives in which the female character is silenced, maybe even locked away in an attic or a room, and labeled insane.

Ladies of Paradox and of Never-You-Mind

The prayer-poem-lullaby *Blueberry Girl*, written by Gaiman and illustrated by Vess, is a much brighter and cheerful work than *The Wolves in the Walls*. The speaker of the prayer-poem addresses three female figures, seen on the first page, and pleads for good fortune and good sense for the blueberry girl in the future. There is no single blueberry girl in the art, which represents a myriad of girls, of different races, hair colors, and ages. The narrative is structured in the form of a prayer, an idea that came from Neil Gaiman's friend and collaborator Tori Amos, to whom he dedicated the work (Campbell 253). The written narrative does not reveal who the narrator is. Through the juxtaposition of visual and written discourses in the story, however, it is possible to infer that the speaker is a soon-to-be or new mother. The illustration on the title page shows an expectant mother, praying for her unborn daughter.[1] The image shows a pregnant woman in a blue dress, caressing her belly, sitting among blueberry shrubs with wild hares watching inquisitively at a distance. The same image appears at the end of the story, in its entirety, on the page containing the final line of the prayer (28–9). This time around she is sitting on a small island, wearing the same blue gown (pulled down to her shoulders as if she had just been breastfeeding), sitting at the base of a strong tree, which reestablishes the connection with the illustration on pages 2–3. The two-page spread shows animals circling her, including birds, squirrels, and even whales— all creatures big and small, from the air, the earth, and the water, that appear throughout the prayer. The animals form a circle around her, all the aquatic beings swimming clockwise around the island, forming a current. At the center of the image, the woman cradles a baby in her arms—this is the same image that appears on the half-title page (1). The two images that open and close the story reinforce the importance of this maternal figure in the narrative and suggest that it is her voice as the speaker. On the page following the end of the prayer, containing both Gaiman's and Vess's dedications, the same blue-clad woman appears again, now with a toddler playing in her arms as she lies in a bed of blueberry shrubs.

The prayer starts with the speaker addressing the "Ladies of light and ladies of darkness and ladies of never-you-mind," and declaring, "this is a prayer for a blueberry girl." The illustration on the left presents a trinity of women, of different ages, races, and attire, framed by a sliver of moon and a ring of stars, rising from the three trunks of a tree in the distance, at the bottom of the page. The towering figures hover with bowed heads and gently closed eyes, and quietly smile over an idyllic scenery of green fields and colorful sunset skies. Opposite this image, a young girl with her arms raised walks along a path from the tree, surrounded by all kinds of wild birds (owls, egrets, pheasants). The position of the three figures and the girl indicate that the women are the ladies the speaker is addressing and the little child is the blueberry girl for whom this prayer is intended. Following the invocation of the gods (a literary feature which frequently began ancient odes) the pregnant mother addresses her prayer to these three goddesses who are reminiscent of different religious traditions without directly corresponding to any in particular.

The written narrative starts off by subverting some of the restrictive dichotomies normally associated with female characters, such as good and evil, darkness and light, especially within the realm of children's tales. The speaker addresses these three female figures, but it does not situate them within those dichotomies, choosing instead to call forth all ladies. The addition of the third category, "ladies of never-you-mind," further resists binary classifications, including all belief systems, even using a sassy undertone—it is none of the reader's business. Those categories are normally imposed on women rather than self-proclaimed, and a lady of "never-you-mind" works as a refusal from the speaker to contribute to a system wherein powerful female figures are always already under an assigned role.

Furthermore, as the visual narrative suggests, the ladies are a trinity, a symbolic number corroborated by the three tree trunks below them, and one favored by Gaiman in his works through the repeated interest in the three-in-one. *Blueberry Girl* is no exception, as it abounds with multiple references of threes. Later in the story, the number three is reinforced again on a page where the written text is once more addressing the ladies directly ("Ladies of paradox, ladies of measure, ladies of shadows that fall") and the visual text displays three fairy-sized babies, crowned with blueberry leaves and fruits, resting within three warm-hued poppies. Intertextually speaking, the reference of a trinity of goddesses to Christian mythology is pretty evident in a narrative making use of the prayer form. Instead of the masculine trinity of the Father, the Son and the Holy Ghost, the three-part god of the Christian faith, the speaker addresses a trio of goddesses.

Perhaps the most prevalent reference the image of three female magical figures evokes is that of fairy godmothers commonly seen in fairytales. The classic model for the fairy godmother comes from Charles Perrault's *Cinderella* (1697), in which the godmother uses her magic to provide Cinderella with the opportunity to attend the prince's ball, and *Sleeping Beauty* (1696), in which the oversight in inviting one of the fairies curses the baby (Clute and Grant 330). *Sleeping Beauty* is particularly relevant to the prayer in *Blueberry*

Girl, for the danger of the spindle is one of the things the speaker asks the ladies to protect the girl from. One of the speaker's first requests of the ladies is to "keep her from spindles and sleeps at sixteen, nightmares at three or bad husbands at thirty," so that "these will not trouble her eyes." In *Sleeping Beauty,* Perrault's first fairy tale, the wicked fairy godmother's curse predicts that the princess will be pricked by a spinning needle and die. To save her, another fairy casts a counter spell that instead puts the princess in a deep sleep for a hundred years, after which a kiss from a prince will wake her up. The relation between spinning and the fairy godmothers in Perrault's fairy tale is an indication of their origin in the Fates from Greek mythology (Clute and Grant 330). The three female Fates spin, measure, and cut the thread of life, controlling a person's destiny. In *Blueberry Girl* the three goddesses addressed by the speaker have great power and, similarly to the complex figures of the Fates, cannot be reduced to manichaeist stereotypes of good and evil, light and darkness. Much like the fairy godmothers, or the three Fates, or even the three witches in Shakespeare's *Macbeth,* in *Blueberry Girl* the three ladies are "ladies of paradox," as the speaker addresses them. Vess's depiction of the ladies adds to that complexity by not purposefully signaling their identities: he does not draw them as Maiden, Mother, and Crone, for instance.

The ladies may evoke the idea of fairy godmothers, but the speaker clearly wishes to avoid the dangers that commonly afflict female protagonists of fairy tales. Besides the direct reference to "spindles and sleep," the speaker is intent on the idea that the blueberry girl stand out from the traditional role of a fairy tale heroine and be independent and make her own choices. Instead of resting the girl's fate in the hands of a prince, or of anybody else for that matter, the speaker asks the ladies to "[h]elp her to help herself, help her to stand, help her to lose and to find." She asks that the ladies protect and guide the blueberry girl, but, more particularly, the speaker wants them to "grant her [their] clearness of sight." This particular request is important because it is the one characteristic specifically associated with the ladies. The request is not simply for clearness of sight, it is for *their* clearness of sight. In this sense, "clearness of sight" expresses the desire of the speaker for the girl to see through appearances and beyond the surface. The traditional fairytale plot is, thus, again unsettled when the innocence of the protagonist will not necessarily be equated with naiveté. Later the speaker reinforces this particular request by implying that there is no one Truth, but rather "truth is a thing she must find for herself, precious and rare as a pearl." The depiction of the three ladies juxtaposes the written and visual discourse, adding new layers to the reading of the characters in a picture book. On the one hand, through the speaker's words, the written narrative describes the complexity of the ladies, how they cannot easily be cataloged. On the other, it is only through the illustrations that one gets the sense they form a trinity of goddesses, an important element of the narrative in terms of intertextual implications. Combined, the two types of discourse evoke new and unique meanings that would not surface if experienced independently by the reader.

"Words written clear on a wall"

Visually, *Wolves* and *Blueberry Girl* are strikingly different, each representative of their respective illustrator's medium, style, and strengths. The romantic visuals of *Blueberry Girl* are in stark contrast to the Gothic postmodern collages of *The Wolves in the Walls*. The two books, however, convey a similar feminist perspective through the complexities of their cross-discursivity. Both posit a rereading of traditional children's stories, such as fables and fairytales, while also responding to more adult references, such as Freud's concept of the uncanny and Greek mythology. Furthermore, the abundant use of metafictive elements, intertextuality, and self-referentiality both in the written language and in the visual text continually adds new layers to the works. Postmodern picture books invite readers of all ages to "generate multiple, often contradictory interpretations and to become coauthors in ways that traditional picture books do not offer" (Pantaleo and Sipe 4). *The Wolves in the Walls* and *Blueberry Girl* are, therefore, epitomes of postmodern picture books, for they invite multiple productions of meaning and challenge the reader to take part in the process and articulate these sometimes contradictory meanings.

Towards the end of *Blueberry Girl*, a line stands out in the flow of the narrative: "Words written clear on a wall." Unlike the rest of the text, where the speaker addresses the ladies directly on the blueberry girl's behalf, this particular line feels more like a statement than a plea. The illustration for the line occupies two pages, establishing its importance within the narrative, with the wall in question starting in the distance on the top left, continuing through the page, across the gutter, and fulfilling the majority of the following page on the right. The winding wall reaches, on the far left, the three-trunked tree that, as discussed previously, is symbolic of the trinity of ladies in the poem. Ultimately, "Words written clear on a wall" is also a metaphor for the cross-discursiveness of picture books and how they produce meaning. As a meta-narrative element, it refers to both the written language, "words written," and the visual one, "clear on the wall," without actually referencing what it is that should be clear. Differently than fairytales or fables, where the story is always bound to an explicit moral, in the narratives of picture books such as *The Wolves in the Walls* and *Blueberry Girl*, the meaning is left open for the reader to infer.

Note

1. *Blueberry Girl* does not have page numbers. For the purposes of this essay, the first page of the story, the half-title page, which shows the woman at the base of the tree with the book title is page 1, followed by the close-up of the woman in blue on page 2, etc.

Works Cited

Aesop. "The Boy Who Cried Wolf." *Aesop's Fables*. N.p. Web.

Anstey, Michele, and Geoff Bull. "The Picture Book: Modern and Postmodern." *International Companion Encyclopedia of Children's Literature*, 2d ed. I. Ed. Perter Hunt. London: Routledge, 2004. 328–339. Print.

Campbell, Hayley. *The Art of Neil Gaiman*. East Sussex: Harper Design, 2014. Print.

Clute, John, and John Grant, eds. *The Encyclopedia of Fantasy*. London: Orbit, 1997. Print.

Desai, Christina M. "Weaving Words and Pictures: Allen Say and the Art of Illustration." *The Lion and the Unicorn* 28.3 (2004): 408–428. Print.

French, Mike. "Interview with Dave McKean." *The View from Here*. n.d. Web. 10 Sept 2014.

Freud, Sigmund. "The Uncanny." *New Literary History* 7.3 (1976): 619–645. Print.

Gaiman, Neil. *Blueberry Girl*. New York: HarperCollins, 2009. Print.

_____. *The Wolves in the Walls*. New York: HarperCollins, 2003. Print.

Gilman, Charlotte Perkins. "The Yellow Wallpaper." *The Norton Anthology of Short Fiction*, 5th ed. Ed. R.V. Cassill. New York: W.W. Norton, 1995. Print.

Hatfield, Charles. "Comic Art, Children's Literature, and the New Comic Studies." *The Lion and the Unicorn* 30.3 (2006): 360–382. Print.

Kiefer, Barbara. "What Is a Picturebook, Anyway? The Evolution of Form and Substance Through the Postmodern Era and Beyond." *Postmodern Picturebooks: Play, Parody, and Self-Referentiality*. Ed. Lawrence R. Sipe and Sylvia Pantaleo. New York: Routledge, 2008. 9–21. Print.

Pantaleo, Sylvia, and Lawrence R. Sipe. "Introduction: Postmodernism and Picturebooks." *Postmodern Picturebooks: Play, Parody, and Self-Referentiality*. Ed. Sylvia Pantaleo and Lawrence R. Sipe. New York: Routledge, 2008. 1–8. Print.

Shakespeare, William. *Macbeth*. Ed. A.R. Braunmuller. Cambridge: Cambridge University Press, 1997. Print.

Shulevitz, Uri. *Writing with Pictures: How to Write and Illustrate Children's Books*. New York: Watson-Guptill, 1985. Print.

"The old man was gone": The Problematic Unity of Tricksters, Gods and Fathers in *Anansi Boys* and *American Gods*

Laura-Marie von Czarnowsky

Neil Gaiman's novels *American Gods* (2001) and *Anansi Boys* (2005) have a complicated relationship. While they share a core theme (the problematization of godly fatherhood), feature the same character (Anansi), and take place in the same fictional universe (where forgotten gods roam contemporary America), they differ wildly in scope, tone, and structure. As Andrew Lawless notes, "Like siblings, destined to be described in connection with each other, *Anansi Boys* and *American Gods* share common genes ... but have gone in different directions." When *Anansi Boys* was heading towards release, Gaiman said that he "worried a bit when [it] was being sold as if it was the *American Gods* sequel. And I kept walking around going (cough, grumble) it's, uh, not" (Gaiman in Crispin).

Gaiman began work on *Anansi Boys* before he wrote *American Gods*. The story opens with U.S.–born Londoner Fat Charlie coming to terms with his father's sudden death. Gaiman originally conceived the material in a conversation with British comedian Lenny Henry in the mid-nineties, when Henry complained about the lack of black people in horror movies. Gaiman began to plan a potential script for a horror story with black characters, but because he thought of casting his friend Henry as the protagonist Fat Charlie, it was "going to be funny. Because Lenny's funny" (Gaiman in Campbell 232).[1] However, writing *Anansi Boys* proved difficult.[2] Gaiman states:

> It wasn't alive, and I wasn't sure who these characters were. The only one who seemed interesting was Mr Nancy, and he wasn't much of a character, in that he was going to die before *Anansi Boys* started, or just as it started. So, I put it on the

back burner, not really being sure what it was. Then when I went to write *American Gods* ... it was fun to go and get Mr Nancy and put him in as a visiting guest star from something that I hadn't yet done! [Gaiman in Lawless].

Once *American Gods* was published, earning Mr. Nancy his debut appearance, Gaiman wrote the award-winning children's novella *Coraline* before finally returning to *Anansi Boys*. Prompted by his editor Jennifer Brehl, Gaiman decided to change the format and the text developed from a film script to a novella, expanding finally into a fully fledged novel (Lawless). Even with the changed medium, the text still retained much of Lenny Henry's voice. This culminated in Henry reading the audiobook version of the book, but more significantly, manifested in *Anansi Boys* having a very different tone from *American Gods*: it is a true comedy, and as such ends happily, with plenty of weddings and good humor.[3] One of the key features that generates the text's humor is the choice of deity that roams its pages: Mr. Nancy is none other than an American incarnation of Anansi; spider god, culture hero, charmer extraordinaire.

According to Emily Marshall, the god/folk hero originates among the Asante in Ghana ("Liminal Anansi" 30) and is seen as a figure who brings wisdom and knowledge while simultaneously being "the ultimate hoaxer, a cunning deceiver, a master of lies and malice" ("Anansi Syndrome" 127).[4] This paradoxical nature is one the defining characteristics of the trickster figure. In his seminal work on tricksters, Paul Radin postulates that the trickster

> represents not only the undifferentiated and distant past, but likewise the undifferentiated present within every individual. This constitutes his universal and persistent attraction. And so he became and remained everything to every man–god, animal, human being, hero, buffoon, he who was before good and evil, denier, affirmer, destroyer and creator. If we laugh at him, he grins at us [168–169].

Anansi Boys' Mr. Nancy is the poster boy of tricksters, a character who, despite the fact that he is recently deceased, does a lot of laughing and grinning. His mirth carries the book, which Gaiman has said to be at its core about surviving families, but Mr. Nancy's trickster nature also stands in direct contradiction with a traditional model of fatherhood that prescribes parental authority (Lawless).

One way of analyzing the father's role in his children's lives is to draw on French poststructuralist Jacques Lacan, who argues that a person's real father is also an embodiment of a male, gendered, paternally governed culture, i.e. what Lacan calls the symbolic order. Lacan thus discusses a double mode of fatherhood consisting of a person's actual father and also the larger "socio-symbolic law" he stands in for (Homer 57). Todd McGowan asserts that "[t]hough there always remains a distance between the actual flesh-and-blood father and the symbolic father, the actual father stands in for the latter, attempting to embody symbolic authority" (41). Interestingly, it is an "attempt": the real father may make mistakes that call his personal authority into question. This however does not diminish the way the socio-symbolic law operates and relies on a paternal metaphor in its ongoing implementation (McGowan 41). Sean Homer also forges a link between the internalization of the paternal metaphor and the existence of the Freud's concept of the superego, which governs all notions of morality and thus controls a person's behavior and desires (Homer 57). The abstract notion of a fatherly authority thus becomes synonymous with a person's conscience. The traditional model of fatherhood, drawing heavily on psychoanalysis, thus stands for paternal law, order, and conscience, all authoritatively enforced.

But "conscience" and "order" are not exactly concepts that are easily applied to Mr. Nancy, who dies drunk while singing karaoke and flirting with tourists many years his juniors. Instead, the reincarnated spider god is a different kind of father figure, and McGowan, drawing on Žižek, calls this the "anal" type.[5] This new model substitutes Freud's and Lacan's more authoritative interpretation of fatherhood with one of a joyful father who is obsessive with regard to his involvement in his children's life; he no longer inspires fear and facilitates acceptable behavior from afar, but from up close, where he monitors, but no longer prohibits enjoyment (McGowan 46). This new type of father, notable for his joyful nature, is a figure of desire and enjoyment. By virtue of his proximity to the child, the joyful father has been both rendered vulnerable in that his mistakes can be observed, and untouchable by criticism (because he invites subversion and thus automatically subverts it himself) (McGowan 46, 55). The joyful father is "a 'Teflon' master, to whom no critique can ever manage to stick" (53).

The father figure that roams the pages of *Anansi Boys* is certainly no all-dominating, all-ruling patriarch with an iron fist. Unlike many other mythological figures including Odin, with whom Mr. Nancy shares the stage in *American Gods*, Mr. Nancy is not an awe-inspiring creature and in this he matches the joyful father more than the Lacanian model. Diminutive in size and physical prowess, he is in many ways a "'man of the people' for there are no shrines, no worship for our hero. In the narratives, Ananse is stripped of any divine trait" (Tekpetey 75).[6]

In his contemporary guise as Mr. Nancy, Gaiman's spider god is an elderly gentleman with lemon yellow gloves, a green fedora, an abundant sense of humor and limitless *joie-de-vivre*, who charms everyone but his son. Mr. Nancy plays instructive pranks such as the Presidents' Day trick on his son, cheerfully breaks all the rules in the hospital by marching in with a New Orleans jazz band, and dies with his face in a tourist's décolletage. Charlie, bemoaning his father's lack of conventionality, points out to his fiancée Rosie "that his father was, he had no doubt, still the most embarrassing person on God's Green Earth" and "that he was perfectly happy not to have seen the old goat for several years" (*Anansi* 10f.).[7]

However, this embarrassed state is not permanent and reconciliation with the joyful father is on the horizon once the child grows up. This is one of the reasons why *Anansi Boys* can be productively read as Fat Charlie's coming-of-age story. Even though he is a grown-up during the novel's main plot, he has yet to come into his own. This is finally achieved when he embraces both his father's mythical and peculiar nature and adopts some of Anansi's character traits which he had hitherto suppressed. This is symbolized in two ways: first, Charlie quite literally finds his voice and becomes a singer in the end, following in his karaoke-belting father's footsteps. Second, Mr. Nancy passes his trademark green fedora on to Charlie during a one-off, post-death meeting in the spirit world, thus turning the hat into a family heirloom. Charlie is skeptical and initially refuses the hat, but Mr. Nancy is nothing if not convincing: "Son, all you need to wear a hat is attitude. And you got that. You think I'd tell you you looked good if you didn't? You look real sharp" (398). While Mr. Nancy is no stranger to tricking his son, he is sincere in this point: the hat fits. This moment thus also marks where Charlie is no longer tricked by his father because he is beginning to become a trickster himself.

Once Charlie accepts his father's hat, and thus his symbolic legacy, he joyfully embraces the odd little moments in life rather than finding them embarrassing. Ultimately, the novel shows how Fat Charlie affirms his father's charm, thus also affirming the principle of the "Teflon"-quality his father embodies. All it took for Mr. Nancy to tip the scales was to die, a state that Charlie, initially living in the mundane, non-mythical world, takes to be permanent, but that for tricksters such as Anansi is more a matter of choice.

Anansi thrives on his cleverness and derives his power not from being supernatural, but from outwitting and charming everyone else. This is partly what drew Gaiman to him: "The thing that made me happy was just the idea that really it represents the point where people stop trying to hit their way out of trouble and start trying to think their way out of trouble" ("Neil Gaiman Takes Questions"). Gaiman, who expresses a general fascination with tricksters, further explained that Anansi "seemed a natural. I needed a trickster in *American Gods*, I had a few in there already, but I wanted one we could just like and that was him" ("Neil Gaiman Takes Questions"). Anansi's likeability stems from his wit, humor, and outrageousness: he is so cheeky that one cannot help rooting for him, and the same applies to his contemporary re-imagining Mr. Nancy. Even his death is a party trick, though everyone keeps telling Charlie that his old man is gone for good. But the reader learns in the novel's conclusion that Mr. Nancy can very much return from the dead. As the old god is pondering the comfort of his coffin, he surmises that the grave "is an excellent place to get a little down time. Six feet down, best kind there is. Another twenty years or so, and he would have to think about getting up" (444). The eventual prospect of grandchildren promises to rouse him from the dead, which also shows that despite his absence for most of Fat Charlie's adult life, he is deeply invested in his family. The voluntary death, impermanent as it may be, also points to two related aspects of his character: namely his lack of sensitivity and his ungoverned desire.

Anansi, in both myth and in Gaiman's adaptation, can be read as the very embodiment of desire. In the oral stories analyzed by Marshall and included in modified form in *Anansi Boys* and *American Gods*, Anansi is all about the immediate fulfillment of his wishes. Every whim must be met, and it must be met promptly, irrespective of the logicality or cost. If he wants food or sex, then Anansi will get both immediately. If he wants recognition, he will trick a larger animal or tell a story about a previous trickery. If Anansi is angry, he will hurt the person who caused his anger. In his absolute lack of patience, Anansi behaves like a little child and thus the problematic relationship between the god and his paternal potential becomes apparent, for the father figure usually governs desire rather than lets it roam free.

Anansi's bottomless desire has lead Tekpetey, in his essay "Kweku Ananse: A Psychoanalytical Approach," to argue that the trickster god can be read as a personification of Freud's id (74). Tekpetey further argues that the other two elements of the Freudian psychoanalytical model are assumed by the audience of Anansi's tales. Anansi's exuberance and excess, his "unrestrained vitality" (81), has a cathartic function and is then in the manner of the ego and the superego moderated to an acceptable degree by the stories' audience (78). Within the novel, Fat Charlie assumes the function of the superego and Gaiman thus creates a process of role reversal. It is not the child that is in need of behavioral moderation, but the father. Yet Mr. Nancy is both a joyful father and a god, thus his refusal to let Charlie reduce his excesses culminates in an estrangement that is only healed by the old man's (apparent) death.

But Anansi's (and thus Mr. Nancy's) excessive nature does not automatically make him a bad father because it is one of the deity's character hallmarks that he exists precisely outside of a good vs. bad dichotomy. As Fat Charlie's mother reminisces when speaking about her former husband, "he's not a bad man.... Well, that's not exactly true. He's certainly not a good man" (*Anansi* 16). More to the point, however, is that Mr. Nancy is quiet simply *not a man* at all. Mrs. Higgler, one of the old ladies in Florida who knew that funny Mr. Nancy from down the street was really a god, tells Charlie he "can't judge [his father] like you would judge a man" (45). Different, and as is quite clearly implied, more forgiving standards apply. A godly father is not like a mortal father and all the things Fat Charlie holds against Mr. Nancy, such as the Presidents' Day trick, the nicknaming, and the scandalous way Mr. Nancy died, can be directly attributed to the trickster's wild and exuberant nature. Tekpetey finds that Anansi's limitless "energy can therefore be used indiscriminately ... for constructive and for destructive purposes" (81). While Charlie always thought of his father as destructively humiliating, Mr. Nancy genuinely cares for his son: "Humiliate you? I loved you," he insists (397). Mr. Nancy's humor might have been an embarrassment to Charlie, but it was not intended as such. Gaiman clearly emphasizes construction over destruction, as his modern incarnation of Anansi is exuberant, but not dangerous. Most importantly, this exuberance helps his son to finally come into his own and to accept the trickster within himself.[8] The novel advocates that an Anansi, any kind of Anansi, is necessary to hold darker gods such as Tiger at bay, thus attributing the trickster figure with a protective paternal quality. Once Mr. Nancy semi-dies, his position as a protector of people and stories is vacant and must be filled by his son. This is exemplified in Charlie tricking a dragon who is barring his path in the spirit world:

> The creature laughed, scornfully. "I," it said, "am afraid of nothing."
> "Nothing?"
> "Nothing," it said.
> Charlie said, "Are you *extremely* frightened of nothing?"
> "Absolutely terrified of it," admitted the Dragon.
> "You know," said Charlie, "I have nothing in my pockets. Would you like to see it?"
> "No," said the Dragon uncomfortably, "I most definitely would not."
> There was a flapping of wings like sails, and Charlie was alone at the beach.
> "That," he said, "was much too easy" [410].

This is a typical Anansi narrative in which a physically weaker character has to face off against a big bully, and the god's trademark use of "tricky wordplay and puns" secures the desired outcome (Marshall "Anansi Syndrome" 131). Charlie, in the tradition of his father, relies purely on wit, confidence, and wordplay to reach his goal with ease. One can argue that Mr. Nancy's death was entirely voluntary, and designed to help Charlie reconnect with his mythical side and become braver and happier once more.[9] This reading positions the god's death as a sacrifice for his son. The fact that it also allows Mr. Nancy some much needed downtime is just an added, but cleverly placed bonus.

While *American Gods* also uses sacrifice as a chief plot point, it does so in a different and notably darker way. Again, the sacrifice plays out between a godly father and his son, but the roles are reversed in the sense that it is the son that sacrifices himself for his father. Like Mr. Nancy, Shadow's father is a modern reincarnation of an old god, but one who is by no means as amusing or benevolent as Mr. Nancy.[10] Instead, he plays more into Lacan's conceptualization of the Name-of-the-Father: Gaiman rewrites Odin, whom Martin in his *Old Norse Concepts of the Fate of the Gods* calls "a complicated figure in the Norwegian and Icelandic sources," as he is simultaneously "the god of poetry, the lord of the slain, the god of war and the father of magic," into a variation of a trickster figure (76).

Odin, the All-Father, is a deity whose adventures and downfall are originally recounted in the *Prose Edda* and the *Poetic Edda*, and who, much like his fellow Norse god Loki, has a very successful and prolific life as a character in contemporary media.[11] Martin writes that Loki appears as Odin's "servant and sworn blood-brother, as a trickster, as a diabolical figure, as the *parens monstrorum*" (86). Gaiman extends all of this to Odin's character as well: while Odin is not exactly the most cheerful god to begin with, Gaiman turns him into a monster and that is achieved by having him violate the most basic law of human nature: parents love their children and must protect them.

Functioning as a father figure in a double sense, he is of course a manifestation of Lacan's symbolic father, for what is more symbolic than a god? However he also functions as an actual father as Odin to many sons. The best-known is the thunder god Thor, who is only mentioned in passing in *American Gods*. Wednesday describes him to Shadow:

> Big guy, like you. Good hearted. Not bright, but he'd give you the goddamned shirt off his back if you asked him. And he killed himself. He put a gun in his mouth and blew his head off in Philadelphia in 1932 [416].

Gaiman has placed another, lesser known son at the center of his text: Baldr, whose American reincarnation Shadow is.[12] The Norse god's fate is tragic: beloved by all, but killed by accident by his blind brother, Baldr cannot be saved by his otherwise omnipotent father. However, the myths explain that his eventual return from the dead serves "to bring in the new world order" (Martin 100).

American Gods plays with precisely this element of the myth and turns it on its head. Odin, who as a father is the giver of life, has always planned to use Shadow's death to reinstate the *old* world order, wherein he still had power. During their first meeting, Wednesday offers Shadow a job and includes an unusual caveat in the job description: "In the unlikely event of my death, you will hold my vigil" (40). Shadow agrees, unaware of three important pieces of information: Wednesday is a god, he is also Shadow's father, and the vigil consists of hanging on a tree without food or water for nine days; an experience so gruesome that it can only be designed to kill the vigil-bearer. This is precisely what Wednesday needs: the willing sacrifice of his child. The All-Father, the god of the slain, requires sacrifice. Mr. Nancy, guest-starring in *American Gods*, tries to warn Shadow about the danger of the vigil:

> "Shadow," he called. "You don't really have to do this. We can find somebody more suited. You ain't ready for this."
>
> "I'm doing it," said Shadow, simply.
>
> "You don't have to," said Mr. Nancy. "You don't know what you're lettin' yourself in for."
>
> "It doesn't matter," said Shadow.
>
> "And if you die?" asked Mr. Nancy. "If it kills you?" "Then," said Shadow, "it kills me."
>
> Mr. Nancy flicked his cigarillo into the meadow, angrily. "I said you had shit for brains, and you still have shit for brains. Can't see when somebody's tryin' to give you an out?" [491].

This passage is interesting in a number of ways. On the one hand, it shows that Shadow, much like his half-brother Thor, is absolutely willing to sacrifice himself for the benefit of others, even if it means his own death. Wednesday's children are entirely selfless. On the other hand, when taking Thor's fate into account, it implies that they also share suicidal tendencies. One reading advertises Wednesday's parental potential, the other speaks directly against it. The passage however also juxtaposes Wednesday and Mr. Nancy, and serves to further place this version of the spider god as constructive rather than destructive. Gaiman's Anansi does not care for senseless violence; in fact, he does his best to save Shadow and leaves angrily when his endeavor fails.

Consequently, Shadow follows through with the promise he made and holds Wednesday's vigil. He dies on the tree, and is brought back by the goddess Easter. During his brief stint in the afterlife, Shadow finally realizes that Wednesday is his father and that his sacrifice was orchestrated from his conception onwards. As Wednesday eventually reveals, "there's power in the sacrifice of a son–power enough, and more than enough to get the whole ball rolling" (575).[13] Almost mockingly, he adds: "To tell the truth, I'm proud of you" (575). This is a perversion of the father-son relationship, and one that marks Wednesday, unlike Mr. Nancy, as utterly destructive. What Wednesday expresses is not really pride in Shadow, but pride in the genius of his own plan and its seamless execution.

This ploy (as well as the larger con that positions the old gods against the new ones) positions Odin as a fellow trickster, which however does not necessarily subvert the original myths. According to John McKinnell:

> The protagonist in myths of exploitation is usually Óðinn. [...] he boasts that he knows spells which enable him to win and keep a woman's love; but his own motivation is usually calculating rather than passionate. [...] his usual aim is to beget a son who will be a defender of the gods, a just avenger, or the founder of a human dynasty [147].

Gaiman's Mr. Wednesday too is a man of exploitation: from hapless waitresses to his own son, he takes advantage of everyone he meets. Unlike the Odin of myth, however, he does not care to defend other gods; on the contrary, he wants their sacrifice to sustain his power. And yet, his son takes on precisely the role the Odin of myth had in mind for his progeny. Shadow surpasses his father's plotting and becomes a savior and an avenger. When Shadow not only comes back from the ordeal of the vigil, but also stops the battle of the gods, which Wednesday was relying on to further feed his energy, it is Mr. Nancy who takes care of him, assuming a paternal role that Wednesday never really inhabited: "That was a good job. Proud of you. You done good, kid" (584). This is even more significant because Mr. Nancy explicitly did not want Shadow to risk his life, but admires his perseverance and the outcome anyway. As the spider god and Shadow return to Mr. Nancy's home in Florida, the trickster also returns to his master-of-excess form and takes Shadow drinking and karaoke singing. This causes Shadow to re-examine the spider god with "fascinated embarrassment," thus beautifully prefiguring both Mr. Nancy's death in *Anansi Boys* and the problem of embarrassing fathers that the comedy so successfully deals with (592). Shadow's and Mr. Nancy's evening in the karaoke bar also serves as a father-son bonding moment; the only problem is that is not undertaken by people who are actually related to each other. As Mr. Nancy stands in for Wednesday, Shadow stands in for Fat Charlie, whom Mr. Nancy describes as "a good boy" whom he does not see often enough (594).

Ultimately, even though *Anansi Boys* opens with Fat Charlie describing the relationship to his father as disastrous, Mr. Nancy and his son have much in common and share a complicated, but deep bond. This means that *Anansi Boys* is a novel about reconciliation, whereas *American Gods* is about letting go. *Anansi Boys* eloquently discusses incorporating the personalities of one's parents into one's own, cherry-picking their admirable traits and thus continuing what is best about a family (or, in Anansi's case, his bloodline), while *American Gods* tells the tale of Shadow's liberation from his father's plans. In a way, Gaiman's statement about *Anansi Boys* being about surviving one's family extends to *American Gods* as well, only that here the survival is literal. Shadow successfully lives through and past his father's plans.

McKinnell, speaking about the mythical Odin, finds that he is the "'Father of All,' but is helpless to prevent his own inevitable downfall" (31). This, perhaps more than anything, aligns Odin with the authoritative father. Returning to the intersection of actual and the symbolic father, Shadow effectively destroys the former by devaluating the latter. As McGowan asserts,

> The authority of the symbolic father depends on collective belief in his power. This is why the subversion of this father is a relatively straightforward matter. It consists of simply showing that the father doesn't really have the strength that he pretends to have [53].

Shadow does so by recovering and revealing Wednesday's plot and thus, with no further support to be gained, Wednesday fades into nothingness. In that, it mirrors Fat Charlie's encounter with the dragon, which he leaves saying that "this was too easy" (410). Shadow faces off against two gods, but because he has already lost everything, he has "nothing" in his pockets and this lack of fear, of emotional investment, paradoxically lets him win. He reveals to the other gods that there was nothing going on, and that there is nothing to be gained for anyone but Loki and Mr. Wednesday. Unlike Mr. Nancy, Wednesday really does die. In the novel's postscript, Shadow does however meet the Icelandic version of Odin, hence showing that even if one iteration of the deity has been destroyed, others still roam free. What killed Wednesday then was not so much the wound he suffered, but the cessation of everyone's belief in him as an All-Father. His final con backfired.

Lynn Gelfand rightly notes that Gaiman amplifies "the subtler trickster qualities associated with the Norse God," but in the end, Gaiman negates both Wednesday's paternal *and* his trickster potential (227). As a father, he has failed by being willing to sacrifice his son for his own gain. As a trickster, he is lacking an essential component because "[t]he universal characteristic of Trickster is his humorous take on a situation and the resolution of that situation through humor. Humor is the energy which upsets the apple cart" (Tannen 137). Wednesday is like a person whose laugh does not reach his eyes; the affable nature he occasionally presented was nothing more than a trick, and it needs more than one trick to be a true trickster. Tekpetey postulates that

Anansi tales serve "as tension-relieving aesthetic devices," and by helping Shadow, one can argue that Mr. Nancy manages to turn a significant portion of *American Gods* into an Anansi tale and himself into a reaffirming father figure (74).

Gaiman thus advocates a modern kind of father figure: involved, caring, mischievous, and perhaps a little bit embarrassing. *Anansi Boys* is not called *Anansi's Boys* for a reason: rather than being possessive, Anansi describes the infectious charm of the trickster figure. Anansi thus becomes an adjective, a desirable quality that Charlie consequently acquires as well, and that Wednesday, paternal traitor and failed symbolic father, never manages to get a grasp on.

Notes

1. Henry was also involved in prompting Gaiman to write *Neverwhere*. For more information, see Campbell, p. 210.

2. While the writing process was initially problematic, Gaiman says that "the research was the fun bit"(5). He largely drew on an unspecified 1922 book about Jamaican folk stories, which was important "as much for tone of voice as for content, but also because so many of the Anansi stories told today have been cleaned up by being told to children" ("Conversation with Neil Gaiman"). This also mirrors a trend in fairy tales which are too often heavily sanitized and censored in order to be made "suitable" for children. In his short story "Snow, Glass, Apples," Gaiman very much writes against this kind of adaptation, instead amplifying the horror. Gaiman's Anansi too resists political correctness and his outrageous nature informs much of the novel's humor.

3. Henry also participated in the BBC World Service radio play, which Gaiman has since expressed dissatisfaction with because it condensed the narrative into one hour and thus drastically changed the story ("Normal Service").

4. Regarding the physical paradox of Anansi being both spider and person, Tekpetey notes, "Even though Ananse is a spider, he is presented in the stories told about him as an *everyman* or *everyone*, and attention is seldom drawn to his spider nature, his *spider-ness*" (75). In the Anansi tales that intersperse the contemporary plot line of *Anansi Boys*, the narrator points precisely to this complex characterization: "You want to know if Anansi looked like a spider? Sure he did, except when he looked like a man" (54).

5. McGowan uses "anal" in the sense of "obsessive" in this context and he does not develop a connection to Freud's anal phase of child development.

6. Tekpetey deliberately uses the Akan spelling "Ananse" rather than "Anansi." In some of the African, Jamaican, and American versions, the trickster usually goes by Anansi, making this the more conventional spelling.

7. Gaiman, himself a father of three, notes that "every father is embarrassing. It just comes with the territory. I have a daughter that is so embarrassed by me that in order to not embarrass her if I'm taking her to school, I have to turn off the music in the car before the door opens so that the kids cannot hear whatever it was that was playing because, 'Oh my God Dad, that is so embarrassing'" (Gaiman in Flanagan).

8. Mr. Nancy's benign nature is one area where he differs from both Anansi the mythological figure, and Wednesday, the other godly father in Gaiman's mythological novels.

9. Charlie's mythical side is externalized in his magically created brother Spider. As the novel progresses, the two brothers interact more and more, and Charlie too draws on magic, while Spider becomes a little more ordinary. Interestingly, the two are not merged into one person again, even though they started as such. Charlie was only robbed of his magical side when Mrs. Dunwiddy, a witch from the neighborhood, was so annoyed with his troublemaking that she pulled the magic out of him and sent it away. The magic took the shape of Spider, who consequently became a person in his own right.

10. Mr. Nancy's and Mr. Wednesday's names are deliberately constructed in a similar way. Neither operate on a first name basis, thus retaining the honorific "Mr..". Furthermore, they play with a connection with the days of the week, for as Marshall points out that "amongst the Asante Anansi had a day-name, and was named Kwaku Anansi, meaning Wednesday-born" ("Liminal Anansi" 31). Similarly, Mr. Wednesday derives his week name from the Germanic version of his name Wotan, which then became Wotansdaag and was anglicized as Wednesday.

11. The *Prose* and the *Poetic Edda* are two thirteenth-century Icelandic books that recount Norse mythology.

12. Shadow's own mythology as Baldr is also one of the central topic of Gaiman's novella "The Monarch of the Glen," published in his anthology *Fragile Things* in 2006.

13. Mr. Hinzelmann is yet another deity whom Gaiman positions between fatherhood (Hinzelmann is a symbolic father of Lakeside) and tricksterhood. Like Wednesday, the initially benevolent seeming Hinzelmann requires blood sacrifice to maintain his power.

Works Cited

Campbell, Hayley. *The Art of Neil Gaiman*. New York: Harper Design, 2014. Print.

"A Conversation with Neil Gaiman." *Anansi Boys*. By Neil Gaiman. New York: HarperCollins, 2008. Print.

Crispin, Jessica. "An Interview with Neil Gaiman." *Bookslut*. October 2006. Web. 25 May 2014.

Flanagan, Mark. "Neil Gaiman Interview." *About.com Contemporary Literature*. 9 September 2005. Web. 25 May 2014.

Gaiman, Neil. *American Gods. The Author's Preferred Text*. London: Headline Review, 2005 [2001]. Print.

_____. *Anansi Boys*. London: Headline Review, 2006 [2005]. Print.

_____. "Neil Gaiman Takes Questions on *Anansi Boys*." NPR, the Bryant Park Project. 9 June 2008. Web. 25 May 2014.

_____. "Normal service will be resumed as soon as possible." Neil Gaiman's Journal. 23 June 2010. Web. 5 May 2014.

Gelfand, Lynn. "The End of the World as We Know It: Neil Gaiman and the Future of Mythology." *The Mythological Dimensions of Neil Gaiman*. Eds. Anthony S. Burdge, Jessica Burke and Kristine Larsen. Crawfordville: Kitsune Books, 2012. 223–239. Print.

Homer, Sean. *Jacques Lacan*. New York: Routledge, 2005. Print.

Lawless, Andrew. "Using Genre to Effect." *Three Monkeys Online*. 1 August 2005. Web. 25 May 2015.

Marshall, Emily Zobel. "'The Anansi Syndrome': A Debate Concerning Anansi's Influence on Jamaican Culture." *World Literature Written in English* 39.1 (2001): 127–136. Print.

_____. "Liminal Anansi: Symbol or Order and Chaos. An Exploration of Anansi's Roots Amongst the Asante of Ghana." *Caribbean Quarterly* 53.3 (2007): 30–40. Print.

Martin, John Stanley. *Ragnarok. An Investigation into Old Norse Concepts of the Fate of the Gods*. Assen: Van Gorcum & Comp, 1972. Print.

McGowan, Todd. *The End of Dissatisfaction? Jacques Lacan and the Emerging Society of Enjoyment*. Albany: State University of New York Press, 2004. Print.

McKinnell, John. *Meeting the Other in Norse Myth and Legend*. Cambridge: D.S. Brewer, 2005. Print.

Radin, Paul. *The Trickster: A Study in Native American Mythology*. New York: Schocken Books, 1956. Print.

Tannen, Ricki Stefanie. *The Female Trickster: The Mask That Reveals. Post-Jungian and Postmodern Psychological Perspectives on Women in Contemporary Culture*. London: Routledge, 2007. Print.

Tekpetey, Kwawisi. "Kweku Ananse: A Psychoanalytical Approach." *Research in African Literatures* 37.2 (2007): 74–82. Print.

"You heard her, you ain't blind": The "Haunting" Presence of *Their Eyes Were Watching God*

DANIELLE RUSSELL

"You got tuh *go* there tuh know *there*. Yo' papa and yo' mama ... can't tell yuh and show yuh ... everybody's got tuh ... find out about livin' fuh theyselves."—Zora Neale Hurston, *Their Eyes Were Watching God*

"EACH PERSON WHO EVER WAS OR IS OR WILL BE HAS A SONG. It isn't a song that anybody else wrote ... it has its own words."—Neil Gaiman, *Anansi Boys*

Neil Gaiman's "Note" on the dedication page of *Anansi Boys* offers an intriguing but cryptic "tip [of] his hat respectfully to the ghosts of Zora Neale Hurston, Thorne Smith, P. G. Wodehouse, and Frederick 'Tex' Avery." The haunting presence of Hurston's work in Gaiman's novel is particularly striking. Referring to *Folklore, Memoirs, & Other Writings* (which contains Hurston's folklore collections and her autobiography), Gaiman acknowledges, "I came across Hurston while researching folklore for *American Gods*. She was quoted everywhere, and once I looked her up, I realized I had to read everything she ever wrote. She is an amazing source for African-American folk stories, and her writing is an absolute delight" (quoted in Spinrad "ReadMe"). Hurston's influence on Gaiman, the "Note" confirms, was not limited to *American Gods*. Her ground-breaking literature on African American and Caribbean folklore is well documented and, although Gaiman does not draw on a particular tale, Hurston's exploration of the trickster figure is evident in *American Gods* and *Anansi Boys*. While it is unclear whether or not Gaiman achieved his goal of reading "everything she ever wrote," there is a strong suggestion in *Anansi Boys* that he has read Hurston's *Their Eyes Were Watching God*. Charles McArthur

Taylor dismissively categorizes "the Zora Neale Hurston influence" in *Anansi Boys* as "a series of warmed-over 'folk' fables in which animals act out various human follies" (30). Such an approach fails to recognize both the narrative potential of folklore *and* the influential power of Hurston's fiction.

Published in 1937, *Their Eyes Were Watching God* follows Janie Crawford's journey of self-discovery. Although Hurston marks each phase of Janie's development by her involvement with a particular man, she resists the formula of a woman finding "Mr. Right" who will make everything right. Having survived two oppressive marriages (Logan Killicks physically isolates her and Joe Starks socially isolates her), Janie meets the man who will reintroduce her to the community. Tea Cake, however, will not survive. Janie must shoot her rabid lover in order to avoid his fate. While Janie must leave the community in order to grow, it is equally important that she return to it. She shares her hard-earned wisdom with her friend Phoeby (who will then carry the tale to the community).

Their Eyes Were Watching God and *Anansi Boys* make for an unlikely comparison, yet the parallels between the novels demand attention. Initially, Janie and Fat Charlie are silenced and oppressed; each must discover an authentic voice in order to achieve a complete life. In this quest for a voice, each must avoid the temptation of becoming a domineering voice (like Janie's second husband Joe Starks or Fat Charlie's adversary Tiger who lays claim to all the stories). By the end of their respective novels, Janie and Fat Charlie speak for, and to, their communities; their stories are life-affirming tales. Hurston's innovative use of the oral, communal tradition of folklore is also woven into *Anansi Boys*.

Gaiman clearly recognizes and appreciates Hurston's experimental approach; both *Their Eyes Were Watching God* and *Anansi Boys* are "speakerly texts." The term is defined by Henry Louis Gates, Jr., as a "text whose rhetorical strategy is designed to represent an oral literary tradition" and "produce the illusion of oral narration" (181). Despite the fact that both authors employ third person narrators, oral (and aural) communities are crucial to their stories. Each of their central characters must "find out about livin' fuh theyselves" (Hurston 183); in the process, Janie Crawford and Fat Charlie learn to "sing their own song" (Gaiman 164).[1] The paths Janie Crawford and Fat Charlie take to discover their songs and learn about living are quite different. Janie endures two oppressive marriages and the loss of her true love. The son of a god, Fat Charlie must battle magical adversaries as well as his own insecurities. And yet, both characters draw upon folklore to empower themselves: Janie's resource is a communal, cultural knowledge while Fat Charlie must discover his lost personal history (that is at the heart of that cultural knowledge) and claim his own "god-voice" (Gaiman 79).

Fat Charlie and Janie live fragmented existences until crucial catalysts enter their lives. The division is both internally and externally imposed. Whereas her first husband, Logan Killicks, physically isolated Janie through the remoteness of his farm and the austerity of his lifestyle, Joe Starks alienates Janie from the community along class lines. He makes good on his promise to show her "what it was to be treated lak a lady" (Hurston 28). Joe makes a concentrated effort to isolate her: he forbids her to make speeches, proclaiming "mah wife don't know nothin' 'bout no speech-makn.' Ah never married her for nothin' lak dat. She's uh woman and her place is in de home" (40–41). Nor does he allow her to join in conversations, despite the fact that "Janie loved the conversation and sometimes she thought up good stories ... but Joe had forbidden her to indulge. He didn't want her talking after such trashy people" (50). Janie's silence, at this point, is an obligation imposed by her domineering husband; to keep the peace, she holds her tongue. It is a means of staving off trouble.

Fat Charlie opts for silence as a way of staving off embarrassment, not violent criticism. He seeks to deny, or at least avoid, those all-too-humbling human foibles—both his own and his father's—that lead to "a parade of indignities, each one of which made his toes curl involuntarily" (5). His father's appearance prompts the fantasy that "the earth would open and swallow him up, or failing that, that he might suffer a brief, merciful and entirely fatal heart attack" (9). Clearly, Fat Charlie's father is his most excruciating source of humiliation but the discomfort is not restricted to the personal: "if something that even looked like it might be embarrassing was about to happen on his television screen Fat Charlie would leap up and turn it off ... [or] he would leave the room on some pretext" (18–19). If this was the extent of his response to embarrassment, Fat Charlie would merely be socially awkward. However, he allows it to reach a debilitating level. Caught singing in the office—and complimented no less—Fat Charlie's cheeks burn and he dodges human contact by focusing on his paperwork (60). In fact, his daydream is "to be able to sing without embarrassment, somewhere there were never any people around to hear him" (61). Fear severely limits Fat Charlie; he denies himself the pleasure of his talent because of his dread of an audience.

Janie attempts to utilize silence strategically by becoming her own audience. She learns to manipulate language and silence as survival tactics. In the face of Joe's all-encompassing world view, his wife "didn't change her mind but she agreed with her mouth" (59). Duplicity protects Janie both from Joe's temper and her own self-betrayal. She "pressed her teeth together and learned to hush" (67). This stance of outwardly agreeing while inwardly rebelling creates a divided life. Janie protects herself by adopting a mask in public:

[She] watched the shadow of herself going about tending store and prostrating itself before [Joe], while all the time she herself sat under a shady tree with the wind blowing through her hair…. After a while it got so common she ceased to be surprised. It was like a drug. In a way it was good because it reconciled her to things. She got so she received all things with the solidness of the earth which soaks up urine and perfume with the same indifference [73].

Janie's silence is a kind of self-medication: numbing herself allows her to function. It does not, however, allow her to thrive. The "reconciliation" is a delusion. This divided life cannot be sustained and, in fact, it is through a public speech that Janie challenges Joe's authority to define her.

Janie's shadow life begins with an act of violence. Joe slaps her and her image of him "tumbled down and shattered," leaving Janie with "an inside and an outside … suddenly she knew how not to mix them" (68). Unbeknownst to him, Fat Charlie's divided life also begins with a violent sundering of self. In denying his own song, Fat Charlie also splits himself into an "inside and an outside," but he will soon discover that he is literally living a divided life. What he initially mistakes for a photo of himself—"aged perhaps five or six years old, standing beside a mirrored door, so it looked at first glance as if two little Fat Charlies [were] side by side"—leads to the discovery that he has a brother (30). Yet Spider is not just any old brother: he is the one who "got all that god stuff" (33); "he was slick, he was fly, he was smart" (51); "there was something larger-than-life about him … [that] made Fat Charlie feel awkward and badly constructed and slightly foolish" (56). In short, Spider is everything Fat Charlie wishes to be, and, it turns out, could be. Fat Charlie discovers that Spider is a part of himself. Mrs. Dunwiddy confesses, "I pull Spider out of you, to teach you a lesson…. I break him off from you. All the tricksiness. All the wickedness" (234–235). Fat Charlie and Spider are the embodiment of a divided self. Unlike Janie, the division is forced onto Fat Charlie but he too must step out of his shadow life—of his own fears, of the intimidating divinities who are his father and brother—and claim the right to determine his own identity.

In both novels, the turning points hinge on speech acts which lead to violence. Janie is provoked by Joe's insults and retaliates; vengeance is hers, albeit at a price. In response to Joe's taunts about her age, Janie asserts:

"Naw, Ah ain't no young gal no mo' but den Ah ain't no old woman neither. Ah reckon Ah looks mah age too. But Ah'm uh woman every inch of me, and Ah know it. Dat's uh whole lot more'n *you* kin say. You big-bellies round here and put out a lot of brag, but 'tain't nothin' to it but yo' big voice. Humph! Talkin' 'bout *me* lookin' old! When you pull down yo' britches, you look lak de change uh life."

"Great God from Zion!" Sam Watson gasped. "Y'all really playin' de dozens tuh-night."

"Wha-whut's dat you said?" Joe challenged, hoping his ears had fooled him.

"You heard her, you ain't blind," Walter taunted [75].

This act of social and sexual exposure effectively deflates Joe's public presence. Silent, submissive Janie yields to her anger and takes no prisoners. Joe's attempt to reassert his masculinity is inarticulate, and ultimately ineffectual: "he struck Janie with all his might and drove her from the store" (76). Despite the fact that she is irrevocably alienated from her husband, the act of defending herself is liberating for Janie.

Fat Charlie's speech act is equally careless. In an effort to rid himself of Spider, Fat Charlie strikes a deal with the Bird Woman. He asks her to make Spider "go away and leave me alone. I don't want you to hurt him or anything" (152). She rephrases his statement, eliciting the more ominous: "I give you Anansi's blood line" (153). Such is Fat Charlie's disconnect from his own life, that he fails to realize that *he* is part of that blood line. The subsequent violence is focused on, but not limited to, Spider. Fat Charlie inadvertently unleashes Tiger's desire for vengeance through his careless conversation with the Bird Woman. Much like Janie's action, Fat Charlie's ill-conceived act of self-defense is ultimately liberating. Rectifying the chaos he has unwittingly instigated requires Fat Charlie to develop the powers he has denied—to accept Spider's assertion that he is "Dad's son" too (241).

While Janie and Fat Charlie initially appear to be empowered by their speech acts—Janie is ignored by Joe and Fat Charlie's luck seems to change, his confidence grows—the pair remain in a precarious state of limbo. Janie has a final, verbal confrontation with her husband on his death bed. Despite recognizing his reluctance to hear her out, Janie insists on being heard: "Ah knowed you wasn't gointuh lissen tuh me. You changes everything but nothin' don't change you" (82). She accuses him of oppressing her: "Mah own mind had tuh be squeezed and crowded out tuh make room for yours in me" (82). Most significantly, Janie recognizes the danger of his dream to "be a big voice" at the expense of his humanity (27). She tries to make him see that "you got tuh pacify somebody besides yo'self if you wants any love and sympathy in dis world. You ain't tried tuh pacify *nobody* but yo'self. Too busy listening tuh yo' own big voice" (82). The insight comes too late for Joe (and therefore smacks of cruelty) but it is a warning to Janie. Widowhood affords her the opportunity to redefine herself, but she needs to discover a different kind of language: enter Tea Cake.

If Joe Starks represents the language that wounds, then Tea Cake symbolizes the healing power of words. As their relationship grows, "new thoughts had tuh be thought," Janie tells her friend Pheoby, "and new words said.... He done taught me de maiden language all over" (109). Looking like the "love thoughts of women," Tea Cake is the "bee" to her "bloom" that Janie has been waiting for since she was sixteen (101). Equally important is the fact that Tea Cake's entrance enables Janie to break from the isolation imposed by Joe. Tea Cake helps to socialize Janie. He reintroduces her to the community through laughter and conversation, not as combat, but play: "they played away the evening.... Everybody was surprised at Janie playing checkers but they liked it. Three or four ... coached her moves and generally made merry with her in a restrained way" (97). The social interaction is Janie's first, tentative step towards a new identity.

With lives on the line, social interaction for Fat Charlie carries a greater intensity. He and his brother are being stalked by Tiger and his human cohort (the sociopath Grahame Coats). In this context, language takes on a heightened importance. Despite the serious situation, the language Fat Charlie must master also resonates with laughter. Confronted by an armed Coats, Fat Charlie joins the hotel entertainers, singing "to buy himself some time" (278). Oddly enough, the formerly frightened young man "smiled and he sang, and as he sang he knew, without any shadow of a doubt, that everything was going to be all right" (279). Nor is the reassurance limited to Fat Charlie; the song reaches the captive Spider: "somewhere someone was singing.... And the song made Spider smile. He found himself wishing that he still had a tongue: he'd stick it out at the tiger.... The thought gave him strength" (281). Galvanized by the song, Spider taps into his own strength and sense of humor; the two are connected as Fat Charlie will soon discover. Like Janie, he must step out of his stance of silence and claim the power and pleasure of his own voice.

In his quest to rescue Spider, Fat Charlie must "slay" a dragon. Accessing his trickster lineage, Fat Charlie enacts a new Anansi story full of "wit and trickery and wisdom" as he finally grasps what his father has known: that the stories encourage people to "*think* their way out of problems" (252–253). Building on the creature's assertion that he is "frightened of nothing," Fat Charlie asks, "Are you *extremely* frightened of nothing?" The dragon concedes it is "absolutely terrified of it." Fat Charlie then drives home the punch line with a challenge, "You know ... I have nothing in my pocket. Would you like to see it?" (303–304). This final blow defeats the dragon and it departs without consuming Fat Charlie. The shift in power is the result of Fat Charlie's new-found sense of humor and ability to manipulate language. Continuing on his mission, for the first time in his life, he composes a tune:

> Charlie had always wanted to make up songs, but he never did, mostly because ... someone would have asked him to sing it, and that would not have been a good thing, much as death by hanging would not be a good thing. Now, he cared less and less, and he sang his song to the fireflies, who followed him.... He hoped the fireflies were enjoying it: their light seemed to be pulsing and flickering in time with the tune [304].

Fat Charlie begins to embrace the creative value of language at this point. Rather than allowing the fear of performing to stifle his desire, he confidently indulges in the creative act. Interestingly, he considers the effect his song is having on the fireflies. In so doing, Fat Charlie avoids Joe Starks's mistake of becoming a "big voice" unwilling to "pacify nobody" (Hurston 82). In asserting his own voice, Fat Charlie takes into account the needs of his audience. His personal expression is not an act of oppression; unlike Joe's determination to impose his worldview on his audience, Fat Charlie's song even incorporates the fireflies.

Fat Charlie and Janie recognize the need for a sympathetic audience *and* a sympathetic speaker. Confronted with life-threatening situations, both characters must adapt their words to the needs of their listeners. On trial for shooting Tea Cake, Janie "had to remember ... she was not at home" as she explains the events; her fear is not conviction but "misunderstanding. If they made a verdict that she didn't want Tea Cake and wanted him dead, then that was a real sin" (178–179). Janie shapes her testimony to her audience—the white judicial system—and maintains her liberty. There is another, more intimate audience which she must address in order to be truly free: the members of the Black community who "were there with their tongues cocked and loaded, the only real weapon left to weak folks" (176). Janie's official testimony does not sway this audience; instead she must use a symbolic language to impress upon them the depth of her love for Tea Cake and her sorrow over his death. Tea Cake's funeral is an elaborate affair fit for "the son of Evening Sun" (180). It functions as a bridge between Janie and the community: "Sop and his friends had tried to hurt her but she knew it was because they loved Tea Cake and didn't understand ... the day of the funeral they came with shame and apology in their faces. They wanted her quick forgetfulness. So they filled up and overflowed the ten sedans that Janie had hired.... And Tea Cake rode like a Pharaoh to his tomb" (180). The richness and sincerity of the ceremony reconciles the community and Janie. She maintains her sympathy for their suffering and they extend their sympathy for her pain.

Both in life and in death, Tea Cake teaches Janie about the healing power of language. Fat Charlie's father fulfills a similar function in his life. Initially, Fat Charlie fails to see the value of his chief source of embarrassment but he learns to draw upon him as a source of wisdom and strength. Confronting his dead father, Fat Charlie discovers, "the important thing about songs is that they're just like stories. They don't mean a damn unless there's people listenin' to them" (293). The sight of his audience terrifies Fat Charlie and he can only issue "a small croaking noise." He considers fleeing until he spots his father: "The old man winked when he caught Charlie's gaze. It wasn't much, but it was enough" (320). Reinvigorated, Fat Charlie launches into song and saves the day. He assumes, not his father's mantle, but his trademark fedora—which soon becomes *his* trademark fedora (331). The reconciliation of father and son is further symbolized by a scene involving Fat Charlie and his son Marcus. It echoes a previous exchange between Fat Charlie and his father. Having sung with the very mermaid his father tried to point out to the child Fat Charlie, "Charlie began to do a sand-dance in his bare feet, soft-shoe shuffling through the sand" (333). Instead of viewing his father as an embarrassment (as Fat Charlie did), Marcus joins in: "together the man and the boy danced their way back up the sand to the house, singing a wordless song that they made up as they went along" (334). The book ends with father and son in harmony, signaling that Fat Charlie has made peace with his own father.

The journey to that harmony is therapeutic, not only for Fat Charlie and those close to him, but also for the world. In claiming the "stories," Fat Charlie prevents Tiger from doing so. It is a key victory for more than Anansi's line. Tiger's stories, Fat Charlie's father asserts, "began in tears, and they'd end in blood, and they were the only stories that people of this world knew" (252). The dark and hopeless nature of the stories is particularly troubling. He continues, "People take on the shapes of the songs and the stories that surround them" (252). The stories shape reality—a point reinforced by Fat Charlie's pivotal performance. Despite "really, *really* never" liking Rosie's mother, Fat Charlie and Spider brave the "beginning of the world" to help heal her (318). Fortified by his father and supported by Spider, "He sang of names and words, of the building blocks beneath the real, the words that make worlds, the truths beneath the way things are; he sang of appropriate ends and just conclusions for those who would have hurt him and his. He sang the world" (321). The scope of the song is expansive. Fat Charlie begins with the call to "listen to my life" but ends by creating a "world" that incorporates "all the creatures listening" (321).

The power to create a world is literal for Fat Charlie but Janie's power also has the potential to provoke change. She tells her story to her "kissin' friend" Pheoby, who is "eager to feel and do through Janie, but hating to show her zest for fear it might be thought mere curiosity" (6). More than merely sympathetic, Pheoby wishes to immerse herself in Janie's account of her experiences. She is clearly moved by the narrative, proclaiming, "Ah done growed ten feet higher from jus' listenin' tuh you, Janie. Ah ain't satisfied wid mahself no mo'" (182–183). Janie's story is a catalyst for her listener, although, at this point, her reaction is "tuh make Sam take me fishin' wid him after this. Nobody better not criticize yuh in mah hearin'" (183). Pheoby's vision for herself is rather limited but her defense of Janie is significant. Janie has designated Pheoby to share her story with the curious community: "You can tell 'em what Ah say if you wants to. Dat's just de same as me 'cause mah tongue is in mah friend's mouf" (6). Confident in her hard-won knowledge, Janie entrusts her narrative to a sympathetic speaker.

Discussions of *Their Eyes Were Watching God* frequently consider the development of Janie's voice—her movement from self-denying silence to self-asserting speech. "The tongue Janie wields," asserts John Lowe, "is honed by humor and the ability to 'talk that talk,' for she achieves maturity, identity, and independence through the development of a voice, one that treats narrative as a repository and display piece for her hard-won, humorously expressed wisdom" (157). The assessment could easily be applied to Fat Charlie as well: he too discovers that his voice—one that resonates with humor and wisdom— is a crucial part of the development of mature identity. Given this emphasis on self-articulation, it is rather curious that neither Gaiman nor Hurston opts for a first-person narrator. The choice of narrator in each of the novels almost creates the impression of form undermining theme—almost.

Their Eyes Were Watching God and *Anansi Boys* employ third-person narrators but they also incorporate signals that they are "oral" texts.[2] Hurston introduces the premise that Janie is relating her story to Pheoby at the end of the first chapter. The next chapter, however, shifts to third-person, then to Janie's narration with "Pheoby's hungry listening help[ing] Janie to tell her story" (10). With this observation, the narrative returns to a third-person narrator. Janie's "voice" re-enters the novel (for three paragraphs) as she shares her newfound insights with Pheoby but the novel ends with a third-person narrator (182–183). Hurston offers a tantalizing glimpse of Janie as the narrator of her life (albeit through the intervention of another narrator) but opts not to grant Janie the authority of first person narration. Gaiman maintains the third-person mode throughout his narrative but there are brief glimpses of the oral tradition in his work too. When the text moves from Fat Charlie's story to Anansi's, it shifts into a more conversational tone through the use of second person; for example: "NOW, PROBABLY YOU KNOW SOME ANANSI STORIES. PROBABLY there's no one in the whole wide world doesn't know some Anansi stories" and "Seeing we were just at a funeral, let me tell you a story about Anansi, the time his grandmother dies. (It's okay: she was a very old woman, and she went in her sleep. It happens)" (36–37). The passage both acknowledges an audience (implying a spoken text) and seeks to reassure it. The influence of traditional folklore is readily apparent in such moments but the oral qualities of the novel range beyond folktales.

The inclusion of African American verbal patterns is more overt in *Their Eyes Were Watching God* but the form is present at a key point in *Anansi Boys*.[3] When Fat Charlie sings to the creatures, he effectively defuses Tiger's verbal challenge that "the songs aren't yours" in the words of his song and by co-opting Tiger's sound:

> Tiger roared in anger, and Charlie took the roar and wound his song around it. Then he did the roar himself, just like Tiger had done it. Well, the roar began just as Tiger's roar had, but then Charlie changed it, so it became a really goofy sort of roar, and all the creatures watching from the rocks started to laugh.... Like any impersonation, like any perfect caricature, it had the effect of making what it made fun of intrinsically ridiculous. No one would ever hear Tiger roar again without hearing Charlie's roar underneath it [321–322].

Fat Charlie silences Tiger by claiming, and reframing, his formerly terrifying roar. The "goofy" substitute is another instance of Gaiman drawing upon a Black oral tradition. Fat Charlie vanquishes his adversary through a powerful "dis." Geneva Smitherman, in her study of Black vernacular patterns asserts, "when you 'dis' someone, you discount, discredit, disrespect that person—a dis is an insult" (*Talkin That Talk* 223). It is a verbal exchange designed to disempower your opponent. Smitherman's work emphasizes the playful, non-threatening nature of the interaction between social equals. "In the Black Oral Tradition," contends Smitherman, "a dis also constitutes a verbal game, played with ritualized insults. The disses are purely ceremonial which creates a safety zone" (*Talkin That Talk* 223). *Anansi Boys* moves beyond the "purely ceremonial." The "game" in Gaiman's novel is too intense to afford a "safety zone"; Fat Charlie and Tiger are engaged in combat, not a ritualized exchange. Smitherman's elaboration on the safety mechanism is significant: "since the signifier employs humor, it makes the put-down easier to swallow and gives the recipient a socially acceptable way out ... they can just laugh along with the group" (*Talkin and Testifyin* 118). In this instance, Fat Charlie uses humor to his advantage; he elicits cutting laughter. Tiger cannot (or will not) employ the "socially acceptable way out"—lacking a sense of humor, he cannot summon it to his aid, nor is he part of the group. The scene is reminiscent of the encounter between Janie and Joe in which she counters his insult about her body by exposing his sexual inadequacies. By turning the laughter against their adversaries, Janie and Fat Charlie essentially emasculate Joe and Tiger. Hurston and Gaiman both utilize the strategy of "dissing" to empower the disempowered.

Janie and Fat Charlie play to the audiences beyond their adversaries. Janie's error in cutting tobacco generates some "good-natured laughter at the expense of women" among the men congregated on the porch. Joe's admonition to Janie, however, changes the atmosphere: "Don't stand dere ... wid yo' rump hangin' nearly to yo' knees!" The initial reaction is laughter, "but people go to thinking and stopped. It was funny if you looked at it right quick, but it got pitiful if you thought of it awhile" (74). His harsh words turn her into an object of pity; Janie quickly returns the favor and Joe's shortcomings as a man are exposed. Janie claims the power of speech, enlisting the aid of the audience to render Joe an object of pity. He is deflated by the awareness that she was "laughing at him, and ... putting the town up to do the same" (76). The mocking laughter sounds Joe's death knell.

Fat Charlie enlists the aid of his audience in a less aggressive manner but he too isolates his opponent from the group. As he "sang the world,"

> all the creatures listening began to clap and to stomp and to hum along; Charlie felt like he was the conduit for a great song that took in all of them. He sang of birds, of the magic of looking up and seeing them in flight, of the sheen of the sun on a wing feather in the morning. The totem creatures were dancing now, the dances of their kind [321].

Fat Charlie's song does not pander to his audience. Instead, Fat Charlie's acknowledgment of the various creatures is a process of inclusion—a kind of reconciliation since his father has provoked most, if not all, of them.[4] The interaction can be classified as a "call-response" exchange. "The African-derived communication process of call-response," Smitherman explains, involves "spontaneous verbal and non-verbal interaction between speaker and listener in which all of the speaker's statements ('calls') are punctuated by the expressions ('responses') from the listener" (*Talkin* and *Testifyin* 104). The creatures respond to Fat Charlie's "calls" with a variety of non-verbal "responses." Smitherman identifies "clapping hands," "stomping feet," "laughing," and "moving around (sometimes in a dance-like fashion)" as common non-verbal responses which are "co-signing (affirming, agreeing with speaker)" and "encouraging (urging the speaker to continue in the direction he has started)" (*Talkin and Testifyin* 106–107). Fat Charlie voices the song but it becomes a collective enterprise. He both feeds, and feeds off, his audience's reactions.

Their Eyes Were Watching God highlights the exchange between speaker and audience with the observation that "Pheoby's hungry listening helped Janie to tell her story" (10). The implication is that Pheoby has been providing non-verbal responses to Janie. The text does not, however, provide them. The various silences in Hurston's novel—for example, we are not given Janie's response to Tea Cake's abuse or her testimony in the courtroom—complicate the interpretation of Janie as a speaker. She has no problem allowing Pheoby to speak for her to the larger community. Departing with Tea Cake alienated Janie from her community; telling her tale to Pheoby is the first step in the process of reconciliation. On the first page of the novel, Hurston establishes the community that Janie returns to: "These sitters had been tongueless, earless, eyeless conveniences all day long.... They became lords of sounds and lesser things. They passed nations through their mouths" (1–2).[5] This is clearly a speech community, and while Janie does not stop to tell her tale to them, she makes Pheoby the bearer of her tale. Voicing her experiences is a shared act with Pheoby (and by extension, the reader); Michael Awkward interprets it as "an example of an Afro-American pattern of verbal communication that represents collective interaction rather than individual dictation" (55). In this framework, storytelling is a means of reconciling the community in a manner similar to Fat Charlie's singing. Janie, however, does not speak directly with a larger audience.

Hurston and Gaiman choose a third-person narrator rather than having Janie or Fat Charlie speak their own stories. Clearly, the characters master the art of telling "big stories" (Hurston 134) and "magical songs that made worlds" (Gaiman 322) and yet their actual words are withheld. "The reader who is conscious of [the oral literary] tradition," Lorraine Bethel contends (in reference to *Their Eyes Were Watching God* but equally applicable to *Anansi Boys*), "will experience the novel as an overheard conversation as well as a literary text" (180). The journeys of Janie and Fat Charlie are surprisingly similar: each character learns the necessity of accessing a communal, oral culture. The distance between the novels of Hurston and Gaiman is further diminished by the influence of folklore in general, and the verbal patterns of the African American oral tradition in particular. Hurston draws upon her own cultural resources while Gaiman accesses them through her "big stories."

Notes

1. As a child, Janie Crawford is called "Alphabet" "cause so many people had done named me different names" (9). The three "marriages"—because she left her first hus-

band, it cast doubt on the legitimacy of her subsequent marriages—alter her last name (Killicks, Starks, Woods) but the name that remains constant, and is used by her friends, is Janie. Fat Charlie struggles to escape his nickname by introducing himself as "Charles or ... Chaz" (2–3). By the end of the novel, "nobody ever calls Charlie 'Fat Charlie' anymore, and honestly, sometimes he misses it" (331).

2. Clearly, they are written texts, but they also draw upon oral tradition.

3. See, for example, pages 59–66 for the verbal play of the men on the store's porch or the fast-paced banter around a card game on page 128; neither episode contributes to the plot or character development in any significant way.

4. The more obvious need for reconciliation might be Fat Charlie's—Spider was once a part of him. He explains to Spider: "'We're more like two halves of a starfish. You grew up into a whole person. And so,' he said, realizing it was true as he said it, 'did I'" (311).

5. In *Mules and Men*, Hurston links lies and nations with creation: "'Zora,' George Thomas informed me, 'you come to de right place if lies is what you want. Ah'm gointer lie up a nation'" (21).

Works Cited

Awkward, Michael. *Inspiring Influences: Tradition, Revision, and Afro-American Women's Novels*. New York: Columbia University Press, 1989. Print.

Bethel, Lorraine. "'This Infinity of Conscious Pain': Zora Neale Hurston and the Black Female Literary Tradition." *All the Women Are White, All the Blacks Are Men, But Some of Us Are Brave*. Eds. Gloria T. Hull, Patricia Bell Scott and Barbara Smith. New York: The Feminist Press at the City University of New York, 1982. 176–188. Print.

Callahan, John F. *In the African-American Grain: The Pursuit of Voice in Twentieth-Century Black Fiction*. Urbana: University of Illinois Press, 1988. Print.

Gaiman, Neil. *Anansi Boys*. New York: HarperCollins, 2005. Print.

Gates, Henry Louis, Jr. *Signifying Monkey: A Theory of African-American Literary Criticism*. Oxford: Oxford University Press, 1988. Print.

Hurston, Zora Neale. *Mules and Men*. 1935. Bloomington: Indiana University Press, 1978. Print.

_____. *Their Eyes Were Watching God*. 1937. New York: Harper and Row, 1990. Print.

Lowe, John. *Jump at the Sun: Zora Neale Hurston's Cosmic Comedy*. Urbana: University of Illinois Press, 1994. Print.

Smitherman, Geneva. *Talkin & Testifyin: The Language of Black America*. Detroit: Wayne State University Press, 1977. Print.

_____. *Talkin That Talk: Language, Culture and Education in African America*. London: Routledge, 2000. Print.

Spinrad, Paul. "On the Bookshelves of the Digerati: ReadMe." Wired 9.08. Aug. 2001. Web. 24 Aug. 2014.

Taylor, Charles McArthur. "Fat Charlie's Angel." *The New York Times Book Review* 9 October 2005: Arts and Entertainment: p. 30. Print.

The Jungle, the Graveyard and the Feral Child: Imitating and Transforming Kipling Beyond Pastiche

Jennifer McStotts

> "I learned from Kipling. At least two stories of mine (and a children's book I am currently writing) would not exist had he not written."—Neil Gaiman, Introduction to *Rudyard Kipling's Tales of Horror and Fantasy*

> "Read. As much as you can. As deeply and widely and nourishingly and irritatingly as you can. And the good things will make you remember them, so you won't need to take notes."—A.L. Kennedy

Most writers agree that mastering their craft requires being an avid reader. Even more, some take learning from other writers' work a step further into the act of imitation. Michael Moorcock advises, "Find an author you admire ... and copy their plots and characters in order to tell your own story, just as people learn to draw and paint by copying the masters" (Maloney). The word "copy" is cringe-worthy, but the act of reinterpreting characters is becoming increasingly common; consider the number of Sherlocks employed in investigations on pages and screens in the last decade. Imitation can be a valuable tool for a writer, a prompt, but it is worthwhile for readers to turn a critical gaze on what makes an imitation a rip-off and what transforms work into something higher.

As a reader, Neil Gaiman is a Kipling fan, as he notes in many interviews. What he admires about Kipling's "The Gardener" can be said of his own *The*

Ocean at the End of the Lane: "It's a story about loss, and lies, and what it means to be human and to have secrets, and it can and does and should break your heart" ("Introduction" xi–xii). Kipling's *Jungle Book* stories and Gaiman's *The Graveyard Book* are inextricably linked; Gaiman rarely omits the connection when discussing his inspiration or writing process.

Both authors are fathers writing stories for their children (and for others' children) based on the same scenario: what happens to a child in danger, separated from his parents, and raised by an unorthodox surrogate family? Both stories ultimately reassure; there will be danger and adventure, but the heroes will endure. What then does *The Graveyard Book* add to the reader's experience and to the canon of children's literature? Scholars have examined *Graveyard* in the contexts of Gothic children's literature (Koppensteiner; Dunford), intellectual virtue lessons (Rice, Barry, and McDuffie-Dipman), and contemporary orphan narratives (Mattix). What do Gaiman and *The Graveyard Book* gain by imitating a classic and re-interpreting the much-used feral child trope?

Mowgli and Bod: Defining the Feral Child

Feral means "of, pertaining to, or resembling a wild beast; brutal, savage," (*OED*) though "feral child" is often more broadly defined as one deprived of human contact, typically from a very young age. Anthropologist Mary-Ann Ochota documents and debunks cases of "boys and girls who have grown up outside the normal structures of family and society, who have survived life in the wild or in the company of animals" ("Feral Children"). In mythology and literature, this isolation occurs in many different ways. For example, Roman twins Romulus and Remus were abandoned by their family to die in the river Tiber. Daniel Waters and Sam Hamm, the writers of *Batman Returns* (1992), imitated this plot device when they reimagined the villainous Penguin; unlike Bob Kane's original bird-loving mobster, this Oswald Cobblepot was abandoned in the sewers by his parents because of his deformity. In other instances, the hand of fate or Nature herself takes the child; Edgar Rice Burroughs's Tarzan lost his mother to disease and his father in an ape attack after the family was marooned in coastal Africa. Occasionally the child himself abandons society; J.M. Barrie's Peter Pan flew out his window as an infant leaving home to live in Kensington Gardens.

For many fans of English literature, Kipling's Mowgli may be the strongest evocation of the feral child archetype. What most people think of as *The Jungle Book* is actually two collections published one year apart and totaling fifteen stories, only eight of which involve Mowgli. He appeared first as an adolescent in the 1893 short story "In the Rukh," which tells of a forest ranger's encounter with a jungle-raised young man. Kipling published it with unrelated stories in *Many Inventions*, then went on to write three additional stories about Mowgli that were published in magazines in 1893 and 1894. These stories describe how Mowgli was separated from his parents during a tiger attack, taken in by the wolf pack, named, raised, and educated in the jungle. Kipling collected these stories in 1894 with four similar anthropomorphic tales of India under the title *The Jungle Book*. A year later he published another volume, *The Second Jungle Book*, with three unrelated jungle tales and five Mowgli stories, in which the feral child has grown into a young man and grudgingly returns to civilization.

For most Kipling readers, *The Jungle Book* refers to all of these stories in aggregate, but for many Americans the same title is more likely to evoke the eponymous 1967 Disney adaptation, which was animated, made into a musical, and has a very different in plot. There have been over a dozen adaptations of *The Jungle Book* since 1942, on stage and on screen, animated and live-action (with two adaptations now in development by Walt Disney Pictures and Warner Brothers Entertainment). In addition, Mowgli inspired numerous feral child stories, including Pamela Jekel's *The Third Jungle Book*, a pastiche collection of storylines Kipling referenced in his writing but left unwritten and Jekel's original plots.

Gaiman mentions Kipling's influence on *The Graveyard Book* in his Newbery Medal acceptance speech in reference to a particular Sussex cemetery he visited as a child and as a young parent:

> It would become the starting place, along with a Kipling story about a jeweled elephant goad ["The King's Ankus"], for my story "The Witch's Headstone." Although it's chapter four, it was the first chapter I wrote of *The Graveyard Book*, the book I had wanted to write for over twenty years.
>
> The idea had been so simple, to tell the story of a boy raised in a graveyard, inspired by one image: my infant son, Michael—who was two, and is now twenty-five, the age I was then, and is now taller than I am—on his tricycle, peddling through the graveyard across the road in the sunshine, past the grave I once thought had belonged to a witch.

Gaiman's child of the graveyard, Nobody "Bod" Owens, is orphaned but not feral in the traditional sense. After his family's murder, Bod crawls to a cemetery and finds ghosts; unlike most of his literary cousins, Bod was raised with human culture and language. Both Mowgli and Bod are orphaned by attackers, one a tiger, the other an otherworldly assassin. Both are adopted by dedicated parents, educated by devoted tutors, and destined to return to their original worlds.

While Mowgli struggles with human civilization, initially rejecting it, Bod leaves the graveyard to attend school willingly (eagerly even) and regrets that he is unable to remain there safely. Bod veers most from the feral child archetype in terms of his education. That existence among the living is *not yet* safe for him is a plot point, not a matter of character or theme. "The dead are not the people to be afraid of in this world—it's the living that can hurt you," as Hayley Campbell writes in *The Art of Neil Gaiman*, and so long as that danger is greater than Bod's ability to deal with it, he must stay close to home regardless of his ability to pass among the living (240). In contrast, Mowgli's wildness means both that he cannot pass in the villages of man outside the jungle and that he remains conflicted over joining the world of man. Mowgli resists, but Bod turns optimistically toward his new life.

Ultimately, a comparison of Mowgli and Bod reveals how their similarities serve an imitative purpose while the greatest differences stem from or reflect thematic significance. In other words, where Gaiman deviates most from Kipling represents the greatest weight in message or effect. This is not to say deviation represents a choice while imitation represents laziness or over-reliance on the source material. With a complex work like *The Graveyard Book*, imitation is as much an intentional choice as it is a revealing act of appreciation for the work that inspired it. The possible combinations of imitation, inspiration, homage, adaptation, and transformation are myriad; it would be too limited even to define these possibilities as a spectrum, especially given the intermixture of new ideas or aspects of the material that are not directly connected to Kipling's work, in this case. Close imitation is at worst theft, at best a flattering homage, but in between—as in *The Graveyard Book*—is a universe of borrowing, exaggeration, reflection, and reversal. *The Graveyard Book* can be unpacked to reveal where the writing is imitative and evocative of Kipling—mostly in character design and use of feral child tropes—and where it is transformative—more universal themes instead of morals, Bod's gravity in place of Mowgli's ferocity, and a less tortured, more optimistic resolution.

Story Structure: Fable, Fantasy or Fairy Tale

Kipling was an Englishman who lived in and set many works in India, an outsider commenting on a foreign culture he felt an intense kinship with. At their core, the stories of *The Jungle Book* are fables, anthropomorphic tales with lessons like Baloo's Laws of the Jungle, with complex social and political commentary threaded throughout. The codes of conduct of various species throughout these Kipling collections—from the aforementioned Laws of the Jungle to the seals' Rules of the Beach—are examples of the author's deeper commentary about the varied forms of so-called civilization. As the human in the fable, Mowgli embodies the tension between man and nature: "Mowgli can stare down any wolf in his pack, but he also goes to live with human parents for a time, who wonder if he might be their long lost son. One of his best friends—Bagheera the panther—understands the boy's plight entirely, having been kept by humans in a cage as a cub, thereby gaining an understanding of both worlds himself" (Asher-Perrin).

Unlike *The Jungle Book, The Graveyard Book* is not laden with sociopolitical commentary, which marks the true difference of the works: thematic contrast. *The Jungle Book* sets man against nature, evokes cultural relativism, and questions the merits of civilization, while *The Graveyard Book* is nonprovocative on these issues. Here is a place Gaiman did not imitate: he sets out no code of the graveyard. The parameters of how the graveyard society functions ("a graveyard is not normally a democracy" [27]) and of how Freedom of the Graveyard works are not illuminated. In short, any codes that would govern graveyard civilization or the culture of the afterlife are left off the page. *The Graveyard Book* is not about unpacking this kind of dichotomy; regardless of tame versus wild, good versus evil, we have all been children and we all eventually pass on. In this way, Gaiman's themes are universal.

The Graveyard Book is a wainscot fantasy. Wainscoting, a type of wall paneling, describes in this context fictional societies that are hidden, literally or metaphorically. A wainscot fantasy therefore focuses on this difficult-to-detect society living in the interstitial spaces of primary reality. According to Kerrie Anne Le Lievre:

> In wainscot fantasy a particular relationship exists between two cultures which share the same physical space. The dominant culture—the culture the text's readers are presumed to share—is mundane, large, and presumed to hold power over its environment, but is largely unaware of the existence of the wainscot culture. The wainscot culture is fantastic in some way, but also small (often literally tiny, but also in terms of numbers) and marginal, vulnerable to the power the dominant culture can exercise over its environment (which includes the wainscot culture) and therefore fearful of attracting the dominant culture's attention [26].

The stories that defined the term "wainscot fantasy" began with Mary Norton's *The Borrowers*, a series of five books following that title and running from 1952 to 1982. As tiny human-like creatures, the Borrowers live beneath floorboards and behind walls, and their greatest defense lies in invisibility; diminutive size is both a weakness and a tactical benefit. This dynamic of dominance and fear creates space for social critique and analogy. Although many wainscot fantasies involve miniature societies, not all do. For example, the premise of Michelle Lovretta's *Lost Girl* (Prodigy Pictures, Inc., 2010–) anchors on a fantasy race (the Fae) deeply concerned with covering up evidence of their existence and maintaining the status quo by not attracting attention. Wainscoting appears throughout speculative fiction from H.P. Lovecraft's Cthulhu cults to Gaiman's own *Neverwhere*, but its use in *The Graveyard Book* places an important twist on *The Jungle Book*. In the latter, there is no plot tension or conflict regarding whether the jungle civilizations will be discovered by mankind, but such tension is central to the mystery of Bod's parents' murders.

One might argue *The Jungle Books* are wainscot fantasy; Kipling imagined a nonmagical but still fantastic society of sentient animals with culture, language, and laws, and this world exists in the wild spaces of our own reality (or right underneath our noses, as in "Her Majesty's Servants," where the human narrator recounts animal conversations in a military encampment). Still, the world of animals is not a wainscot society; it is neither clandestine nor hidden. People have studied animal behavior for as long as we have had the capacity to do so; it was a matter of mortal necessity to understand predator patterns and to predict prey behavior.

In contrast, *The Graveyard Book* includes multiple levels of wainscot societies, both imitative and transformative, but only the Consortium of Jacks have contact or conflict with mainstream, dominant society. The dead continue their unique existence beyond the graveyard's "spike-topped iron railings" and "high brick wall" (13) in the same manner as little people secretly living in walls, except they need not fear discovery by the living.[1] The villains of the piece, the Jacks, function as a hidden society, yet their exposure is in play. The same is true of the ghouls, though it is these interstitial societies that necessitate the existence of the Honor Guard—"We guard the borderlands. We protect the borders of things" (303)—suggesting a more complex magical system.

Nevertheless, Gaiman sets aside all of these worlds, their interactions, politics, and magics, focusing on Bod and the mysteries surrounding him. The only scenes in which Bod does not appear are the short "Interlude" about the Convocation of Jacks and two brief scenes of Silas and the Honor Guard. To imitate *The Jungle Book* as a whole, Gaiman could have explored numerous stories without Bod or the graveyard; after all, of Kipling's fifteen collected stories, only eight involve Mowgli. Gaiman envisioned both an homage to Kipling's short stories and a novel: "I wanted the book to be composed of short stories, because *The Jungle Book* was short stories. And I wanted it to be a novel, because it was a novel in my head. The tension between those two things was both a delight and a heartache as a writer" (Newbery Acceptance Speech). Ultimately, there are immediate parallels between isolated jungle stories and individual graveyard chapters, but on the whole *Graveyard* has a rearranged and more unified arc.

Moreover, Gaiman's stories are less lesson-oriented than Kipling's; they are not fables, but are they children's literature? Such a genre label raises fundamental questions about what it means to be children's literature, and Gaiman's oeuvre is particularly ripe for analysis of which aspects speak to children and which speak most to adults. Scholar Yukino Semizu seeks to develop a systematic paradigm of assessing adult readers' reactions to children's and YA literature. Her analysis roughly divides reader reactions into what she calls "direct adultness"—thinking about our own ideas of childhood as we read—and "indirect adultness"—thinking about the experience of the child we will be reading the book with or mediating the book to (19). Some stories, according to Semizu, also use a "safety ring"—a narrative device that protects the child reader from anything too-adult within the story (20). For example, a character who is a victim of sexual violence might have amnesia, so that the child narrator (and child reader) are never exposed to the details of the trauma, allowing a children's book to walk the line on adult topics. While that is an extreme example, Semizu references various others, including how Gaiman's narrator does not provide details of how an orphaned toddler would, realistically, survive in a graveyard. Gaiman used Silas who can come and go from the graveyard as the mechanism for gathering food and clothes for the growing boy.

According to Semizu, where the safety ring is an "honest" device, it fits the greater narrative structure. She describes other uses as "dishonest" and "manipulative," untrue to the setting or plot of the book. She considers Gaiman's *Graveyard*, particularly the aspect described above, an example of this dishonest "exploitation" of the ring (222). She claims the prospect for Bod's survival "is never explained in the way that is congruent with the setting of the story," though she does not specify why this explanation is inadequate (316). Her conclusion hinges on applying Neil Philip's claim that failing to attend to detail in this way offers child fantasy readers only a "simplistic daydream not a literary experience" (82). Philip's larger argument reads: "successful fantasy uses the 'other' to explore the familiar, not to escape from it. And to do that well requires a rigid grip on the familiar so that the distortion introduced by the fantasy element involves an extension not a diminution of understanding" (82–83). While Semizu claims Gaiman's grip on the familiar is inadequate here to sustain the narrative, she does not support this assertion, nor explain how it might cause a "diminution of understanding."

Whether the level of detail Gaiman devotes to the mechanics of Bod's survival is enough could be dismissed as a matter of opinion, but it raises questions about the necessity of a threshold of realism to assess children's literature, especially fantasies, *as* literature. If Kipling had devoted great detail to explaining how Mowgli was fed in the early years of his jungle life, the book might have been considered too violent for children in that era. He only touches on how Mowgli survived other elements, such as exposure, in a few lines of banter about how exposed the "man-cub" is and whether he needs to borrow another animal's hide (180). One possible reason readers do not long for more explanation from Kipling may be because realism would require a level of graphic detail that would take the story out of the realm of children's literature; it would violate the safety ring.[2] Critics like Semizu apply an unfair double standard to "fantasies"—those that involve the supernatural or magical—in comparison to works that are subtly fantastic, like Kipling's, or realistic. Aspects of the graveyard are explained in sparse detail not because it is a children's book, nor as part of the safety ring (dishonest or otherwise), but because this is Gaiman's style and because the book is an homage to Kipling, who offered only cursory details about how Mowgli hunted, lived, and survived.

Moreover, the fairy-tale affect of Gaiman's work defies excessive exposition. This affect—the impression or disposition of the work—evokes a fairy tale, as described by Kate Bernheimer, specifically through abstraction in and depthlessness of the text (McStotts 196–197). Neither Kipling nor Gaiman identify the precise time or place in which their works are set—not even a decade or a region. The points of view are both limited third-person. The texts are neither specific nor deep in detail, character psychology, or thematic meditation, though Kipling's thematic commentary is more developed and closer to the surface of the text. Ultimately, a child reader can ponder themes threaded through a text—man versus nature, life versus afterlife, what it means to be an orphan—without multidimensional realistic detail or complexity of fantastic explanations. *The Graveyard Book* is more than a fairy tale interpretation of Kipling's *Jungle Book*. While Gaiman acknowledged Kipling as a source of inspiration, repeatedly and with reverence, a detailed analysis shows the plot and characters are not strictly parallel.

Imitation: It Takes a Village and a Villain

Upon close reading, *The Graveyard Book* imitates *The Jungle Book* primarily in how the feral child is raised. The adoptive mothers, for instance, are strikingly similar—fiercely protective she-wolves, literally in *The Jungle Book* and metaphorically in *The Graveyard Book*. The mothers are introduced in *The Jungle Book*'s first collected story, "Mowgli's Brothers," and in *Graveyard*'s first chapter, "How Nobody Came to the Graveyard." In response to Father Wolf questioning whether she wants to keep the baby, Mother Wolf replies:

> "He came naked, by night, alone and very hungry; yet he was not afraid! Look, he has pushed one of my babes to one side already. And that lame butcher would have killed him and would have run off to the Waingunga while the villagers here hunted through all our lairs in revenge! Keep him? Assuredly I will keep him. Lie still, little frog. O thou Mowgli—for Mowgli the Frog I will call thee—the time will come when thou wilt hunt Shere Khan as he has hunted thee" [9].

Mrs. Owens has a similar reaction after promising to protect the baby:

> "His mama gave the boy to me," said Mrs. Owens, as if that was all that needed to be said.
> [Josiah Worthington:] "My dear woman..."
> "I am not your dear woman," said Mrs. Owens, getting to her feet. "Truth to tell, I don't even see why I am even here, talking to you fiddle-pated old dunderheads, when this lad is going to wake up hungry soon enough—and where am I going to find food for him in this graveyard, I should like to know?" [22].

There are multiple passages in both first chapters in which these alpha females demonstrate maternal instinct, protectiveness, and a no-nonsense disregard for the objections of men. Both feel forced to defend their choice to bring an outsider into their community. Despite the close character and plot parallels, Gaiman does not borrow Kipling's dialogue or even closely parallel any particular lines. Also, Bod's mother need not physically defend Bod as Mother Wolf must; Mrs. Owens sweeps the infant into her embrace, which makes him disappear so that the killer Jack cannot see him, while Mother Wolf, "Raksha [The Demon]," must stand off against the tiger, Shere Khan (8).

After these opening introductions of the boys and adoptive families, both authors include a scene in which the boy is presented to the pack or community. These scenes introduce the major teaching figures for the boys: (1) the bear Baloo who vouches for Mowgli and the panther Bagheera who seconds, purchasing Mowgli's life for the price of a freshly killed bull, and (2) Silas who names himself Bod's guardian and takes responsibility for bringing him sustenance.

At different points in these first stories, the babies make eye-contact with and laugh at their new parents. The lines are not syntactically parallel, but the imitation is close: Mowgli "looked up into Father Wolf's face, and laughed" (7) upon first seeing him, and when Mrs. Owen meets Bod and attempts to stroke his hair (she cannot because she is incorporeal), and Bod "giggled with delight" (14). These moments show the babies imprinting on their adoptive parents, seemingly not traumatized. Moreover, turning the narrative cameras on them at their most innocent and trusting sets up a sharp contrast for later moments in which the power of the babies' gazes becomes important. Yet the latter is where the narratives differ. Mowgli, as a young child, "discovered that if he stared hard at any wolf, the wolf would be forced to drop his eyes, and so he used to stare for fun" (14). This demonstrated his inherent strength but also speaks to Kipling's views of man's supremacy and hubris. In contrast, Gaiman places this moment after Bod's naming, as Silas holds him: "It was then that, as if responding to the name, the child opened its eyes wide in wakefulness. It stared around it, taking in the faces of the dead, and the mist, and the moon. Then it looked at Silas. Its gaze did not flinch. It looked grave." Like Mowgli, Bod is fearless when faced with a new situation, but he is not demonstrating nor abusing his power. Mowgli will grow to be a hunter and leader, and Kipling reveals this potential early on, while Gaiman gives his feral child different strengths, including an emotional strength camouflaged by Gaiman's pun.

As both books progress, close reading reveals further parallels. In "Kaa's Hunting," Baloo disciplines his pupil Mowgli using corporal punishment. During one lesson, Baloo instructs Mowgli on the language of the jungle for his protection, and he defends his methods to Bagheera:

> "Better he should be bruised from head to foot by me who love him than that he should come to harm through ignorance," Baloo answered very earnestly. "I am now teaching him the Master Words of the Jungle that shall protect him with the birds and the Snake People, and all that hunt on four feet, except his own pack. He can now claim protection, if he will only remember the words, from all in the jungle. Is not that worth a little beating?" [29].

The same lesson is reinterpreted in the third chapter of *The Graveyard Book*, "The Hounds of God," when Silas leaves Mowgli with a substitute teacher of sorts, the werewolf Miss Lupescu. Her methods are similar to Baloo's but less violent; she calls Bod "ignorant," and most importantly, the material she covers in her lesson is analogous to what Baloo teaches Mowgli: "for two days she taught him nothing but ways to call for help in every language in the world, and she would rap his knuckles with her pen if he slipped up, or forgot" (71–72). Gaiman's adaptation of the corporal punishment from Kipling is a softening that reflects modern sentiments. Nevertheless, both boys rebel against their teachers and consequently are taken from their homes—Mowgli by the *Bandar-log* (the monkey people) and Bod by ghouls—to their kidnappers' cities (the Lost City and Ghûlheim), wilder and more dangerous than the rest of the jungle and graveyard. It is their teachers who rescue them.

The Graveyard Book affirms the adage "it take a village to raise a child," even if that village is populated by ghosts (Rice, Barry, and McDuffie-Dipman 35). Beyond the parallel surrogate parents of both books, there are comparable minor characters throughout and conflations and role shifting amongst major characters. In "Kaa's Hunting," Baloo and Bagheera cooperate with Kaa the rock python to rescue Mowgli from the *Bandar-log*. In the parallel *Graveyard* chapter, "The Hounds of God," Lupescu rescues Bod in cooperation with anonymous night-gaunts, but in the absence of Silas. While she has this solo appearance of significance, Miss Lupescu does not receive as much narrative attention as Silas, unlike Baloo and Bagheera who appear with approximate equivalence. Eventually within the Mowgli stories, Kaa takes on an advisory role to Mowgli of near equal weight to Baloo and Bagheera; in short, the three animals' roles are conflated primarily in Silas and secondarily in Miss Lupescu. (In fact, Silas serves Bod in a godfather-like role as Mr. and Mrs. Owens appear very little after the opening chapter. Similarly, Baloo, Bagheera, and even Kaa spend more page-time with Mowgli after the first chapter than Father and Mother Wolf.) The two members of the Honor Guard (Haroun the ifrit and Kandar the mummy) who join the battle against the Jacks with Silas and Lupescu, unbeknownst to Bod, have no character development or jungle parallel. Mowgli's wolf brothers are not translated into the graveyard, and the villagers who believe they are Mowgli's parents have no *Graveyard* equivalent. Instead, Gaiman populates the graveyard with more female characters, including both the ghostly witch Elizabeth "Liza" Hempstock and Bod's only living friend, Scarlett Perkins. Liza's role in helping Bod in the village in "The Witch's Headstone" could be analogized to Kaa's involvement with the *Bandar-log*, but Mowgli has no companions among men as Bod has Scarlett.

The sharpest distinction between Gaiman's tale and its source text is in the rearrangement of the villains' roles. While Jack Frost and Shere Khan seem from their character introductions to be parallel, the latter does not serve as antagonist beyond the third Mowgli story. Instead, the dhole or "Red Dogs" represent the large penultimate conflict. At the corresponding place in Bod's narrative, the Consortium of Jacks has been mostly eliminated, but secretly, off-stage, and by someone other than Bod. Nonetheless, as Mowgli cleverly entrapped the dog pack, Bod tricks and vanquishes the remaining Jacks, including his nemesis.

The closing episodes of both stories represent the internal battles of the feral child—whether and how to return to the world. The basic arcs are the same: a child is orphaned; he grows to learn and to realize his own strengths, which include both the abilities of his unique upbringing and the inherent cleverness of his character; he defeats his enemies using the latter skills; and he begins to be drawn by forces beyond his control away from his adoptive home and family and back to his original world. Both Mowgli and Bod wrestle with what it means to be who and what they are. This manifests as Mowgli argues with his jungle family regarding attacking men:

> "Back! Back and wait! Man does not eat Man!" Mowgli shrieked.
> "Who was a wolf but now? Who drove the knife at me for thinking he might be Man?" said Akela, as the four wolves turned back sullenly and dropped to heel.
> "Am I to give reason for all I choose to, do?" said Mowgli furiously.
> "That is Man! There speaks Man!" Bagheera muttered under his whiskers. "Even so did men talk round the King's cages at Oodeypore. We of the Jungle know that Man is wisest of all. If we trusted our ears we should know that of all things he is most foolish" [217].

Even as Mowgli insists upon being considered a wolf, not a man, he cannot bear to see other men attacked. He is not ready or inclined to wrestle with this internal conflict, which is reflected in Bagheera's contradictory sense that man is at once both the wisest and most foolish. In a more contemplative conservation, Silas and Bod discuss what living means, and why Bod's existence is different than his family and friends in the graveyard:

> Bod shrugged. "So?" he said. "It's only death. I mean, all of my best friends are dead."
> "Yes." Silas hesitated. "They are. And they are, for the most part, done with the world. You are not. You're alive, Bod. That means you have infinite potential. You can do anything, make anything, dream anything. If you change the world, the world will change. Potential. Once you're dead, it's gone. Over. You've made what you've made, dreamed your dream, written your name. You may be buried here, you may even walk. But that potential is finished."
> Bod thought about this. It seemed almost true, although he could think of exceptions—his parents adopting him, for example. But the dead and the living were different, he knew that, even if his sympathies were with the dead [179].

This idea of conflicting sympathies is parallel across texts, and tension between biological and adoptive cultures is natural to the feral child experience. What Gaiman adds is introspection, a thoughtful consideration and compromise far more characteristic of Bod than of Mowgli.

In these twin conclusions, both adolescent boys, now on the cusp of manhood, feel drawn out of their comfortable worlds. For Mowgli, there is frustration that during this "Spring Running" he has lost the ability to lead the animals or even hold their attention. He has lost one of his superpowers, his preternatural command of the jungle, which he had since his first unbroken staring contest. Moreover, his angst at feeling pulled to leave is existential, and he suffers it as a physical trauma:

> "Why did I not die under Red Dog?" the boy moaned. "My strength is gone from me, and it is not any poison. By night and by day I hear a double step upon my trail. When I turn my head it is as though one had hidden himself from me that instant. I go to look behind the trees and he is not there. I call and none cry again; but it is as though one listened and kept back the answer. I lie down, but I do not rest. I run the spring running, but I am not made still. I bathe, but I am not made cool. The kill sickens me, but I have no heart to fight except I kill. The Red Flower [fire] is in my body, my bones are water—and—I know not what I know."
> "What need of talk?" said Baloo slowly, turning his head to where Mowgli lay. "Akela by the river said it, that Mowgli should drive Mowgli back to the Man-Pack. I said it. But who listens now to Baloo? Bagheera—where is Bagheera this night?— he knows also. It is the Law."
> "When we met at Cold Lairs, Manling, I knew it," said Kaa, turning a little in his mighty coils. "Man goes to Man at the last, though the Jungle does not cast him out" [377–378].

Bod's experience is gentler. Upon arriving in the graveyard, he gained abilities and potential: "'You were given the Freedom of the Graveyard, after all,' Silas would tell him. 'So the Graveyard is taking care of you. While you are here, you can see in the darkness. You can walk some of the ways that the living should not travel. The eyes of the living will slip from you'" (38). Bod masters these abilities, described as "Fading and Sliding and Dreamwalking" (37), as he matures, but loses them in the final chapter, a loss described without undue emphasis: first, he is unable to slip (Slide) through overgrown ivy (295), and finally, he is unable to see Silas in the dark chapel (301).

On the whole, Gaiman's changes relate to the different themes of his book, though some of the themes would not necessarily emerge in a child's reading. His real life inspiration—a familiar graveyard in which his son played—merged with one of his favorite *Jungle Book* segments "The King's Ankus" to become "The Witch's Headstone" and decades later *The Graveyard Book*. The ancient treasure-guarding white cobra became Gaiman's Sleer— still ancient, still treasure-guarding, but now supernatural, three-headed, and ultimately a tool for Bod's victory over his personal Shere Khan. While Kipling comments on the curse-like power of wealth, on man's weakness and greed, and on the rise and fall of civilizations, Gaiman covers different territory. As Mowgli takes the ankus from the cobra's lair, so does Bod steal a piece of the Sleer's treasure, a brooch, but the latter does not bring death in the same manner as the former. Mowgli discards the ankus, and the men who find it betray and kill each other to possess it. Bod steals the brooch in order to gift Liza with a headstone, but Abanazer Bolger traps Bod to steal the treasure. Like the unnamed men of Mowgli's jungle, Bolger turns on his accomplice Tom Hustings, but unlike those men, Bolger and Hustings do not die. The boys return the treasures, both more aware of man's greedy and violent nature.

The Sleer reappears in a later chapter—unlike the cobra—as an important part of the climax. In those scenes, the serpent's purpose is to complicate questions of monsters and evil, mortality and murder: the Sleer imprisons and "protects" Jack for eternity, but Bod manipulated the situation so this would happen. Therefore, Bod's action could be seen as vengeful, even akin to murder:

> Scarlett said, "I thought you said the Sleer couldn't hurt people. I thought all it could do was frighten us."
> "Yes," said Bod. "But it wanted a master to protect. It told me so." Scarlett said, "You mean you knew. You knew that it would happen...." "Yes. I hoped it would" [285].

Scarlett believes Bod has become a murderer, that her friend has used evil to commit evil, while Bod believes he has saved them both by turning a mindless monster against the greatest evil he knows. The Sleer may be terrifying, but to Bod, it is an amoral tool for something greater. Not only does he believe his actions were just, he does not believe he committed murder: "I didn't kill anyone.... Look, it's okay. I dealt with them" (286).

Transformation: Rites of Passage

Where Kipling contrasts the jungle with human civilization—specifically Victorian era British and Indian culture, often to the benefit of the jungle—Gaiman contrasts universal concepts: good and evil, life and death. Mowgli must be reminded of his humanity, though what that means is less cut-and-dried than the difference between being dead or alive. Unlike Silas, Bod is very much alive, a truth he must be reminded of throughout:

> Josiah Worthington said, "The dead and the living do not mingle, boy. We are no longer part of their world; they are no part of ours. If it happened that we danced the *danse macabre* with them, the dance of death, then we would not speak of it, and we certainly would not to speak of it to the living."
> "But I'm one of you."
> "Not yet, boy. Not for a lifetime" [163].

Silas's lines about the potential of the living—"You can do anything, make anything, dream anything" (179)—speak not to our child-like selves and Gaiman's child readers. The idea that the adults of Bod's world could be jealous of his potential is a reversal of most childhood perceptions that adults have all the power and control, and therefore the only enviable position. It is a reversal of the adult-child power dynamic.

The narrative arc of *The Graveyard Book* reinvigorates the power of the traditional rite of passage in a feral child story. Both boys lose their birth and adoptive families and their homes, but only Mowgli resists strongly, and embracing adulthood is only painful for him. Bod expresses sadness and regret, but he welcomes the adventure that adulthood represents to him. Mowgli's last act is to sob and sob (379), while Bod "walked into [Life] with his eyes and his heart wide open" (307).

Gaiman describes his own realization as he wrote the closing lines of Mrs. Owens's half-remembered lullaby (a doggerel) that the point of *The Graveyard Book* for him had become the contrast of childhood and parenthood[3]:

> And my eyes stung, momentarily. It was then, and only then, that I saw clearly for the first time what I was writing. I had set out to write a book about a childhood—it was Bod's childhood, and it was in a graveyard, but still, it was a childhood like any other; I was now writing about being a parent, and the fundamental most comical tragedy of parenthood: that if you do your job properly, if you, as a parent, raise your children well, they won't need you anymore. If you did it properly, they go away. And they have lives and they have families and they have futures.

While an author's description of theme is not the *only* interpretation, Gaiman's explanation of his writing experience confirms how he added value by empowering the child character and thereby the child reader. Gaiman captures the pure spirit of a rite of passage: adulthood as a beginning, not an end. Feral child stories have the ability, by their very nature, to be the best possible examples of parenthood. Other contemporary fantasy orphan narratives, such as *A Series of Unfortunate Events* and *Harry Potter*, model children overcoming mistreatment by inadequate or malevolent adoptive parents. In contrast, feral children more often have the best parents and mentors, those who raise their children so well as to make themselves unnecessary, to prove their children's inherent abilities and strength. One possible lesson then, to child readers of *The Graveyard Book*, is their own potential for self-sufficiency.

Conclusions

In recent years, the inclusion of magic and the dark fantastic has increased in the young adult genre. In *The Graveyard Book*, the addition of the fantastic adds value to the feral child narrative. The relocation of the story from jungle to graveyard does more than expand the market. The proximity of the fantastic to the real in stories like *The Graveyard Book* allows for authentic exploration of deeper, older themes.[4]

The core similarities of these stories are the foundation from which to examine their significant differences. Bod is not Mowgli, ghosts are not wolves, and a graveyard is not a jungle, yet the literary resemblance between these books is clear. Why would a sophisticated author reveal and even emphasize the fingerprints of his inspiration and imitation? Illuminating *Graveyard*'s heredity reveals the book's position in the line of Kipling's influence. It places this work close to *The Jungle Book*, but it is *Graveyard*'s own merits that place it in the realm of children's literature. Gaiman demonstrates incredible skill and craft in careful imitation, but it is the transformative elements—elastic themes in place of fable-like morals, Mowgli's cleverness overlaid by Bod's unique gravity, and the optimistic, open resolution—that give *The Graveyard Book* its unique impact.

The long-term cultural influence of Kipling's *The Jungle Book* was undeniably redirected by the 1967 Disney film adaptation. Animated, set to music, and re-interpreted for children, the story of Mowgli's experience in the jungle is radically different for viewers than for readers of the original text. For many, the names of Mowgli's animal mentors will always evoke the image of dancing and singing rather than the lessons of Kipling's fables. It remains to be seen how the live-action adaptation of *The Jungle Book*, due in October of 2015 and also from Disney, will further change the broader cultural memory of Mowgli and Kipling, though the choice to cast Kaa as female is intriguing.

Whether film adaptation will change the popular understanding of *The Graveyard Book* remains to be seen; the script, also a Disney project, is still being written and the director remains in flux, therefore whether the adaptation will be animated or live-action has not yet been determined.[5] *Graveyard* has already been adapted into a two-volume graphic novel by artist P. Craig Russell (2014).

All too often it seems that the standard measure of a book's success now is whether and how soon it becomes a movie, as if this transformation is a rite of passage stories must go through like a child growing up. In the final chapter of *The Graveyard Book*, Mother Slaughter realizes Bod has become a young man and remarks upon the way we grow: "You're always you, and that don't change, and you're always changing, and there's nothing you can do about it" (298). This rings true for contemporary stories; they remain the same, on the page if nowhere else, yet they must change, as they must cross media, whether as authorized adaptation or fan fiction. Regardless, the stories endure on the page, telling readers, "Come back again," like Mowgli's mother in the village saying, "By night or by day, this door is never shut to thee" (374).

Notes

1. Cemetery destruction is specifically eliminated as a plot-risk in *The Graveyard Book*, as the people of Old Town have designated this graveyard as "an official nature reserve" (19).

2. The level of realism, detail, or explanation necessary to tell a story is the author's choice, and whether the chosen level of realism is sufficient from the reader's perspective is a matter of opinion, rather than literary merit. In other words, some readers expect or prefer more realism, others less, and in practice, some are more willing to allow gaps in or suspend disbelief than others.

3. Mrs. Owens' song: "Sleep my little babby-oh / Sleep until you waken / When you wake you'll see the world / If I'm not mistaken ... // Kiss a lover / Dance a measure, / Find your name / And buried treasure ... // Face your life / Its pain, its pleasure, / Leave no path untaken" (306).

4. See Jennifer Hollander for similar arguments.

5. Early rumors placed Henry Sellick in the director chair for the adaptation, which lead to speculation that *The Graveyard Book* would be stop-motion animation like Sellick's adaptation of Gaiman's *Coraline*. In 2013, Ron Howard was in talks with Walt Disney Productions to take over the position.

Works Cited

Asher-Perrin, Emily. "Raised by Apes and Wolves: Fiction's Top 11 Feral Children." Tor.com. 29 September 2012. Web. 29 May 2014.

Campbell, Hayley. *The Art of Neil Gaiman*. New York: HarperCollins, 2014. Print.

Clute, John, and John Grant, eds. "Wainscot." *Encyclopedia of Fantasy*. SFE, June 1997. Web. 29 May 2014.

Dunford, Laura. "The Child and the Gothic Body: A Study of Abjection and Nineteenth Century Influences in Selected Works of Contemporary Gothic Children's Literature." Thesis. University of British Columbia, 2010. Web.

Firman, Courtney Linn. "Fantasy Making the Invisible Visible: Liminality in Neil Gaiman's Neverwhere and American Gods." Thesis. Bucknell University, 2010. Web.

Gaiman, Neil. *The Graveyard Book*. New York: HarperCollins, 2008. Print.

_____. "Introduction." *Rudyard Kipling's Tales of Horror and Fantasy*. Ed. Stephen Jones. New York: Fall River Press, 2008. xi–xii. Print.

_____. "The Newbery Medal Acceptance Speech." American Library Association. Chicago. 12 July 2009.

Kipling, Rudyard. *The Jungle Book: Complete and Unabridged*. 1894 and 1895. New York: HarperCollins, 1994. Print.

"Kipling First Edition with Author's Poignant Note Found." British Broadcasting Corporation, 8 April 2010. Web. 29 May 2014.

Koppensteiner, Jasmina. "The Gothic in Children's and Young Adult Literature." Diss. Universität Wien (University of Vienna), 2011. Web.

Le Lievre, Kerrie Anne. "Wizards and Wainscots: Generic Structures and Genre Themes in the Harry Potter Series." *Mythlore* 24.1 (2003): 25–36. Web.

Maloney, Evan. "The Best Advice for Writers? Read." *The Guardian* 4 March 2010. Web. 4 June 2014.

Mattix, April A. "The Orphan Among Us: An Examination of Orphans in Newbery Award Winning Literature." Diss. University of Pittsburgh, 2012. Web.

McStotts, Jennifer. "Inverting the Fairy Tale: The Value of the Complex Female in 'Chivalry.'" *Feminism in the Worlds of Neil Gaiman: Essays on the Comics, Poetry and Prose*. Ed. Tara Prescott and Aaron Drucker. Jefferson, NC: McFarland, 2012. 192–205. Print.

Ochota, Mary-Ann. "Feral Children." Feral Children. Web. June 2014.

Peterson, Nancy J., ed. *Toni Morrison: Critical and Theoretical Approaches*. Baltimore: Johns Hopkins University Press, 1997. Print.

Philip, Neil. "Fantasy: Double Cream or Instant Whip?" *Signal: Approach to Children's Books* 35 (May 1981): 82–90.

Rice, Suzanne, Arlene L. Barry, and Molly McDuffie-Dipman. "Intellectual Virtue: The Contributions of Newbery Award Winning Books, 2000–2010." *Journal of Thought* 47.4 (2012): 23–38. Web.

Semizu, Yukino. "Adultness in Children's Literature: Toward the Awareness of Adults' Presence in Children's Literature." Thesis. University of Nottingham, 2013. Web.

Wisdom, Strength and Courtesy: Graveyard-Favor Go with Thee

Margaret Seyford Hrezo

"Wisdom, Strength, and Courtesy,
Jungle-Favour go with thee!"
—Rudyard Kipling, *The Jungle Books*

"You're always you and that don't change, and you're
always changing, and there's nothing you can do
about it."—Neil Gaiman, *The Graveyard Book*

"For the heart of the matter is that of recognizing or failing
to recognize who is happy and who is not."—Plato, *Gorgias*

Wisdom, strength, and courtesy are the jungle's wishes for Mowgli when he leaves at 17 for life with human beings. These are also the lessons Nobody ("Bod") Owens learns that he takes with him when he leaves the graveyard for the final time at about 15. Inspired by Rudyard Kipling's *The Jungle Books*, Neil Gaiman's *The Graveyard Book* is the story of a toddler who wanders into a graveyard the night his family is murdered and grows up there. Like Kipling's classic story, it offers a rich variety of themes and multiple points of interpretive access. One theme in this book that often escapes notice is the contribution of the classic understanding of reason to growth in wisdom, strength, and courtesy, that is, in understanding the best way to always be "you." *The Graveyard Book* suggests that a life grounded in the classic (or noetic) understanding of reason is a prerequisite for genuine and continuing growth in these three qualities and for development of orderly individuals and societies.

In telling Bod's story, Gaiman uses his gifts as a storyteller to restore order through imagination (to paraphrase Walt Disney in *Saving Mr. Banks*). In a world often full of random violence, suffering, and pain—indeed with what often only can be considered unmitigated evil, Bod learns that wisdom, strength, and courtesy help him differentiate between individual and societal order and disorder. Further, he sees that these qualities and the order that accompanies them are the foundations of a happy life. As he matures, Bod comes to understand that human beings have "infinite potential" (179). Silas tells Bod: "You can do anything, make anything, dream anything. If you change world, the world will change" (179). However, Bod also learns that without the lessons taught by the classic understanding of reason—without wisdom, strength of character, courtesy to all, and charity, disorder and unhappiness ensue. For when "he had broken all the rules of the graveyard ... everything had gone wrong" (125). Bod's life in the graveyard teaches him that order comes from within and that the only way to develop the qualities that produce an orderly and a happy person is by paying attention to both the visible and the invisible aspects of reality.

The classic (or noetic) experience of reason is related to what the Greeks called *nous*. It begins with Aristotle's *thaumazein*, the experience of awe and wonder in the face of the mystery of existence, that is, with the universal questions of why things exist and why things are the way they are and not different. Noetic reason is more a way of life than a concept or an idea and it dominated western philosophic and political thought until the advent of the Modern Project in the sixteenth century with the thinking of Machiavelli and the rediscovery of Lucretius' writings during the Enlightenment.[1] Those who accept the Modern Project understand reason as pure calculation of the means required to reach a desired end and assume that reality is only what they can see or touch. They see each individual as the sole author of her or his life with no need to think about the consequences of choices or actions for anyone but that particular individual. The goodness or badness, the wisdom or folly, of the desired end is irrelevant. Rationalism is instrumental. The measure of rationality is success in achieving goals. Certainly success is the measure of rationality for the members of the Convocation who seek to destroy Bod and his family (and Scarlett in the process) in order to protect their desire for power. The members of the convocation clad themselves in an impenetrable armor of self-interest. They recognize no existential confusion that prompts a questioning search for order. They have withdrawn from humanity into a second reality in which anything that can be done, should be done. This is the measure of rationality relied on by the final Jack, Jack Frost, in the confrontation with the Sleer: "There can be a new Brotherhood, more powerful than the last. POWER, echoed the Sleer" (281). There is no awe and wonder in the face of mystery in the Modern Project. There only is the desire for power and certainty. The Jacks, like the ghouls, represent all the forces of disorder in the universe and epitomize what happens when individuals follow the Modern Project's logic to its ultimate conclusion—greed, villainy, murder, the unbridled desire for power, and the certainty that only the individual who desires these things matters.

Noetic reason views reality as more than the use of power to gain economic, social, and political gain. It requires paying genuine attention to reality in all its myriad forms. In the face of the mystery of existence, human beings seek answers in both physical reality and non-existent reality (a reality composed of things and experiences which are real, but which we cannot see or touch). Plato and Aristotle articulated *nous* in resistance against the personal and societal disorder of ancient Greece (Voegelin *Volume 12* 266). *Nous* was the symbol of the specifically human attribute that allowed human beings to participate in World Order or World Soul (Divine *nous*)—some essence or thing that transcends physical reality and produces the universe's order. In *Gorgias*, for example, Socrates tells Callicles that "wise men claim that partnership and friendship, orderliness, self-control, and justice hold together heaven and earth, and gods and men, and that is why they call this universe a world order, my friend, and not an undisciplined world disorder" (Socrates 508 a). The claim is that the universe possesses an inherent order—perhaps divine, perhaps not—but decidedly real. That order may not readily be apparent to human beings because they would prefer that the universe accommodate itself to them rather than having to accommodate themselves to it. However, a well-ordered and happy life depends on cultivating friendship, orderliness, self-control, and justice; that is, by living in harmony with the World Order (*nous*) or World Soul (divine *nous*). That individual is "good" or "orderly" and is a force for order or disorder in society as a whole (Voegelin *Volume 12* 266). That person possesses *opsis*, clear-sightedness.

The classic understanding of reason underlies the life of the graveyard with its openness to all parts of reality. Bod symbolizes this openness as the child who walks "the borderland between the living and the dead" (270–271). There is an order to the graveyard, an order imposed by death, and the mere act of the dead adopting a live boy disturbs that order and is the source of much discussion. Further, the Freedom of the Graveyard enjoyed by Bod as he grows up has its limits. When Bod ignores those limits and breaks the rules of the graveyard, he brings the potential for conflict and evil into its space.

It is dangerous for Bod to leave the graveyard or to use what he has learned there (Fading, Sliding, Dreamwalking, etc.) on the living. When Bod is thoughtless or fails to pay attention to "the borders between things" that the Honor Guard protects (303), he threatens the order of the graveyard. Trespassing the border is possible. However, because trespassing that border violates most human beings' understanding of what is real and what is not, moving beyond that borderland puts them in danger of madness. As Silas tells Bod, "People want to forget the impossible. It makes their world safer" (289). Bod compromises the safety of both the graveyard and himself by taking the brooch from the oldest tomb and trying to sell it to buy Liza Hempstock a grave marker. He jeopardizes his safety, Silas' safety, and the safety of the graveyard by drawing attention to himself at school and in trying to stop the school bullies, Nick Farthing and Mo Quilling. And he puts himself and Miss Lupescu in terrible danger by following the ghouls through the ghoul-gate. In these instances Bod mistakes what he wants to happen for what should happen.

Noetic reason, on the other hand, is right reason, the ability to understand truth and the relationship of order to some ground of being—some foundation or anchor for life beyond the search for power, fame, and wealth. As an experience it calls people to pay attention to the world around them, experience the confusion and wonder of that world, take joy in it, and then to turn that joy into responsive and responsible action. It requires an ability to see what is right in front of us and act upon it. Noetic reason demands a balanced consciousness, one that can integrate the needs of the self with those of others, individual desires with the good of the whole.

Thus, noetic reason revolves around wisdom, fortitude, temperance, and charity. In other words, the classic experience of reason demands concern for the ability to forget the self. When an individual truly pays attention to something or someone, that person becomes part of a bigger story or drama of being. The individual is no longer the only and most important story, but learns moderation and proportion. That person can see the story from the inside, as a participant subject to larger forces rather than as the sole author of his or her life. Further, that person no longer possesses total control over the story.

The Graveyard Book is a story steeped in what the political philosopher Eric Voegelin calls spiritual realism. The spiritual realist believes in the reality of the spirit, of experiences that are real but that cannot be explained in empirical terms. She or he sees reality as much larger and all-encompassing than does the Modern Project—the use of personal and state power to satisfy our psychological and material needs and desires. Since the onset of the Modern Project human beings increasingly have drained the spiritual content from the world and replaced it with concern for the material and for technological and scientific progress. However, without the ability to see reality as larger than the physical, modernity lost the ability to see that "2 + 2 = 4," as Dr. Rieux puts it in Camus' *The Plague*. In other words, the Modern Project lost *opsis*, clear-sightedness, the ability to see things for what they are. Instead it focused on abstractions. War, genocide, and plague are abstractions that have little impact on the human mind. People get caught up in the day-to-day issue of staying alive themselves. The problem is not that human beings cannot add; the problem is that they do not see what is right in front of them—the very real fact of millions upon millions of deaths, for example. Only the clear-sighted have the ability to see and comprehend the implications and human costs of events and decisions.

In *The Plague*, Camus writes, "The soul of the murderer is blind; and there can be no true goodness nor true love without the utmost clear-sightedness" (131). This clear-sightedness allows Bod to transform his and suffering, similar to what we all face and the only reward Camus sees for life—into human solidarity. As Rambert states in *The Plague*, "now that I've seen what I've seen, I know that I belong here whether I want it or not. This business is everybody's business" (Camus 209–210).

Silas warns the citizens of the graveyard that "it will take a graveyard" to raise Bod, and they heed his words (23). Raising Bod becomes "everybody's business." Silas becomes Bod's guardian so that the child will have food and clothes. Miss Lupescu, the Hound of God, puts herself into danger in order to save him from the ghouls and ultimately sacrifices her life to save other members of the Honor Guard and protect Bod from the Convocation. Silas risks himself to save Bod from exposure when Mo's policeman uncle picks him up for "being out late" (204) and "breaking things" in Mo's back garden (199). At the end of the book, the entire graveyard works together to foil the Jacks' attempt to murder Bod and Scarlett. The solidarity of the graveyard protects and guides him.

Ultimately, understanding what things are everybody's business, acknowledging the reality of the human experience of mystery, and accepting that human beings originated in some other ground or source than themselves are essential to achieving *opsis*. These three ideas are the building blocks of wisdom. Accepting the reality of the human experience of mystery, of understanding that human beings originated in some other ground or source than themselves, is essential to achieving *opsis*. As G.K. Chesterton (another of Gaiman's favorite writers) maintained in "Everlasting Man," human beings did not create themselves in the first instance and are unlikely ever to know with absolute precision the origin of the human race. In its classic sense reason fosters understandings of that mystery and recognition of the tension in existence produced by living between life and death and between the pull of reason and the push of the physical and emotional passions (Voegelin *Volume 12* 279). Human beings are constantly pulled in two directions simultaneously.

The spirit of the first three chapters of *Everlasting Man* permeate *The Graveyard Book*. Chesterton, like Gaiman, rearranges the way we think about the things we take for granted. He will not allow us to let our thinking get into some rut that ends ultimately in a mud hole. He will not let us over-complicate either the world around us or the place of humanity in the world. In his essay on the cave paintings of France, Chesterton exposes us to the almost terrifying simplicity and elegance that underlies history, and he will not let us dress up our ultimate ignorance. His goal for us is the same as his goal for himself—to see "through the eyes of a child" (Chesterton 163).

"I think," he writes, there is "something a trifle vulgar about this idea of trying to rebuke spirit by size" (Chesterton, 155). Bigger ideas are not necessarily better, more fundamental, or more fixed or certain (205). The understanding of a child is not necessarily any worse than that of an adult. Instead of looking at size or complexity, Chesterton suggests that human beings start at the beginning, which is a mystery. Humanity should just accept that and look at the world with simplicity. "And by simplicity I do not mean stupidity," he clarifies, "but rather the sort of clarity that sees things like life rather than words like evolution" (158).

This is the key to thinking about *The Graveyard Book*. Children think with simplicity. They start at the beginning. They look at things rather than words. They do not impose concepts on life. If it is something they want to pay attention to, they are capable of amazing powers of concentration. They look at the world afresh every time they go outside. They begin with a certain amount of natural clear-sightedness that can either be nurtured or ignored.

That is certainly what Bod does. Gaiman has said that "children's fiction is the most important fiction of all" (Newbery Award). In this he evokes the spirit of Chesterton's notion of seeing the world with the eyes of a child— of someone who possesses understanding and reason but still sees mystery and can accept even dragons, gods, wizards, and fairies as real. Children "walk the borders" of reality and require Honor Guards to protect their borders. They intuitively grasp the in-between nature of human existence.

Readers of *The Graveyard Book* can see this in-between existence in many places. No one has told Bod that reality is purely external, that all else is imagination and unreality. It is the dead, who are "as they were in life," that have difficulty accepting the possibility of a living child among them until the Lady on the Grey, whom "each of us encounters ... at the end of our days," arrives and cautions them that "the dead should have charity" (30). It is Scarlett, who has been taught by her parents that Bod is an imaginary friend and that her experiences in the graveyard with him are purely imaginary, that has difficulty with mystery and the in-between nature of human existence (60). She will be able to think of Bod's actions during the climactic scenes in the graveyard only as murder, so Silas must erase her memories of Bod and of all that has happened in order for her not to go mad. Bod, on the other hand, can accept the mystery in which he lives as normal. He adapts easily to the idea that Master and Mistress Owens will be his parents and Silas, who is neither dead nor alive but has the Freedom of the Graveyard, will be his guardian and obtain food and other necessities the graveyard itself cannot provide. As Avi writes, "in a world where the truth is often hidden, fantasy reveals reality" (Kurkjian 496). What Nobody "Bod" Owens sees and experiences in *The Graveyard Book* is very real, even if it cannot be perceived by any other living person. He can see what is right in front of him and learns to embrace mystery and transcendence as normal because he has experienced multiple levels of reality, both spiritual and the physical.

The Danse Macabre (or Macabray, a playful mispronunciation) of chapter five that occurs when the winter flowers bloom underscores the in-between nature of human existence and its ultimate mystery. The dance, in which the living join hands with the dead, demonstrates the universal commonality of the human journey through life, its fragility, and the futility of anchoring a life in the search for tangible things. It is "a line dance that had been ancient a thousand years before" (159). The song that accompanies the dance contains the refrain, "*Rich man, poor man, come away. / Come to dance the Macabray*," suggesting the inevitable (144). In the end, the Lady on the Grey tells Bod that everyone will dance the Macabray (161). All but the undead, like Silas, participate in the dance and live in-between life and death. And all ultimately will ride with the Lady. They live in-between in accordance with the spell Liza uses to save Bod from Abanezer Bolger's shop:

> Be hole, be dust, be dream, be wind
> Be night, be dark, be wish, be mind,
> Now slip, now slide, now move unseen,
> Above, beneath, betwixt, between [132].

Certainly the unthinking malevolent evil and animosity represented by the Jacks of All Trades in *The Graveyard Book* is mysterious, transcendent, and spiritual—and is just as blind as is the soul of the murderer Camus refers to in *The Plague*. The Jacks can see only the need to get what they want, Bod's death, to ensure the future of the Convocation and "keep everything running tickety-boo for another five thousand years" (271).

For Gaiman as for Camus, a full, ethical, and hopeful life requires understanding that "it will take a graveyard" (23) and that being able to "walk into life" with "eyes and heart wide open" (307) necessitates attunement to all levels of being, all aspects of reality. For the spiritual realist the "order of the spirit" is a living reality, even though it is not a reality that can be named or put in a box. And it is the product of noetic reason.

Only what Voegelin calls a "balanced consciousness"—an understanding of what it means to be human, how human beings treat one another, and the place of humanity in the universe based in humility, wisdom, strength, and courtesy—successfully can negotiate the tensions of an in-between life. This is the life that Bod knows that he lives and that most of the rest of humanity lives but does not acknowledge.

It is a balanced consciousness that Silas, Miss Lupescu, and the inhabitants of the graveyard seek to encourage in Bod. What they really teach him is to see what is right in front of him, to pay attention and be clear-sighted. Even in the darkness of the tomb, the one holding the burial site of someone even older than the Celts, and on the evening of the Macabray, Bod can see what is happening—what is really going on. Openness to and participation in both seen and unseen realities gives him *opsis*. But the natural clear-sightedness of the child must be nurtured by paying attention.

During the time he lives in the graveyard, paying attention is the most important lesson Bod learns. He does best when he is paying attention to what is right in front of him and others are not. This is what happens on his first visit with Scarlett to the tomb that was made even before the Celts arrived. A men enters the tomb who is "well-preserved, but still like something that had been dead a long time" with skin painted or tattooed with "purple designs and patterns" (52). The Indigo Man announces that he guards "the place from all who would harm it!" (53). Bod notices that Scarlett can see the Indigo Man who guards the tomb's treasures even though she cannot see the dead man on the tomb's floor. And thus Bod deduces the Indigo Man is imaginary because Scarlett can see him and she "can't see dead people" (54). Unlike two grave robbers who had preceded them, including one whose body is still there, Bod does not panic. Failing to scare the boy, the Indigo Man disappears and is replaced with the Sleer. Bod hears, "WE ARE THE SLEER" but Scarlett hears nothing (55). Bod deduces that the Sleer "can't touch" them, and states, "All you can do is scare" (56). The children leave the chamber unharmed.

Bod is only in danger when he fails to pay attention. When Bod is about 10, Silas goes on a journey leaving his charge in the care of Miss Lupescu. She requires the boy to memorize lists of information he considers useless and brings him unfamiliar foods to eat. Frustrated by Silas' absence, Miss Lupescu's strictness, and the feeling that his parents "do not understand him," Bod stomps "off into the graveyard feeling unloved and underappreciated" (73). Bod is so wrapped up in his sense of injustice and loneliness that he does not pay attention to what is in front of him. Attentive readers know from the chapter's first page that there is a ghoul-gate in the cemetery. Ghouls were on the list of the "different kinds of people" Miss Lupescu had been trying to teach him, along with the cries of various creatures. However, when the ghouls appear, Bod fails to recognize them for what they are and follows them through the ghoul-gate. Even the ghouls notice the boy's lack of attention: "Bod said, 'What *are* you people?' 'Ghouls,' said the Bishop of Bath and Wells. 'Bless me, somebody wasn't paying attention was he?'" (82). Bod's abduction by the ghouls shares many parallels with Mowgli's failure to "see" the nature of the *Bandar-Log* that preceded his abduction to the Lost City (Kipling "Kaa's Hunting" 25–53). The *Bandar-Log* monkeys are silly creatures without understanding, without order, whose only notion of truth is "we all say so" (Kipling 44). The ghouls are equally silly and pretentious. But both the ghouls and the monkeys are very dangerous. As one of the "Maxims of Baloo" states, "*There is none like to me!" says the Cub in the pride of his earliest kill; / But the jungle is large and the Cub he is small. Let him think and be still*" (Kipling 25).

Ghûlheim (the home of the ghouls), with its angles that are all wrong so "that the walls sloped crazily, that it was every nightmare he had ever endured made into a place" is not the place of order the ghouls claim it to be and is the very opposite of the graveyard (82). There can be no peace, no wisdom, no courtesy, and no moderation within its confines. Once there, Bod will be utterly lost. He will have no self, even though he would consider himself "more important than kings and queens, than presidents or prime ministers or heroes" (81). Like the Lost City of the *Bandar-Log*, Ghûlheim is the seat of injustice and disorder; the ultimate place of folly and bad judgment. Both Mowgli and Bod, however, have paid enough attention to know to try to get help. Mowgli, whom Baloo has taught the cries of the various animals, asks Chil the Kite for help in alerting Kaa and Bagheera, who then rescue him. Bod finally remembers the cry of the Night-Gaunts who alert Miss Lupescu and help rescue him.

The ability to differentiate between order and disorder depends on paying attention. Paying attention allows us to see all that is right in front of our eyes and to perceive what is there with a clear-sightedness the Greeks called *opsis*. They understand that "the death of the spirit was the price of progress.... The more fervently all human energies are thrown into the great enterprise of world-immanent action, the farther the human beings who engage in this enterprise move away from the life of the spirit" (Voegelin *New Science* 195). Fewer see the close connection between the act of paying attention and the development of *opsis*. However, growing up in the graveyard Bod learns the lessons valued by the classic understanding of reason, most importantly to pay attention and see with a clearness of vision because "wherever you go, you take yourself with you" (104).

Thus, no longer inexperienced and foolhardy, Bod is prepared when he is called up to save Scarlett and himself from the Every Man Jack who gather together to finish the job of killing Bod because of a prophecy that "there would be a child born who walked the borderland between the living and that dead" (271). That child would prove to be the end of the Convocation of Jacks.

One day Scarlett gets on the wrong bus after school and finds herself at the graveyard where she is befriended by a Mr. Frost who does headstone rubbings. He eventually becomes friends with her mother as well. Mr. Frost, however, is Jack Frost—the man Jack who murdered Bod's family. He is living in Bod's old home and entraps Bod and Scarlett under the pretense of helping Bod understand his family's story. They escape only to find four other Jacks at the front door. Like the ghouls, the members of the Convocation—many of whom the story tells us have high places in government, the police, and "other places besides"—are forces of disorder with consciousnesses formed to serve only their passions and appetites (268). They are unbalanced souls that seek to dominate others and to control both their own stories and those of others, rather than participate in the drama of being. They exhibit the polar opposite of noetic reason. For the Jacks, reason is merely the ability to calculate the best manner in which to achieve power and wealth. Bod is able to save himself and Scarlett because he has paid attention and because of the love of the graveyard's inhabitants. The Jacks, however, doom themselves because their single-minded pursuit of the teenagers blinds them. They cannot see what is in front of them or pay attention to the dangers of the graveyard. Two of the Jacks fall through the ghoul-gate and another falls into a grave and cannot get out. The Sleer, protector of the grave hoard, take Jack Frost when his desire for power and control of the treasure motivate him to name himself its master. In saving Scarlett and himself, Bod displays all the lessons he has learned growing up in the graveyard. He has paid attention. He has developed *opsis* and formed a balanced consciousness.

Ultimately, however, Bod, like Mowgli before him, must make his life among living human beings. As Bod approaches 15 he notices a change in his relationship with the graveyard. It is harder and harder for him to see all he used to see and the inhabitants seem to avoid him. He no longer can see in the dark as the dead do. Mother Slaughter tells him, "You're always you and that don't change, and you're always changing and there's nothing you can do about it" (298). It is time for Bod to leave and live in the human world. But he will keep much of the graveyard with him as he fulfills his desire to "see life." "I want to hold it in my hands. I want to leave a footprint on the sand of a desert island. I want to play football with people. I want ... I want *everything*," he declares (304). Bod is ready and prepared to live a full life. Silas has been his guardian as long as Bod needed protection. Now, however, the Jacks are gone and Bod is old enough to protect himself. It is time to experience the world of the living and participate in the drama of being from its perspective.

The key to understanding Bod's change is in the lullaby Mistress Owens sings when he leaves the graveyard:

> Kiss a lover,
> Dance a measure,
> Find your name
> And buried treasure ...
> Face your life,
> Its pain, its pleasure,
> Leave no path untaken [306].

This lullaby contains everything evoked by the idea of awe and wonder at the mystery of life, the need to pay attention and be clear-sighted, the acceptance of all reality, expectation, wisdom, temperance, fortitude, and charity. One of the lessons of *The Graveyard Book* is that we are our stories. We help write our stories; we are pure possibility. However, that infinite possibility has ethical borders because of the type of reason—noetic reason—Gaiman embeds in his plots. Those ethical borders are important because they help us achieve the *opsis* of a balanced consciousness.

In his Newbery Medal acceptance speech for *The Graveyard Book*, Gaiman says that he had once forgotten "what fiction was to me as a boy ... an escape from the intolerable, a doorway to impossibly hospitable worlds where things had rules and could be understood.... I remembered. I would not be the person I am without the authors who made me what I am" (9). Chesterton and Kipling are among those authors. Although Bod will forget much of what he experienced in the graveyard—as it becomes a "place" instead of his "home" (304), he will not forget either the graveyard's inhabitants or its lessons. He no longer possesses the Freedom of the Graveyard. However, Bod has achieved a sense of himself as both an individual and as a participant in the larger story of life, and he will hold onto the lessons he learned there. Its inhabitants are the authors of who he is. They have taught him to understand that there is only one story—the story of human beings living in between the pulls of life and death. It is through incorporating our lives into a larger reality and relying on noetic reason that we know our "selves" as part of that larger story. We give up our egoism, adopt a reflective distance from which to evaluate our choices, and can see ourselves as part of a larger whole. As Bod goes off to "leave no path untaken," he understands that life is "an adventure of decision on the edge of freedom and necessity" (Voegelin *Israel* 1). He is well-prepared to "see life" and "to hold it in [his] hands" (304). Wherever he goes, however he changes, and whatever challenges he meets Nobody Owens will pay attention and live a life of wisdom, strength, and courtesy.

Note

1. In political philosophy modernity begins with the writings of Machiavelli. The Modern Project is a term that is often used to pull together the ideas found in modern political thought. Modern ideologies such as liberalism, conservatism, and Marxism and the modern idolization of science and the state blind us to the tension inherent in living and confine us to a world defined by the limited categories of political "realism." In the world as described by the Modern Project, "power" means force or competition for domination over others and "knowledge" comes purely from sense impressions.

Works Cited

Camus, Albert. *The Plague*. New York: Vintage, 1991. Print.

Chesterton, G.K. *The Collected Works of G.K. Chesterton, Volume II: The Everlasting Man, St. Francis of Assisi, St. Thomas Aquinas*. Rutler Azar and George Marlin, eds. San Francisco: Ignatius Press, 1986. Print.

Gaiman, Neil. *The Graveyard Book*. New York: Harper, 2008. Print.

_____. "Newbery Medal Acceptance Speech: Telling Lies for a Living...and Why We Do It." *Children and Libraries* (Summer/Fall 2009): 7–10. Radford University Library. Radford, VA. 30 November 2013.

Kipling, Rudyard. *The Jungle Books*. New York: Macmillan, 1964. Print.

Kurkjian, Catherine, Nancy Livingston, Terrell Young, and Avi. "Worlds of Fantasy." *The Reading Teacher* 59.5 (February 2006): 492–503. Radford University Library. Radford, VA. 3 April 2014.

Plato. *Gorgias*. Indianapolis: Hackett, 1986. Print.

Voegelin, Eric. *The Collected Works of Eric Voegelin Volume 11: Published Essays 1953– 1965*. Ed. Ellis Sandoz. Columbia: University of Missouri Press, 2000. Print.

_____. *The Collected Works of Eric Voegelin Volume 12: Published Essays 1966–1985*. Ed. Ellis Sandoz. Baton Rouge: Louisiana State University Press, 1990. Print.

_____. *The Collected Works of Eric Voegelin Volume 25: The New Order and the Last Orientation*. Ed. Jürgen Gebhardt and Thomas A. Hollweck. Columbia: University of Missouri Press, 1999. Print.

_____. "The New Science of Politics." *The Collected Works of Eric Voegelin Volume 5: Modernity Without Restraint*. Ed Manfred Henningsen. Columbia: University of Missouri Press, 2000. Print.

_____. *Order and History Volume I: Israel and Revelation*. Baton Rouge: Louisiana State University Press, 1958. Print.

_____. *Order and History Volume III: Plato and Aristotle*. Baton Rouge: Louisiana State University Press, 1957. Print.

"Nightmare in Silver" (2013)

"We've upgraded ourselves": Gaiman's Resurrection of the Cybermen

Emily Capettini

In an interview with Collider.com, Neil Gaiman reveals that he first turned down an invitation to write a second *Doctor Who* episode, but Steven Moffat's request to "[make] the Cybermen scary again" convinced him (Radish). Gaiman continues, "Patrick Troughton was my Doctor," adding that he found the quiet nature of the Cybermen "very off-putting" (Radish). To viewers familiar with Troughton's era of *Doctor Who*, particularly "The Moonbase" (1967) and "Tomb of the Cybermen" (1967), Gaiman's comment may not come as a surprise. Much of what viewers see in Gaiman's 2013 episode, "Nightmare in Silver," can be traced back to Troughton's adventures. As for the Cybermen being "scary again," the monsters had horrifying characteristics, but most reviewers agree that these characteristics got lost in the new series. As most reviewers note, "Gaiman has dipped right back to their earlier days ... when the Cybermen were still able to get under your skin (hello, *Tomb of the Cybermen*)" (Brew). Alasdair Watkins adds, "the very thing that makes [the Cybermen] so fascinating is also what tends to undercut them as villains ... [they] prize survival above all else." The emphasis on survival is different from the main priority of another *Who* villain, the Daleks. Watkins is aware of this rivalry, stating, "Cybermen aren't just Daleks with legs," and echoing Simon Brew's observation in another review: "For such an iconic *Doctor Who* monster, they've always struck us as one of the least scary in recent times." The Cybermen have been historically low on the scale of *Doctor Who*'s scary monsters.

On the surface, it seems peculiar to claim a race of robot-like aliens who harvest humans for spare parts is not as terrifying as aliens determined to kill everyone, but Brew, Watkins, and Gaiman challenge this notion. The Cybermen have long been considered secondary to the Daleks, which is clear in Brew's comments and even in "Doomsday" (2006), when the Daleks seem much more capable of decimating Earth than the Cybermen. Yet one cannot hold the Daleks and the Cybermen to the same standards, for while the Daleks cruise around yelling their intentions and killing everyone, all early stories featuring the Cybermen depend on the slow, quiet invasion. In "Tomb of the Cybermen" (1967), actual, living Cybermen do not appear until awakened by the antagonist. Perhaps what makes the Cybermen "off-putting" instead of terrifying is that they began as a more topical villain. In much the same way he did in his previous episode, "The Doctor's Wife" (2011), Gaiman looks to *Doctor Who*'s past in order to invent its future.[1] Critics are split on the narrative success of "Nightmare in Silver," but Gaiman clearly succeeds in making the Cybermen scary again. He does so by tapping into their early past during Troughton's era and returning the Cybermen to their quiet, "off-putting" selves in a very Gaimanesque fashion.

Before analyzing "Nightmare in Silver," it is worth noting that *Doctor Who*'s seventh series already owes a debt to Troughton's tenure as the Doctor, 1966–1969. Villains, costume choices, and Smith's acting allude to the original series with Troughton. The most notable villain with ties to the Troughton era is the main antagonist The Great Intelligence, last seen onscreen in "The Web of Fear" (1968).[2] Episodes like "Cold War" (2013) also feature the Ice Warriors, who first appeared in 1968.[3] In costume, Smith and Troughton regularly wear bowties as their respective Doctors. In series seven, Smith's tweed blazer is swapped out in favor of a long, dark jacket that is visually similar to Troughton's black frock coat. Considering that series seven also marks the return of the Ice Warriors and The Great Intelligence, the visual similarity in costumes is more than coincidental.

Additionally, Smith's acting is influenced by Troughton. In a 2010 interview, Moffat told *Doctor Who Monthly* that after Smith was given the role of the Doctor, he went back and watched the classic series, for "of all the [actors they] saw, he probably knew the show least" (Spilsbury 18). After Smith had watched "Tomb of the Cybermen," which he now cites as a favorite, he called Moffat and "was on the phone for about 20 minutes … just raving about it, about how brilliant it was … and how much he loved Patrick Troughton" (Harp; Spilsbury 18). Smith's affection for Troughton's Doctor is evident in his mannerisms as well as the script. For example, in "Closing Time" (2011) the Doctor (Smith) cheerfully comments to a friend, "Oh, you've redecorated. I don't like it." This moment is a reference to "The Three Doctors," in which the Doctor

(Troughton) looks around the new TARDIS interior and says, in the same tone, "I seen you've been doing the TARDIS up a bit. I don't like it." In many ways, *Doctor Who*'s season seven has already presented viewers with a wealth of visual and narrative parallels between Smith and Troughton. "Nightmare in Silver"'s debt to the original series, including a reinvention of the Cybermen based on the first several Cybermen stories, fits in well with season seven's aesthetic.

Though the Daleks may be *Doctor Who*'s most iconic villain, they lack an immediate, detailed origin story like the Cyberman have.[4] One reason for this discrepancy between the Daleks and the Cybermen may be Kit Pedler. Pedler, "a surgeon and research scientist" and "head of the Electron Microscopy Department of the University of London" was brought on as a scientific advisor to *Doctor Who* in 1966 (Hearn 38–40). "The Tenth Planet," the Cybermen's debut and the last serial to feature William Hartnell as the Doctor, was written by Pedler and Gerry Davis. The episode grew out of concerns about medicine "[becoming] a matter of machines," a future in which humans were hooked up to a computer, rather than being cared for by doctors and nurses (40). If humans were "totally cybernetic," there was a possibility that their souls would be lost (40). Marcus Hearn calls Davis's and Pedler's collaboration "methodical" and emphasizes its "commitment to realism"; a contrast to Terry Nation's "instinctual approach" to creating the Daleks (40). It is impossible to separate the Cybermen from contemporary anxieties about humanity versus advancing technologies. Gaiman's "Nightmare in Silver" reminds us of these original concerns, particularly when the Cybermen match wits with humans.

In his quest to reinvent the Cybermen, Gaiman revives the tactics the Cybermen use in early stories like "Tomb of the Cybermen" and "The Moonbase," such as the use of Cybermats and Cybermites, quiet invasion, and manipulation. "Nightmare in Silver" opens in a "slightly kitsch-y," abandoned amusement park, a location "so Gaimanesque ... it may as well stalk about wearing black and not brushing its hair" (Mellor). Impresario Webley, a kind of con artist, curator, and magician, greets the Doctor and companions Clara, Angie, and Artie after they arrive on Hedgewick's World, "the biggest and best amusement park there will ever be" ("Nightmare in Silver"). He invites them into his exhibit, and this is when the antagonist is revealed:

> WEBLEY: Now, let me demonstrate to you all, the wonder of the age, the miracle of modernity. We defeated them all a thousand years ago ... but now he's back to destroy you. Behold—the enemy!
> DOCTOR: Cyberman! Get down!
> [title credits]

WEBLEY: No need to panic, my young friends. We all know that there are no more living Cybermen. What you are seeing is a miracle. 699th wonder of the universe as past displayed before the Imperial court. And only here to destroy you ... at chess! An empty shell, and yet it moves ["Nightmare"].

The sort of stock storytelling one would expect from a magician accompanies Webley's big reveal of the Cyberman. Webley's rumpled appearance, beaten up top hat, and wrinkled frock call to mind another of Gaiman's characters: *Neverwhere's* marquis de Carabas. The marquis is dressed in "a huge dandyish black coat that was not quite a frock coat nor exactly a trench coat, and high black boots beneath his coat, raggedy clothes" (Gaiman 40). Though Webley works in illusions and there is something uncanny about the marquis's skills, the sartorial similarities carry a certain Gaiman quality. This sort of raggedy Victorian look is also present in Gaiman's previous *Doctor Who* episode, "The Doctor's Wife." Idris's clothing, a corseted dress with a bustle, is also dirty and worn. Webley fits the part of a Gaiman character.

On Hedgewick's World, as the Doctor examines the "empty shell" and Webley continues his pitch, the camera alternates between the Doctor and companions and metallic, beeping insects. These insects are later identified as Cybermites, upgraded Cybermats. Cybermats, appearing as recently as "Closing Time" (2011), are converted infants, who are "too small" for conversion into a whole Cyberman ("The Crystal of Cantus"). Instead, "their organs are harvested and used to create ... a Cybermat," which "will assist [the Cybermen] in [their] advance through the galaxy" ("Crystal"). Though it initially seems these tiny spies have gone unnoticed, the Doctor later tells Clara that he wants to stay so he can collect "funny insects" ("Nightmare"). The claim that the Cybermen are extinct cannot be believed, and audiences by now are well aware of *Doctor Who*'s troubled history with the word "extinct."

The dramatic irony surrounding Webley's assurance that the Cybermen are dead reflects much of *Doctor Who*'s history with supposedly extinct races, but more specifically calls to mind "Tomb of the Cybermen." The Second Doctor and companions Jamie and Victoria travel to Telos, a Cybermen planet. There, they encounter an archeological dig, "searching the universe for the last remains of the Cybermen," who "died out many centuries ago" ("Tomb"). Like Webley, most of the expedition members are confident there are no more living Cybermen. Professor Parry, the expedition's leader, later clarifies that the Cybermen "have been dead for the last 500 years" ("Tomb"). The Cybermen have been defeated or become extinct and humans without firsthand experience of Cybermen have gone in search of remains. As one may expect, the expedition does not go well.

Parry constantly uses the terms "died out" and "extinct," but the Doctor uses notably different language: "Perhaps the Cybermen aren't quite as dormant as you imagine," he says ("Tomb"). The use of "dormant" instead of "extinct" keeps the Cybermen as a constant threat, like a dormant volcano. The most significant difference between "Nightmare in Silver" and "Tomb of the Cybermen" is in the 1967 story, humans have gone looking for Cybermen and hope to find remains, whereas Webley's claim that "uniforms give me the heebie-jeebies" and his poorly-lit exhibit indicate a desire to hide his collection of three "dead" Cybermen ("Nightmare"). More obviously, the soldiers stationed on the planet are skeptical of the presence of Cybermen, though they do possess a basic supply of anti–Cybermen weapons: one anti–Cyber gun, a handful of hand-pulsars that knock out Cybermen if close enough, and a bomb that will implode the planet. Captain Ferren tells Clara that "even one anti–Cyber gun is a miracle," and a rare weapon in a punishment platoon's possession suggests humanity's continued caution about Cybermen ("Nightmare"). Though the expedition in "Tomb of the Cybermen" is an archeological trip, there is still no thought as to what they will do if Cybermen appear. In contrast, even a platoon stationed somewhere so they "can't get into trouble" is equipped to deal with the threat of Cybermen ("Nightmare").

Within both narratives, the Cybermats and Cybermites play an equally important role. In both episodes, the first appearance of the Cybermen is their scouts: the Cybermats. These creatures first appear in "Tomb of the Cybermen." Victoria, upon discovering an inactive Cybermat, proclaims she has found a fossil and puts it in her purse. When Klieg wakes the interred Cybermen, the Cybermat becomes active and attacks Klieg's partner, Kaftan. Yet, the Cybermats are not a major threat at this point in the episode. There is only one, and it is quickly destroyed when Victoria shoots it. Despite this, the Cybermen are able to "use the power of cybernetics" through the Cybermats. They upgrade humans, including a member of the archeological expedition, Toberman ("Tomb"). The "power of cybernetics" is a nod to the Cybermen's origins and the anxieties about advancing technologies they represent. A single Cybermat's presence indicates a much larger problem. Multiple Cybermats are capable of converting humans. The Cybermats attack the expedition while they sleep, sneaking up through a ramp too small for the Cybermen to get through. A quiet attack like this one is characteristic of the early Cybermen, but was not a frequent part of their return in the new series.

Unlike their later appearances in "The Rise of the Cybermen" (2006) and "The Next Doctor" (2008), the attacks in "Tomb of the Cybermen" are silent, and the conversion of human to Cyberman is much less ostentatious.

Though the quiet kidnapping of Torchwood employees is much like the tactics in "Tomb of the Cybermen," what is far more memorable are the rows and rows of conversion units and humans filing in, only to be heard screaming while being dismembered ("Army of Ghosts," "Doomsday"). Furthermore, a teaser for "The Next Doctor" signals the Cybermen as the main enemy before they are even seen. The teaser shows shots of the main cast interspersed with text, but the only sound is the familiar hydraulic stomping that was characteristic of the Cybermen from 2005 to 2011 ("The Next Doctor" promo, BBC). These incarnations of the Cybermen announce their presence, unlike the 1960s versions. Though there is some terror in a marching group of Cybermen, the thought that they may be concealed in plain sight is far more unsettling.

It is no coincidence that the Cybermen reverted to sneaking around and creeping up on victims quietly in "Nightmare in Silver." In the same interview with Collider.com, Gaiman outlines what, to him, made the Cybermen so terrifying. As a child, he first saw the Cybermen in their second appearance, "The Moonbase." Gaiman states, "I was much more scared of them, in a way, than the Daleks because they were quiet and they slipped in and out of rooms. It was very off-putting" (Radish). They were so off-putting that when it came time to reinvent them, although Gaiman "[loved] the design of the clanky clanky Steampunk Cybermen," the noise was dropped (Radish). As a result, the Cybermen from "Nightmare in Silver" have much more in common with their original counterparts.

Gaiman cites "The Moonbase" when he mentions the quiet invasion. In the episode, there are multiple shots of the Cybermen walking quietly into a room, picking up an unconscious crewmember and slipping out ("The Moonbase"). So effective is this invasion that none of the characters, or the audience for that matter, see a whole Cyberman until the end of the first episode ("The Moonbase"). The single shots of arms and hands underline the fact that the Cybermen's presence on the Moon remains unknown. While viewers may figure out that the problems plaguing the base are due to the Cybermen, their presence is only glimpsed.

In addition to kidnapping, the Cybermen have been infecting crewmembers in an even less detectable way: introducing a virus into the base's sugar supply that makes infected crew members puppets of the Cybermen ("The Moonbase"). This sort of attack is similar to sending small conversion units to convert people into machines, as in "Tomb of the Cybermen." So not only does this tell audiences that the Cybermen are a danger, but it also indicates that one may be unaware of the danger until it is too late to prevent infiltration.

These stealth tactics and quiet, methodical invasions are how the Cybermen survive and return in "Nightmare in Silver."

The "funny little insects" the Doctor notices in "Nightmare in Silver" are in line with the first-strike Cybermats from "Tomb of the Cybermen" and "The Moonbase." Alone, Webley begins to reorganize the chessboard when the supposedly dead Cyberman grabs his wrists. Cybermites flood out of the Cyberman's eyes like maggots on a corpse, swarming up Webley's arms. The camera angle then changes to Webley's back and audiences hear "Upgrade in progress" ("Nightmare"). Later, when the Doctor boards the Valkyrie, the Cyberman spaceship, a half-converted Webley throws Cybermites on the Doctor so the Cyber Planner may convert him. Once more, this conversion—luring people away from the group and upgrading them almost silently—draws inspiration from the 1960s Cybermen.

The Cyber Planner's attempt to convert the Doctor also follows in the same manner of the invasions in "The Moonbase" and "Tomb of the Cybermen." The Doctor seems to be unaware of the danger the Cybermites possess until it is too late. He picks one up and carries it on board the Valkyrie and is alarmed only when he sees that Webley has handfuls of Cybermites ("Nightmare"). In fact, this invasion and regrouping of the Cybermen is perhaps the slowest in *Doctor Who*'s history, marking a thousand-year gap. In "The Moonbase," the Cybermen were last seen almost a century prior ("The Invasion"). In "Tomb of the Cybermen," the gap is 500 years. However, while the Cybermen have been waiting for the opportunity to launch an attack in "The Moonbase," the Cybermen in both "Tomb of the Cybermen" and "Nightmare in Silver" wait for humans to find them. The Cybercontroller tells Parry's expedition of this plan:

PARRY: How did you know that we would come to release you? You could have remained frozen forever.

CYBERCONTROLLER: The humanoid mind. You are inquisitive.

DOCTOR: Ah, I see, a trap. A very special sort of trap, too.

PARRY: What do you mean, special trap?

DOCTOR: Don't you see? They only wanted superior intellects. That's why they made the trap so complicated.

CYBERCONTROLLER: We knew that somebody like you would come to our planet someday.

DOCTOR: Yes, and we've done exactly as you've calculated, haven't we? ["Tomb"].

The Cybermen in this episode carefully construct a plan that will draw humans. More specifically, this trap was designed so that only "superior intellects" would make it to the actual tomb. In "Nightmare in Silver," Cyber-Webley reveals that the Cybermen kidnapped people from Hedgewick's World for "spare parts" to repair "critically damaged units" ("Nightmare"). Here, the lure is the amusement park, because the Cybermen need "a child's brain with its infinite potential" ("Nightmare"). Like the Cybermen's tomb, the amusement park was designed for the kind of humans the Cybermen required. It is fitting that the Doctor, with his limitless and predictable curiosity, is lured aboard the Valkyrie and is then recognized as being the best choice for the Cyber Planner.

Previous stories, as well as "Nightmare in Silver," have established that the Cybermen only seek out humans for conversion. In a truly terrifying moment, when the Doctor tells Cyber-Webley that his Time Lord brain is biologically useless to them, Cyber-Webley answers, almost cheerfully, "Oh, that was true a long time ago, but we've upgraded ourselves" ("Nightmare"). The amount of knowledge that the Doctor possesses is a great danger to the universe in the hands of the Cybermen, who are already quite adept at manipulating humans and now, more worryingly, Time Lords.

What is most unsettling about this characterization of the Cybermen lying in wait is that it implies there could be Cybermen hiding anywhere, waiting to kidnap people for upgrades. Finding Cybermen in a Cybermen's tomb is not wholly unexpected, but the amusement park is another issue, for it reminds viewers of how individuals can disappear, even in large groups of people. The amusement park underlines what might be the most terrifying aspect of the Cybermen. Cybermen are once-humanoid creatures who, as a result of continual upgrades to extend their lifetimes, removed all emotions ("The Tenth Planet").[5] The fact that Cybermen are at once like and completely different from humans mean they straddle an interesting split in science fiction narratives. In their overview of science fiction and life sciences, Joan Slonczewski and Michael Levy note:

> The great adversary [in contemporary science fiction] is no longer an alien superpower, but the enemies within—cancer, AIDS, and bio-weapons—as well as the accidental results of genetic manipulation, and our own lifestyle destroying our biosphere. The engineering challenge of the future is less a matter of machines replacing living organisms than of machines imitating life's complexity [174].

The Cybermen, it is vital to remember, are not only an alien superpower, but also represent an enemy within: mortality and the damaging consequences of subverting that mortality. In a different sense, after a human is upgraded and becomes a Cyberman or a puppet of the Cybermen, she or he also becomes the enemy within a group, often infiltrating humans who have not yet been converted to further Cybermen. In "The Moonbase" and "Tomb of the Cybermen," humans that have been taken over by the Cybermen are returned to their places in order to infiltrate. In "Nightmare in Silver," Cybermen are inside the Doctor's head. The Doctor and the Cyber Planner vie for .238 percent of the Doctor's brain, and whoever wins the chess game wins the Doctor's consciousness and knowledge ("Nightmare"). Despite a lack of emotions, the Cybermen still have enough humanity left to be able to accurately predict human (and Time Lord) actions and manipulate accordingly. All Cybermen stories hinge on this uncanny ability, which is often exacerbated by humanity's lack of direct experience with Cybermen and how humanity responds to an almost undefeatable enemy.

"Tomb of the Cybermen" shows the most obvious human errors when people are faced with Cybermen. Financing the expedition is Eric Klieg, a member of the Brotherhood of Logicians, a group dedicated to "logic and power" ("Tomb"). Despite this emphasis on logic, Klieg, like Webley, makes poor decisions. In search of power to back their plans, Klieg infiltrates archeologist Parry's expedition to Telos ("Tomb"). The Doctor asks Klieg if he thinks the Cybermen will agree to help, and Klieg answers, "Of course, I shall be their resurrector" ("Tomb"). Oddly, Klieg fails to note the Cybermen's key characteristic: the Cybermen are completely devoid of emotions. What has long made the Cybermen such a dangerous enemy is this absence, or, as co-creator of the Cybermen, Gerry Davis, put it, a lack of souls. Instead, Klieg assumes that the Cybermen will see the logic of the situation: he has brought them back after 500 years, and they should show due deference. Klieg values logic above all else, and the Cybermen are a logical race. This partnership should work, yet the irony is that Klieg does not think to consider the Cybermen's perspective. The narrative of "Tomb of the Cybermen" turns on a lack of experience interacting with the Cybermen. However, the consequences of this mistake result in six deaths, a small body count compared to later stories, which marks a split between "Tomb of the Cybermen" and "Nightmare in Silver."

"Nightmare in Silver," despite its use of familiar tactics and tropes from the 1960s stories, emphasizes consequences to raise the emotional stakes and show just how dangerous the Cybermen are. Instead of Klieg, the characters are Webley, Porridge (the missing Emperor), and a group of inexperienced soldiers lead by the competent Captain Ferren. To be fair, the only people unalarmed by the mention of the Cybermen are those who have never heard of them: the companions Clara, Angie, and Artie. Though the Cybermen are threatening in "Tomb of the Cybermen" and the tomb has dangers aplenty, including electrified doors, the solutions in "Nightmare in Silver" are very different. As Porridge tells Clara, they defeated the Cybermen by destroying the entire Tiberian Spiral Galaxy and all of its inhabitants, which included the Cybermen. This drastic solution calls to mind nuclear warfare, and it is not apparent that the ends justify these means. The consequences of killing "a billion trillion people" are still visible: there is a black, blank spot in the sky where the galaxy once was ("Nightmare"). The Doctor also keeps directing Clara not to let "anyone blow up [the] planet" ("Nightmare"). This moment is funny, due to Smith's lighthearted delivery, but it is also serious, for the Doctor has some experience when it comes to blowing up a planet in the interest of saving the rest of the universe. Gaiman mentions that this is an idea he "loved": "Planets are expendable, but a Cyberman, if you can't destroy it immediately, is not. It's going to be very, very hard to destroy" (Radish). No doubt part of the threat of these new Cybermen is their speed. In the episode, the Cybermen move so fast, they blur. This speed upgrade is part of their new threat: they can move too quickly to stop, as seen when a Cyberman whips through a group of humans and kidnaps Angie. It is not difficult to see why this Cyberman would pose an undefeatable threat if not destroyed immediately.

After the Cyberman kidnaps Angie in "Nightmare in Silver," the Doctor has two requests of Clara:

DOCTOR: Stay alive until I get back and don't let anyone blow up this planet.
CLARA: Is that ... something they're likely to do? ["Nightmare"].

Clara already knows the last Cyberwar ended after the Tiberian Spiral Galaxy was blown up, but the thought of destroying one planet still shocks her and is meant to shock viewers, as well. It is also unintentionally amusing to think of Clara, who is currently babysitting Angie and Artie, as the main obstacle to planetary destruction. In a similar vein, the Doctor's last reminder to not blow up the planet is delivered to the whole platoon and sounds like a reprimand: "And you lot.... No blowing up this planet!" ("Nightmare"). The combination of humor and gravity in these moments serves to underline the almost incomprehensible nature of destroying a planet or galaxy. The suggestion that a planet, or galaxy, is more easily destroyed than a race inhabiting it is unsettling. The sacrifice of "Nightmare in Silver" does not line up at all with the deaths in "Tomb of the Cybermen," and indicates larger, more far-reaching consequences for humanity in their fight against Cybermen.

In addition to their quick invasions, the Cybermens' upgrades are a new threat and no doubt why there is so much talk of imploding planets. These instant upgrades happen multiple times in the span of one episode. Prior to

"Nightmare in Silver," such upgrades would take years and typically happen off-screen, between Cybermen stories. Like Pedler and Davis in their creation of the Cybermen, Gaiman turned to modern technology for inspiration: "my phone doesn't look anything like what it looked like five years ago, and that didn't look anything like what it looked like 10 years ago.... I thought, 'Cybermen talk about upgrading, so let's watch them upgrade'" (Radish). Gaiman, like Pedler, reinvented the Cybermen as a topical villain by looking to modern technology for inspiration. Upgrades for modern technology occur far more frequently than ever before, so it seems logical that a Cyberman thousands of years in the future would have the capability to upgrade on the spot.

While there are many parallels to the 1960s Cybermen, there is a lot of Gaiman in this episode, too. Louisa Mellor points out that the "slightly kitschy tourist attraction" of an abandoned amusement park and a high stakes board also make appearances in *American Gods*.[6] The language of the episode is also very fitting in both *Doctor Who* and Gaiman's prior works. The episode opens with the Doctor proclaiming he has a "golden ticket" to the best amusement park in the universe:

> DOCTOR: Well, here we are, Hedgewick's World. The biggest and best amusement park there will ever be, and we've got a golden ticket, eh? Eh? Fun!
>
> CLARA: Fun?
>
> ANGIE: The stupid box can't even get us to the right place? This is like a moon base or something?
>
> DOCTOR: Well, it's not the moon.
>
> ARTIE: Actually, I think it does look like the moon ... only dirtier.
>
> DOCTOR: Hey, guys, it's not the moon, okay? It's a Spacey Zoomer Ride, or it was ["Nightmare in Silver"].

First, the golden ticket is a reference to Roald Dahl's *Charlie and the Chocolate Factory*, a children's novel about a reclusive and whimsical candy-maker with whom the Doctor no doubt feels a close kinship. The golden ticket in *Doctor Who* unlocks a day of adventure at an amusement park that turns out to be as fraught with dangers as Wonka's factory. Mellor cites this moment as an example of Gaiman's recurring "[acknowledgement] that many stories have gone before it."

The name of the ride also fits in with the language of *Doctor Who* and Gaiman's inspirations. The "Spacey Zoomer Ride" is not quite as serious as contemporary space-themed amusement park attractions, such as Walt Disney World Resort's MISSION: Space. Mellor notes that this title and other names in the episode have "hints of Adams and Terry Pratchett," "a Zaphod Beeblebrox the Fourth kind of silliness." The name fits right in with a show whose most-famous line is arguably, "People assume that time is a strict progression of cause to effect, but actually, from a nonlinear, nonsubjective viewpoint, it's more like a big ball of wibbly-wobbly ... timey-wimey ... stuff" ("Blink"). The Spacey Zoomer Ride's juxtaposition with the more technical aspects of "Nightmare in Silver," such as the Cybermen's upgrades, is in keeping with the madcap humor of the show.

Not unlike the Spacey Zoomer Ride is Natty Longshoe's Comical Castle. Neither Spacey Zoomer nor Natty Longshoe's Comical Castle seem out of place in this "slightly kitsch-y" amusement park. After the Cyberman kidnaps Angie, the platoon assembles their anti–Cybermen weapons and begins to look for a base. In yet another balance of humor and horror, Captain Ferren pulls out a collapsible metal pointer and presents Clara with the possible bases, all illustrated on the park's map:

> FERREN: The Beach, Giant's Cauldron, Natty Longshoe's Comical Castle.
> CLARA: Real castle? Drawbridge, moat?
> FERREN: Yes. But comical ["Nightmare"].

The map is brightly painted with garish colors and the rides are not to scale, as is typical for an amusement park map. In a military setting, it is humorously out-of-place. Meanwhile, Ferren and Clara evaluate each attraction's suitability, including "comical" alongside defensive (drawbridge and moat). Clara and Ferren are faced with the return of an alien race with a body count of over a billion trillion, yet are briefly preoccupied with how "comical" fits into a defensive strategy.

"Nightmare in Silver" also centers on the creepy or unseen horror of the everyday. People (especially children) sometimes get lost in enormous crowds, often in places like malls and amusement parks. Being quietly kidnapped and used as spare parts for alien robots, however, possesses a singularly Gaiman quality. To take commonplace disappearances and infuse them with something otherworldly is how Gaiman creates eerie or terror in the everyday. This motivation is present in his other works, such as the world of London Below in *Neverwhere* and the manipulative Jacks of All Trades in *The Graveyard Book*. "Nightmare in Silver" is yet another example of Gaiman's excellent ability to take old stories and create something new that remains true to but is not limited by its origins.

Related to this idea of the terror in the everyday is fearing the wrong thing. That is, being distracted by a fear of something nonthreatening and missing the actual threat. In "Nightmare in Silver," Artie sits alone in the dark. He says aloud, "I'm not scared. If you're wondering. I just think ... I ought to turn the lights back on" ("Nightmare"). As he runs to the light switch, the camera pans around the dimly lit space and shadowed wax figures. Artie turns on the light and looks around the room, relieved. A few seconds later, a Cyberman grabs him. The bait-and-switch horror here is clever: while the wax figures are creepy, Artie's fear of them blinds him to the real threat. The Cyberman attacks Artie in a fully lit room, thus inverting the trope of only dark spaces carrying threats. Perhaps what makes this moment so scary is that the Cyberman does not care if it is seen, for, as shown later, it is almost impossible to stop.

From a critical standpoint, "Nightmare in Silver," did well. Most reviewers agree that Gaiman was successful in making the Cybermen scary again, but the narrative strength of "Nightmare in Silver" is less successful. Brew comments that the episode "feels like it needed more space," though the "sheer ambition" of the narrative "slightly tempers the episode," while Sarah Crompton adds, "a large chunk of it took place inside the Doctor's head ... [and] this gave Matt Smith a brilliant opportunity for some dexterous and compelling acting ... but the acting masterclass went on a bit long." Watkins, in a review that sums up both Brew's and Crompton's concerns, comments, "This episode has far more blanks than a wholly successful story really should, but the sheer scope of Gaiman's ambition makes up for it." While the story was too much for under an hour, its ambitious concept and the successful reinvention of the Cybermen make the episode worth watching.

Though Neil Gaiman's second episode of *Doctor Who* does not quite live up to the high bar set by "The Doctor's Wife," it still marks an ambitious and adventurous contribution to *Doctor Who*. By returning to the characteristics of Patrick Troughton's Cybermen enemies, Gaiman revitalizes the Cybermen, making them formidable foes with their Cybermats and Cybermites, talent for manipulating humans, capacity for instant upgrading, and far-reaching consequences. Gaiman's success in returning the Cybermen to their original, terrifying selves makes the episode a strong contribution to the fiftieth anniversary season and promises more Cybermen stories to come.

Notes

1. For more on "The Doctor's Wife," see Emily Capettini, "'A boy and his box, off to see the universe': Madness, Power, and Sex in 'The Doctor's Wife,'" *Feminism in the Worlds of Neil Gaiman: Essays on the Comics, Poetry and Prose*, ed. Tara Prescott and Aaron Drucker (Jefferson, NC: McFarland, 2012).

2. The Great Intelligence's first appearance in "The Snowmen" (2012) references

the Troughton era. Jenny states that it is unlikely they are in danger of a "disembodied intelligence that thinks it can invade the world with snowmen" ("The Snowmen"). Vastra adds, "Or that the London Underground is a key strategic weakness" ("The Snowmen"). The Great Intelligence first appears controlling robotic Yetis in "The Abominable Snowmen" (1967), which later invade London via the tunnels of the Underground in "The Web of Fear" (1968).

3. "The Ice Warriors" aired November 11–December 16, 1967.

4. The Daleks' origin story did not get a detailed examination until the 1975 serial, "Genesis of the Daleks."

5. Their origin story in "The Tenth Planet" is that they are from Mondas, a twin planet of Earth. Presumably the reason for upgrading only humans was due to biological similarity.

6. In *American Gods*, the characters ride an otherworldly carousel and play life-or-death checkers.

Works Cited

"Army of Ghosts." *Doctor Who, Season 2*. Writ. Russell T. Davies. Dir. Graeme Harper. BBC, 2007. DVD.

"Blink." *Doctor Who, Season 3*. Writ. Steven Moffat. Dir. Hettie MacDonald. BBC, 2008. DVD.

Brew, Simon. "Doctor Who Series 7: Nightmare in Silver Review." *Den of Geek*. DoGTech, 11 May 2013. Web. 15 July 2014.

Crompton, Sarah. "Doctor Who: Nightmare in Silver, BBC One, Review." *The Telegraph*. Telegraph Media Group, 11 May 2013. Web. 15 July 2014.

"The Crystal of Cantus." *Bernice Summerfield 6.5*. Writ. Joseph Lidster. Dir. Gary Russell. Big Finish Productions, March 2006. mp3.

"Doomsday." *Doctor Who, Season 2*. Writ. Russell T. Davies. Dir. Graeme Harper. BBC, 2007. DVD.

Gaiman, Neil. *Neverwhere*. New York: Avon, 1996. Print.

Harp, Justin. "'Doctor Who' Matt Smith: 'Patrick Troughton's my favorite Doctor.'" *Digital Spy*. Hearst Magazines UK, 29 July 2011. 28 July 2014.

Hearn, Marcus. *Doctor Who, the Vault: Treasures from the First 50 Years*. New York: Harper Design, 2013. Print.

"The Invasion." *Doctor Who*. BBC One. BBC, London. 2 November–21 December 1968.

Mellor, Louisa. "Doctor Who, Neil Gaiman, and Where Nightmare in Silver fits." *Den of Geek*. DoGTech, 11 May 2013. Web. 15 July 2014.

"The Moonbase." *Doctor Who: The Moonbase*. Writ. Kit Pedler. Dir. Morris Barry. BBC, 2014. DVD.

"The Next Doctor" promo. Advertisement. BBC One. 2008. Television.

"Nightmare in Silver." *Doctor Who: Season 7, Part 2*. Writ. Neil Gaiman. Dir. Stephen Woolfenden. BBC, 2013. m4v.

Radish, Christine. "Neil Gaiman Talks DOCTOR WHO Episode 'Nightmare in Silver,' Evolving the Cybermen, Creating the Cybermites, His View on the TARDIS and More." Collider.com, 9 May 2013. Web. 15 July 2014.

Slonczewski, Joan, and Michael Levy. "Science Fiction and the Life Sciences." *The Cambridge Companion to Science Fiction*. Ed. Edward James and Farah Mendlesohn. Cambridge: Cambridge University Press, 2003. 174–185. Print.

Spilsbury, Tom. "The Time Is Now!" *Doctor Who Magazine*. 3 March 2010: 18–25. Print.

"The Rise of the Cybermen." *Doctor Who, Season 2*. Writ. Tom MacRae. Dir. Graeme Harper. BBC, 2007. DVD.

"The Tenth Planet." *Doctor Who: The Tenth Planet*. Writ. Kit Pedler and Gerry Davis. Dir. Derek Martinus. BBC, 2013.

"Tomb of the Cybermen." *Doctor Who: The Classic Series*. Writ. Kit Pedler and Gerry Davis. Dir. Morris Barry. BBC, 2014. m4v.

Watkins, Alasdair. "*Doctor Who:* 'Nightmare in Silver.'" *The A.V. Club*. Onion, 11 May 2013. Web. 15 July 2014.

What Neil Gaiman Teaches Us About Survival: Making Good Art and Diving into the Ocean

Monica Miller

As in much of Neil Gaiman's work, the vision of childhood in his 2013 novel *The Ocean at the End of the Lane* is not a rosy time of innocence. Rather, the novel's epigraph by Maurice Sendak captures Gaiman's darker vision of childhood: "I remember my own childhood vividly.... I knew terrible things. But I knew I mustn't let adults know I knew. It would scare them." For children, suffering and joy coexist in registers from the quotidian to the mythic. Gaiman illustrates that what makes survival possible for children is that they do not understand that these registers are supposed to be separate. What allows his child protagonist to survive is the fact that he does not question the thresholds between the mythic and the everyday. Instead, he crosses and re-crosses these boundaries, maintaining his identity while helping to save the world.

The novel demonstrates one of the primary strategies for survival that Gaiman explains in his widely celebrated "Make Good Art" speech: "If you don't know it's impossible it's easier to do."[1] In this speech, which he gave to the 2012 graduating class at Philadelphia's University of the Arts, Gaiman acknowledges both the pain and the pleasure of the artist's life—and by extension, life in general. According to Gaiman, the goal of being an artist is "the moment that you feel that, just possibly, you're walking down the street naked, exposing too much of your heart and your mind and what exists on the inside, showing too much of yourself. That's the moment you may be starting to get it right." We reach such moments through the unrelenting pursuit of art. When we fail, we should make art. When we succeed, we should make art.

Though the unnamed narrator of *The Ocean at the End of the Lane* is an artist, he does not explicitly describe his art. Rather, it is his story which illustrates what it means to "expose too much of your heart and your mind and what exists on the inside." Within the frame story of a middle-aged man returning to his childhood home for a family funeral lies a tale of childhood terror, guilt, and survival involving not only infidelity and suicide but also mythic encounters with otherworldly beings, both nurturing and destructive. *The Ocean at the End of the Lane* is a beautifully-crafted illustration of the possibilities of adult healing through a willingness to remember, reconstruct, and temporarily return to the worlds of childhood.

Opening with the narrator's drive to his childhood home after attending his father's funeral, the story swiftly moves to his memories of life there and the neighboring Hempstock Farm. He remembers meeting the neighbor girl Lettie Hempstock at the age of seven, the same day that his family's tenant is found dead in the stolen family car, a victim of suicide after losing all of his money gambling.[2] His death is the first in a series of unfortunate events, including a new nanny (Ursula, a human manifestation of an evil force unleashed into this world by the narrator's feelings of loneliness after the tenant's suicide) who seduces his father. Even more shocking than stumbling upon the primal scene of his father engaged in sexual activity with the nanny is the narrator's vision of the dead man's face, which he inadvertently glimpses while peeking into the car, trying to locate his comic book. He is saved by Lettie Hempstock, who offers to bring him back to her house while his father deals with the police.

The women of Hempstock Farm provide the narrator maternal nurturing within physical, emotional, and even magical dimensions. This is evident in one of his first exchanges with Lettie, which highlights how firmly connected material sustenance is to the emotional, spiritual, and other, more abstract, aspects of the human psyche. When the narrator asks Lettie, "Do you think he killed himself?" Lettie replies, "Yes. Do you like milk? Gran's milking Bessie now" (19). This exchange not only allows Lettie to quickly change the subject from the disturbing death and distract the narrator from his traumatic encounter, but it also highlights a central theme of the novel, that survival requires sustenance on many levels simultaneously. When the narrator returns to the farm as an adult, the Hempstock women provide him not only solitude at the magical "ocean," but also tea and a cheese and tomato sandwich (172).

More than simply a Proustian agent of memory, food is an essential element for being able to inhabit the multiple dimensions within the novel. Certainly, the Proustian element of memory is a strong undercurrent: upon taking a bit of the cheese and tomato sandwich, the narrator reports, "It was good, really good. Freshly baked bread, sharp, salty cheese, the kind of tomatoes that actually taste like something. I was awash in memory" (172). However, such sensory details are equally capable of bringing one back from abstractions. After engaging in the battles with the demonic Ursula Monkton as well as the fantastic "hunger birds" which threaten to destroy all of the heavens and earth, the Hempstock women feed the narrator spotted dick, a comfort food which nourishes his soul as much as his body. Reflecting on that meal, the narrator muses,

> I do not miss childhood, but I miss the way I took pleasure in small things, even as greater things crumbled. I could not control the world I was in, could not walk away from things or people or moments that hurt, but I found joy in the things that made me happy. The custard was sweet and creamy in my mouth, the dark swollen currants in the spotted dick were tangy in the cake-thick chewy blandness of the pudding, and perhaps I was going to die that night and perhaps I would never go home again, but it was a good dinner and I had faith in Lettie Hempstock [149].

The sensory immediacy of the comfort food allows the narrator to ground himself in the present and fully inhabit a sense of safety; the material sustenance reinforces the sense of emotional security. As a regionally specific food, the spotted dick provides a strong connection to his home as the intense flavors and textures of these foods focus his senses, a focus which he can then utilize for the task at hand. For a narrator who was previously afraid to go to sleep without the lights, the strong sense of home, kinship, and safety which this last meal of sorts provides allows him to find courage he was not aware he was capable of.

Earlier in the novel, the narrator learns that the dead man owed money to many people, including many friends. Lettie is somehow able to access the man's point of view, from which she reports:

> He took all the money that his friends had given him to smuggle out of South Africa and bank for them in England, along with all the money he'd made over the years mining for opals, and he went to the casino in Brighton, to gamble, but he only meant to gamble with his own money. And then he only meant to dip into the money his friends had given him until he had made back the money he had lost [21].

His last moments on earth were full of such longing for money that his hunger awakened Ursula Monkton, a being in another dimension. By the nearly eternal Hempstock scale, creatures such as Ursula register as no more powerful than "a flea," but in the narrator's recognizably human sense of scale, Ursula's power is titanic (70). The narrator feels responsible for her allowing her access to the realm of earth, as she gains access to human form through him. Although Lettie assures him that Ursula cannot harm them, Ursula's fantastic threatening display in her otherworldly form so terrifies him that he momentarily doubts Lettie, letting go of her hand in order to shield himself from Ursula's threats. Letting go of Lettie's hand allows Ursula to use his body as a bridge to this world. Once Ursula gains access to a human form, she moves in with his family, ingratiating herself with his father and sister and menacing the narrator with threats of destroying his parents' love for him as well as locking him away forever.

Although Lettie is capable of doing battle with Ursula directly, she chooses to invite Ursula's natural enemy—the scavenging hunger birds—to take her on. Unfortunately, by inviting these uncontrollable, powerful, otherworldly scavenger creatures to eliminate Ursula from the narrator's world (something like releasing ladybugs in a garden infested with aphids) Letttie unwittingly endangers earth, and she must ultimately turn to the power of her older female relatives to finally banish the dangerous creatures and restore the world. However, the cost of restoring the narrator's world is Lettie's immediate life. After Lettie does battle with the hunger birds, she appears dead, though Old Mrs. Hempstock explains that "she's not dead.... She's been given to her ocean. One day, in its own time, the ocean will give her back" (164). However, at the time of the narrator's present-day visit, she has yet to return— according to Old Mrs. Hempstock, Lettie is "sleeping ... [and] healing. She's not talking yet" (174). However, she is present in her ocean, and is apparently satisfied with the results of her sacrifice.

Throughout these battles, Lettie remains aware of the toll being taken on the narrator and does what she can to take care of him. After facing the demons unleashed by Ursula, for example, Lettie shows maternal concern by observing that the narrator must be hungry. Indeed, he realizes,

> I was so hungry, and the hunger took my head and swallowed my lingering dreams.... I was scared of eating food outside my home, scared that I might want to leave food I did not like and be told off, or be forced to sit and swallow it in minuscule portions until it was gone, as I was at school, but the food at the Hempstocks was always perfect. It did not scare me [147].

The Hempstock women's facility with providing nurturing food exemplifies what Gaiman insists upon in *Make Good Art*, that creation is necessary for survival. Cooking and sewing are domestic arts, necessary not only for physical comfort and survival but also to give pleasure, a reason for living.

According to Gaiman, creation and creative expression is crucial for survival, regardless of the kind of threats being faced. In his speech, Gaiman says,

Husband runs off with a politician? Make good art. Leg crushed and then eaten by mutated boa constrictor? Make good art. IRS on your trail? Make good art. Cat exploded? Make good art. Somebody on the internet thinks what you do is stupid or evil or it's all been done before? Make good art. Probably things will work out somehow, and eventually time will take the sting away, but that doesn't matter. Do what only you do best. Make good art.

Art heals all; the act of creation is available to anyone for any problem, no matter what the problem's register. The Hempstocks understand and embrace this philosophy throughout the novel, but particularly through their creativity in the domestic arts. For example, Ginnie Hempstock responds to the threat of apocalyptic destruction by making a shepherd's pie, certainly a form of "good art." As the hunger birds bear down on her chosen world, threatening to obliterate it, she makes stunning food by scratch—"shepherd's pie, the mashed potato a crusty brown on top, minced meat and vegetables and gravy beneath it"—and though she speaks in "low, urgent tones" to Lettie, her long-range perspective allows her to express a sense of optimism because she is capable of creation: "'Stuff and nonsense,' she said. 'They're all mouth, they are'" (147).

While Gaiman explains the necessity for creation in *Make Good Art*, he illustrates the relationship between creation and hunger in *The Ocean at the End of the Lane*. In the novel, the source of evil is unassuaged hunger. The most dangerous creatures in the novel are, in fact, "hunger birds." Gaiman recognizes that people have a number of hungers which must be fed: for food, certainly, but also for honesty and love. All of these are absent in the narrator's home, from his father's burnt toast to his father's affair with the nanny. Hunger is such an enormous drive that it is a source of great power for those who are able to feed it. Certainly, the nourishment the narrator receives from the Hempstocks forges a tremendous bond between the narrator and these maternal figures. However, the ability to feed hunger is a powerful one, and the potential for such strong bonds can be quite dangerous. In fact, once Ursula takes over the cooking, the narrator nearly starves, preferring to go hungry rather than submit to her.

The rest of his family, however, allows her to feed them, and this danger quickly becomes apparent. Under Ursula's power, his father's temper (which the boy already feared) swells into sheer terror. Before Ursula, "he never hit me. He did not believe in hitting" though the narrator was still "terrified of him when he was angry (67). His face (angular and usually affable) would grow red, and he would shout, shout so loudly and furiously that it would, literally, paralyze me. I would not be able to think" (66–67). Once Ursula becomes a part of their household, however, she not only cooks for the family, but also provides companionship for the narrator's father and sister after his mother takes a job outside the home. Feeding these needs allows Ursula to control the family and put the narrator in danger. At one point, his father loses his temper more than he ever has, to the point of almost drowning his son in the bathtub in anger: "The bathwater was cold, so cold and so wrong. That was what I thought, initially as he pushed me into the water, and then he pushed further, pushing my head and shoulders beneath the chilly water, and the horror changed its nature. I thought, *I'm going to die*" (72, emphasis in original). Ursula not only deprives him of food but also of his father, his father's love, and the certainty of a secure home. She not only engages in a sexual affair with his father but also feeds his father's temper in ways which lead him to physically abuse his son.

Ursula herself owes her physical manifestation in this world to hunger, and she herself is hungry, deprived of her own home. She enters the novel's reality in response to the opal miner's hunger—however, she misreads his need, which he thinks about and expresses in his suicide note as a hunger for money, which he imagines is at the root of his problems. Upon his death, Ursula provides money for many people in the vicinity—but as this money is the product of neither creation nor imagination, it fuels problems, rather than solves them. The narrator awakens with an antique silver shilling stuck in his throat, his sister accuses him of throwing coins at her, one neighbor accuses his wife of prostitution after finding bills in her purse, and another neighbor "goes mad" after discovering that her mattress is full of money, refusing to get out of bed, afraid of theft (30–31). If only the opal miner had managed to meet the Hempstocks—they would have fed him in their warm, comforting kitchen and helped him face his demons, rather than end his life.

Although food is a central agent in this regard, it is certainly not the only domestic article which plays a role in other realms. Art gains its power through the combination of creation and imagination, which is manifest in much of the domestic arts in the novel. Some of the most striking magic uses sewing, as Lettie and her grandmother actually alter time using scissors, needle, and thread. Taking the dressing gown that the narrator donned after his father's attempted drowning, Old Mrs. Hempstock cuts out pieces of fabric in which these events evidently reside: "*Snip! Snip! Snip!* went the black scissor, and the irregular section of fabric that Old Mrs. Hempstock had been cutting fell to the table." Ginnie Hempstock picks up the bits of fabric, observing, "*That's* your dad and you in the hallway, and *that's* the bathtub. She's snipped that out. So without any of that, there's no reason for your daddy to be angry with you" (97, emphasis in original). To the boy's—and the reader's—amazement, his parents freeze at the moment of cutting, and once Old Mrs. Hempstock sews the edges back together, indeed, their memories of the evening are gone, replaced by Old Mrs. Hempstock's suggested memories which she stitches into their memory with her needle and thread and the narrator's dressing gown.

The Hempstock women are a feminist reimagining of the three Fates, or the divine feminine. Kristine Larsen characterizes the traditional divine feminine as a "passive, oppressed feminine principle in nature" and Gaiman's women as a progressive manifestation of "more modern, and far more powerful, 'liberated' quantum cosmological goddesses, agents of change who have the ability to traverse, create, and even destroy entire universes" (265). According to Larsen, "rather than merely representing the moon or stars," these new deities

> travel between dimensions and create and/or destroy entire universes.... Gaiman puts a fresh and empowering face on the Great Mother and her reproductive powers. Gone is the Newtonian concept of a singular, linear, mechanistic universe; the universe is now replaced by the chaotic, roll-the-dice multiverse of Einstein, Guth, and Everett [261].

Although the Hempstock women remember the time of Cromwell and claim a heritage which is recorded in the Domesday book, they are able to live in the present world—even using milking machines and indoor plumbing. And while the trio of Lettie, her mother Ginnie, and her grandmother Old Mrs. Hempstock is an obvious manifestation of the maiden/mother/crone archetype, by the end of the novel, the confused narrator ultimately sees only one Hempstock woman, admitting, "It's funny. For a moment, I thought there were two of you. Isn't that odd?" The woman before him replies, "It's just me," and adds, "It's only ever just me" (177), a comment which emphasizes the "quantum" nature of the otherworldly Hempstocks.[3]

The narrator's confusion continues, as he believes that this is the first time he has visited the Hempstock Farm since his childhood, he discovers that he has, in fact, returned several times since and experienced similar reveries of reminiscence at critical points in his life similar to the grief he is currently facing. The novel's reconstruction of the story of his childhood functions as a multivalent act of recovery. On the most basic level, the novel illustrates the recovery of narrative, creation as an act of memory. However, recovery is functioning in another way here, as the narrator's recovery of this forgotten memory of his childhood also functions in his process of grief, in his working through and recovering from the trauma of his father's death.

Memory can be a strategy for gaining control over history and time, as well as a key to recovery, especially as the slippage between "recovery" as healing from trauma and "recovery" as a discovery of repressed or forgotten memories highlights. Frederick Jameson has explained, we only understand our history through storytelling; when the story becomes inaccessible, the past cannot be worked through or understood. Echoing Jameson, trauma theorists such as Cathy Caruth have similarly pointed to the importance of narrative to processing trauma—as the very nature of trauma itself is "its very unassimilated nature—the way it is precisely *not known*" (4). The key to processing trauma, then, is the ability to incorporate it into the narrative, into the story one tells oneself about the past.

Certainly, this construction of narrative is one of many reasons that it is tempting to read Gaiman as the unnamed narrator. The novel is dedicated "To Amanda, who wanted to know," and Gaiman has explained that his inspiration for the novel was "missing Amanda. I wanted to write something for her, because she was making THEATRE IS EVIL in Australia, and I was in Florida. I took my childhood and the places I lived as a boy, and put them into a story for her" (Gaiman and Palmer). Palmer, an artist and musician married to Gaiman, acknowledges the tremendous courage which Gaiman's artistic accomplishment required of him. In her discussion of why *Ocean* is by far her favorite piece of Gaiman's writing, she notes, "i'm going to plant my hungry art-mouth right on neil gaiman's face and suck the divine force out of him, too: i'm going to gulp magic air from the brave plummet he took in writing and publishing 'ocean'—i saw him, he was shit scared. and he did it anyway" (Palmer). As this novel emerged while Gaiman was mourning his own father, it is tempting to read the narrator as Gaiman himself.

However, it is important to keep in mind that Gaiman's speech exhorts us to make *good art*: not exact replication or memoir. According to Leah Schnelbach, much of the novel's setting, at least, is based on Gaiman's childhood:

> It is set, more or less, on the lane where Gaiman spent his childhood, and deals with a fictional family, the Hempstocks, who first took up residence in Gaiman's imagination when he was nine years old. They showed up soon after he found out that the farm at the end of his lane was mentioned in the *Domesday Book*. The farm had to have people living in it, the boy reasoned, so he thought up many generations of Hempstocks. Years later, various members made appearances in his work—Daisy Hempstock turned up in *Stardust*, and Liza Hempstock in *The Graveyard Book*. In *Ocean*, it is Lettie Hempstock who befriends the narrator and tries to protect him when a dark form of magic is unleashed in his village ["Neil Gaiman Talks about *The Ocean at the End of the Lane*"].

However, it is important to note that the Hempstocks are primarily residents of Gaiman's *imagination*, not the neighboring farm. This is where art as the intersection of creation and imagination becomes key to the importance of art: its strength lies not in the fact that Gaiman recorded the story of his grief for his father as a memoir, but that the effects of his grief were folded into the landscapes of his childhood along with the creatures of his imagination.

Gaiman's comments about his father's death provide a useful companion piece for his *Make Good Art* speech, as they fill in the details for which his speech provides a scaffolding. Gaiman did not write a memoir about losing his father: in his speech, he claims, "I don't think immediate tragedy is a very good source of art. It can be, but too often it's raw and painful and un-dealt-with." Although he admits that "[s]ometimes art can be a really good escape from the intolerable, and a good place to go when things are bad," he makes it a point to caution his audience, "that doesn't mean you have to write directly about the bad thing; sometimes you need to let time pass, and allow the thing that hurts to get covered with layers, and then you take it out, like a pearl, and you make art out of it" (Gaiman "Father's Day"). The artistic process both mirrors and supplements that of grief, as they both require patience and submission. Such surrender is a critical aspect of the healing process, as one must stop trying to force any pattern or design on experience.

Ocean's characters, like the glowing heroine of his two *Doctor Who* episodes, are "bigger on the inside." In *The Ocean at the End of the Lane*, the pond which is really an ocean is an analogue of this phenomenon, reflecting the artist's capacity to "contain multitudes," in Whitman's famous words ("Song of Myself" 1326). The capaciousness of art, of creation, functions as an analogue of the human psyche in its ability to not only contain contradictions and unresolved trauma but also allow the space necessary to recreate, relive, restore, and ultimately recover from trauma. In his attempt to explain his art, the narrator of *The Ocean at the End of the Lane* explains early on, "If I could talk about it, I would not have to do it" (4). As Gaiman explains in his speech, "Life is sometimes hard. Things go wrong, in life and in love and in business and in friendship and in health and in all the other ways that life can go wrong. And when things get tough, this is what you should do. Make good art." The combination of creation and imagination which art requires is ultimately a combination of the material and the sublime; by fusing these two worlds in *The Ocean at the Lane*, Gaiman beautifully illuminates the fact that these worlds are inseparable.

Notes

1. Unless otherwise noted, all quotes from the "Make Good Art" speech are from the published edition of the speech, illustrated by Chip Kidd; this edition is unpaginated.

2. *The Ocean at the End of the Lane* is not the first appearance of the Hempstocks in Gaiman's work. While at work on the novel, Gaiman reported in his online journal that he was "writing a story about Lettie Hempstock. Who may be distantly related to Daisy Hempstock in *Stardust* and Liza Hempstock in *The Graveyard Book*" ("I Took My Love to Hobart in the Rain").

3. That Old Mrs. Hempstock can see subatomic particles only reinforces their particularly quantum nature.

Works Cited

Caruth, Cathy. *Unclaimed Experience: Trauma, Narrative, and History.* Baltimore: Johns Hopkins University Press, 1996. Print.

Gaiman, Neil. "The Father's Day and Invisible Plane Post." *Neil Gaiman's Journal.* June 21, 2009. Web. 1 March 2014.

_____. "I Took My Love to Hobart in the Rain." *Neil Gaiman's Journal.* January 13, 2011. Web. 1 March 2014.

_____. *Make Good Art.* New York: HarperCollins, 2013. Print.

_____. *The Ocean at the End of the Lane.* New York: HarperCollins, 2013. Print.

Gaiman, Neil, and Amanda Palmer. "neil & i answer 'evening with' questions on reddit (warning: contains all sorts of things)." *The Official Website of Amanda Fucking Palmer—Yes It Is.* November 19, 2013. Web. 1 March 2014.

Jameson, Fredric. *The Political Unconscious: Narrative as a Socially Symbolic Act.* 1981. Ithaca: Cornell University Press, 2005. Print.

Larsen, Kristine. "Doors, Vortices and the In-Between: Quantum Cosmological Goddesses in the Gaiman Multiverse." *Feminism in the Worlds of Neil Gaiman: Essays on the Comics, Poetry, and Prose.* Eds. Tara Prescott and Aaron Drucker. Jefferson, NC: McFarland, 2012. 261–279. Print.

Palmer, Amanda. "sharing the cosmic cold sore: a meditation on life, death, and art (and anthony's new book)." *The Official Website of Amanda Fucking Palmer—Yes It Is.* December 22, 2013. Web. 1 March 2014.

Schnelbach, Leah. "Neil Gaiman Talks About *The Ocean at the End of the Lane*." Tor.com. June 20, 2013. Web. 1 March 2014.

Whitman, Walt. *Leaves of Grass.* 1892. New York: W. W. Norton, 1973.

Remembering the Dead:
Narratives of Childhood

Rebecca Long

Neil Gaiman's *The Ocean at the End of the Lane* (2013) is a story about forgetting, remembering, and forgetting again. In many ways and certainly in Gaiman's semi-autobiographical novel, remembering and forgetting are two sides of the same magic. According to Old Mrs. Hempstock, "different people remember differently" (Gaiman 236). Such is the nature of memory, as Old Mrs. Hempstock knows. She is old enough to remember when the moon was made. Gaiman's narrator, on the other hand, must forget his own childhood in order to truly remember it and Gaiman uses this paradox to explore the primal connection between memory and identity which informs the narrative. Identity, from childhood to adulthood, is fundamentally based on and formed by memory. Without a past, without a remembered childhood, one cannot have an identity or a future.

Gaiman's narrator realizes this as he begins his journey into remembrance beside Lettie Hempstock's ocean. Gaiman frequently writes about the importance of stories in everyday life and how they allow us to make sense of the world and our place within it. And if, as Gaiman maintains, people carry worlds within them, they carry stories as well: they carry the myths of those microcosmic worlds. *The Ocean at the End of the Lane* resonates with the power of narrative and promotes the primacy of memory in the development of identity. Using the linked concepts of amnesia and remembrance, Gaiman interrogates the development of human identity and the nature of childhood itself, remembering, re-imaging, and re-narrating the world of childhood.

In many ways, childhood is a constructed space or experience. Childhood is structured by and constituted within "sets of meaning in language" (Lesnik-Oberstein 2). Children create their own realities by telling stories about their experiences even as adults use language to impose structure on those experiences. According to Karen Lesnik-Oberstein, the child as a literary figure symbolizes the possibility "of a redemption of existence from language," of a movement into, through, and out of language to a world that is consistently knowable and recognizable (6–15). The little boy's descent into Lettie's ocean and his emergence out of it are symbols of the potentiality and liminality of childhood as a state of experience. Memory and the narrative language used to recount and retrieve it are intimately linked to the representation of childhood in the text—and to the development of the little boy's identity.

The narrator remembers a childhood in which grownups were something to be feared: figures imbued with terrifying, even monstrous qualities. They do not believe when children tell them the truth and they lie; they have the power to manipulate language and through this manipulation, to compromise and exert control over the childhood experience. Throughout the narrative, the boy equates adults with monsters, precisely because they cannot be known or understood. The narrator himself never truly acknowledges that he has ever grown up. For example, at the funeral at the start of the novel, the narrator reveals that he feels he is only pretending to be an adult. But the narrator remembers a time when he was a monster: a small child who cared for nothing but getting his own way. He tells the reader, "I do not actually remember being a monster. I just remember wanting my own way" (69). Here, the narrator connects monsterhood with a kind of solipsistic selfishness, a focusing inwards of thought and emotion, to the exclusion of all others. He remembers himself as a small, fearless boy who did not know enough about that world to be afraid. Ironically, now that he is older, he has become a "frightened child" haunted by the knowledge of his own vulnerability (69).

In her own way, Ursula Monkton is also child: an ancient child who believes she is a god. Like a child, she desperately wants her own way. She wants the world to be a place where she will be happier. In this context, children, adults, and monsters are very much the same and childhood, adulthood, and monsterhood become mirror images of the same experience.

As an adult monster and a monstrous adult respectively, Ursula Monkton and the little boy's father are relatively free to move within their environment. In contrast, as a child, the little boy is constantly placed or centered in "designated spaces" throughout the text (Jenks 73). Movement out of these spaces becomes an act of trespass or intrusion into adult territory. But the child self that Gaiman's narrator remembers is made conspicuous by his *absence* from these designated spaces: he escapes from the monsters in his home and realizes that the space itself is suddenly lost to him. He does not return home until Ginnie Hempstock brings him back. The little boy is displaced and exiled

from his home as a result of Ursula Monkton's influence and his father's violence against him. Outside the home, he can perceive it as a space which has
been violated. He misses the memory of his home but not the space as it exists
in the present, invaded by a monster. In this context and within the narrator's
story, Bachelard's "house of other days," the childhood home, the nest-like
space associated with the memories and dreams of youth, is lost, as is the
domestic intimacy it once symbolized (*Poetics of Space* 100). The narrator's
memory reconstitutes this lost space as his narrative becomes an act of imaginative reconstruction.

That domestic intimacy is lost in the moment the little boy's father tries
to drown him in the family bathroom. The only thing the little boy can do is
kick out against the older man: the only option is to transgress his father's
authority. The adult narrator remembers that he was "terrified" of his father
when he was angry: terrified as only a small, helpless child can be in the face
of a grown-up's wrath (89). Possessed and influenced by Ursula Monkton, his
father is transformed by his anger and his actions in the bathroom are the
actions of a monster. Slowly, as the traumatic moment unfolds, the ways in
which the little boy measures and understands the reality of his life are violated
and broken. The locked bathroom door is broken open by his father—even
though locked doors stop people from coming in, even though locked doors
are supposed to mean "that you were in there" (95). His father's actions violate
all established rules and domestic protocols. Once a source of trust and security for the little boy, the father has become the monster in the fairy tale. As
he relates this traumatic incident, Gaiman's narrator remembers wondering,
even as his father held him in a grip he could not escape, what his father would
do: would he finally hit him or send him to his room, or shout at him? It is
only when the little boy realizes that his father means to drown him in the
bath that he kicks out at "the horror of something happening against the established order of things" (97). At that moment there are two monsters in his
house: Ursula Monkton and his own father.

The intimacy of his childhood home is never regained: the little boy's
house ceases to function as a safe and homely space the moment Ursula Monkton enters it. As Dylan Trigg writes, "to dwell in a house is to feel oneself to
be in the center of things" (293). The little boy is denied access to the center
of his life by Ursula Monkton and her monstrous presence in his home. Adrift
from the center, he moves towards the farmhouse. The Hempstock home
becomes the new center of his life and in order to save himself, the little boy
begins a series of movements outwards from the farm and then back towards
it. His life thus becomes a movement away from and a return to the center the

farmyard represents; the source of the myth and the memory. The farm or the center becomes a kind of sacred zone within a changing, unstable landscape; it functions as the "zone of absolute reality" in that it allows the narrator to access the truths that he has forgotten (Eliade *The Myth of the Eternal Return*, 8).

For Eliade, "the reality and the enduringness of a construction" or in this case a narrative are secured by the acknowledgement of a central, sacred space and "by the transformation of concrete time into mythical time" (20–21). The ritual re-telling and re-imagining of memory-based narratives establishes this mythical time: time which is by its very nature cyclical and which facilitates the recollection and re-living of past experiences. Any ritual which re-enacts the mythical moment of creation or of destruction "unfolds ... in a sacred reality" (Eliade 21). The narrator's story is precisely such a ritual: he returns again and again to the Hempstock farmhouse, unwittingly performing a narrative ritual that functions as a memorial to the childhood he remembers and relives. His impulse to return to the farmhouse and his urge to express the meaning of his childhood memories through narrative constitute Eliade's "exemplary gesture" (35): the mythical gesture which opens up the world and allows him access to his memories. According to Eliade, this gesture can only occur when the individual performing it is "truly himself" (35). The narrator is only truly himself when he is beside Lettie's pond, when he is remembering the child he once was. Outside of this memorial ritual, his life is passed in "profane time" (35): time without meaning when he does not know his true self or his true past and when he is slowly, inexorably moving back towards the moment of return and remembrance. Remembering and forgetting become elements of a mythic narrative cycle.

In terms of that cycle, the little boy's earliest memory is the story of the scar on the sole of his foot. It is an intimate memory and the scar his body bears as a result of the incident connects him indelibly to that specific moment in time. The scar anchors and confirms his memory. But the little hole which appears after his encounter with the flea that will become Ursula Monkton is new: his body has recorded a new story, created the sign of a new memory. The adult narrator wonders now why his child self did not ask an adult what to do. He does not remember asking adults about anything, "except as a last resort" (64). Not only is there a gap or disjunction between childhood and adulthood, there is also a distance between children and adults within the text and within his memory. His life as a child and his childhood experiences are lived at a distance from his parents and sister. Because of the hole in his foot, because of the gate that is left in his heart, the narrator's child self becomes a symbol of the existence of another world, "a beyond" (Eliade *Myth and Reality* 139). He is the means of "awakening and maintaining consciousness" of that world (139). As such, he is actually—at least while his heart is compromised in this way—an incredibly powerful figure in the mythic landscape of the text. He is keeping the world open: he is the site of a breakthrough of the sacred into the world. He functions, physically and existentially, as a hierophany within the narrative. The narration of his childhood is also the narration of a hierophany, of a manifestation of the sacred or supernatural into the world. In this context, the narration of his childhood becomes a myth.

According to Northrop Frye, in a "true myth" there can be no continuous or meaningful distinction between supernatural and living beings (50). As such, there is really no distinction between Lettie and the little boy: on a fundamental, archetypal level, they are both children. In this mythic tale of memory and forgetting, childhood is the only constant: through the interaction between memory and narration, the past and the present "exist simultaneously" (Stephens 213). Frye also reveals that in all literary verbal structures, the "final direction of meaning is inward" (74). In a narrative sense then, moving towards a conclusion involves moving inwards. Frye does not claim that meaning is reached by this movement inwards but rather that meaning *itself* moves inwards, developing as the narrative develops. Meaning and memory are intimately linked throughout the narrator's tale: the little boy recognizes this in Lettie's ocean when he perceives eternity as an existence spent looking inwards at a series of mirrors. As a symbol of shared knowledge, the ocean is Frye's "communicable unit," the archetype or "typical or recurring image" that connects all forms of narrative on a fundamentally symbolic and imaginative level (99). The "essential action" of a true myth takes places outside of history, outside of time (Knox 65). As such, the narrator's story is, in a sense, *always* occurring, always happening as he continues to remember and Lettie continues to watch him from the ocean. The Hempstocks are the center of the story: the myth originates in the archetypal domestic space the farmhouse represents.

Initially, the narrator recedes further and further back into his memories; he is literally remembering the way back to the child he used to be. Standing in the hall of the Hempstock farmhouse, it all begins to come back to him, establishing the connection between place and memory within the text. The farm becomes a repository of memory, a memorial space that is also an access point for the narrator, a gateway into his childhood and the past. In both narrative and figurative terms he falls into the ocean of memory that Lettie's pond represents and enters a new cycle of remembrance and forgetting. In that act of falling, the narrator remembers and bears witness to the return of his memories. But this remembrance is tempered—or perhaps augmented—by the knowledge that is, by its very nature, ephemeral: contained in this sustained moment of remembrance is the corresponding act of forgetting, of losing, of letting go. The movement away from the farmhouse becomes an act of faith: in the belief that in time, the cycle of remembrance will begin again. The narrator muses that "childhood memories are sometimes covered and obscured beneath things that come later" but they are never truly lost for good (6). The connection between the child that was and the adult that is remains, even if it is forgotten: the child self is not distinct from the adult self but rather both are separated from each other by memory. Memory, because it essentially and necessarily recalls something that is past, something that has *already* occurred, is inherently associated with absence. In remembering, the narrator re-acknowledges the loss of something that is already gone.

So forgetting can be a form of protection, of *self*-protection. In the farmhouse, having escaped from Ursula Monkton, the little boy wakes himself in the darkness. He makes a conscious decision to pull himself out of the nightmare. In the darkness he knows only that the dream has scared him "so badly [he] had to wake up or die" and yet, no matter how hard he tries, he cannot remember what he has dreamed (145). Given the events of the evening, it is hardly surprising that his dreams frighten him. Upon waking—and waking here is akin to saving himself—his mind chooses to forget the distressing nightmare, precisely because he cannot forget his father's violent actions. The little boy's childhood has been betrayed and violated by Ursula Monkton's influence over his father, the man who is supposed to love and protect him. He misses his father and mother: he misses the life he once knew, the home that was once inviolate. In recognizing the vulnerability of his home, the little boy begins to grow up.

In the farmhouse kitchen, holding the fabric of his traumatic evening in his hand, the little boy wonders what will happen if he burns it. Will it have really happened? Will his father have tried to drown him in the bath? Will he forget? Lettie's mother asks him what he wants. "I *want* to remember ... because it happened to me. And I'm still me," the little boy replies (135). He is still himself, no matter what Ursula Monkton has done. Here, the connection between memory, identity and narration is made explicit. If we live and dream through and within narrative, we essentially use narrative to "evaluate experience and present the self" and so storytelling becomes a form of self-affirmation, of self-construction, inextricably bound up with the act of remembrance and the impulse towards the memorialization of experience (Hardy 98). If narrative presents the self in the context of the linear experience of time, narrative itself becomes a form of memory as it moves outwards from the past towards the future. In the wider metanarrative of children's literature the child figure tends to move outwards from the homespace, leaving "the security of the home" and experiencing adventures (Nikolajeva 7). There is then a consequent movement back towards the home; the returning child figure is accepted back and "established order is restored" (7). The child figure is changed; he has shed his immature solipsistic perception of the world. He has grown up—or at least taken a step out of childhood and towards adulthood. In *The Ocean at the End of the Lane*, the concept of home is compromised by the actions of the very figures that should be protecting it: his father's violence and his mother's absence undermine the security of the home. The little boy does not willingly leave the home to embark on an adventure; he flees to escape from a monster who has exposed his home to the fundamentally real and adult concepts of abuse, sex, and manipulation. Returning to the compromised home is equated with being lost.

But in contrast, returning to Lettie's ocean is a homecoming that allows the narrator to find himself again, even if only for the duration of that visit. The first time Lettie takes the little boy to her ocean he sees it only as a pond. As they contemplate its placid surface, the little boy says, "You aren't people" (151). He has begun to realize that there is a disjunction between Lettie's form—the child body she inhabits—and her actual self. She disagrees with the little boy: "Are too," she says (151). She has been eleven "for a very long time": she has been a child existing in a dynamic, mythic paradigm (116). She, her mother, and her grandmother *are* people, but not in the way the little boy has come to expect. He shakes his head. Crucially, it is not because he does not believe her: he shakes his head at the inadequacy of the language he must use to try and articulate his perception of the Hempstocks. "I bet you don't actually look like that ... not really," he ventures (151). As a seven-year-old boy he recognizes the distinction between the exterior physical self and the interior self: what looks out from behind his face when he stares at himself in the mirror. Lettie shrugs in response: initially she does not attempt to verbally reply. She relies on gestures and silences to communicate with him, to help him understand. Theirs is a bond based on faith and physical connection. She eventually tells him that "nobody looks like what they really are on the inside" (151). She does not look that way and he does not; "people are much more complicated than that" (151). In a way, people are like Lettie's ocean: the form which encases them bears no relation to the self they struggle to recognize and maintain.

The little boy asks Lettie if she is a monster like Ursula Monkton. Not only is Ursula Monkton a monster, her form is monstrous: her being bears no relation to the woman's form she wears and the fact that the other children and adults around the little boy cannot perceive this is precisely what makes her monstrous. There is a monster in his house, in the place where monsters should not be. The little boy knows, even as he asks Lettie, that she is not a monster, at least not the same way that Ursula Monkton is. But he is curious. He wants to know who or what she is: he is aware of two categories, people and monsters, and it would appear that this little girl is neither.

Lettie throws a pebble into the pond before she begins to answer. Monsters, she tells him, "come in all shapes and sizes" (151). Just like people. Sometimes, there is very little that separates a monster from a person. And monsters, like people, are scared of things. The little boy is astonished by this: he cannot understand how Ursula Monkton, a grownup, could be frightened of anything. He firmly believes that "grown-ups and monsters aren't scared of things" (152). Unwittingly, the little boy has come to equate monsters with grownups and has created a distinction between them and him. He is not a monster and he is not a grownup, so consequently, both of those things which are Other must somehow be the same or similar. But Lettie speaks with a childlike authority. In the moment before she decides to tell the little boy something important, she stops talking, as though she is contemplating the words she will use. She tells him that "grownups don't look like grownups on the inside" (152). According to Lettie, there is no such thing as grownups: as if grownups belong in fairy tales and not in the real world at all. On the inside, adults "look like they always have" (152). On the inside, adults look like the children they once were. The child self is the essential self. Here again, the direction of meaning is inward: we must look beyond and even through the physical form of the characters in the text to discover their true selves. The physical form may change and age but the self that resides inside remains, in many ways, the same. We have all been seven—and indeed, eleven—years old for a long time.

The two children sit side by side on the wooden bench by the pond, "not saying anything" (152). Their physical togetherness is a sign within the text of the connection they share. The little boy thinks about adults, wondering if they are "really children wrapped in adult bodies, like children's books hidden in the middle of dull, long books" (152). He contemplates the idea that the child self moves further and further away from its own memories as the child body grows and matures but that these memories are never lost: on a certain level, the child self does not age and childhood can always be re-accessed. Thinking this, the little boy still finds himself telling Lettie that her ocean is "just pretending," that it is just a pond and not an ocean at all (152).

He feels, in that moment, as though he is betraying childhood: as though he is acting like a grownup. Disgruntled, Lettie tells him that the pond is "as big as it needs to be" just as he himself, later in the text, will be as brave as he needs to be when he runs towards the hunger birds in order to save the world (153). Now, looking at her, in a physical sense, it seems to him that she is three or four years older than him. In that moment, he realizes that she might be "three or four thousand years older, or a thousand times again" (155). Her form contains her being but it does not define her. The little boy trusts her. He believes in her, as though she is something out of a myth or a fairy tale that has come to life in front of him. He believes in her and in his mind, this means he will come to no harm while he is with her. Lettie's ability to protect him is linked to his faith in her. That faith will ultimately come to define their relationship as he sits in the darkened fairy circle and waits for her return. He cannot know then that Lettie Hempstock will return, ultimately, not to him but to her ocean after she sacrifices herself, her actual self, to save his life.

The river Lethe might run into Lettie's ocean. If that mythic river accepts the memories of the dead as they cross it into a final paradise, then it stands to reason that it becomes a receptacle for those memories. In gazing into the pond, Gaiman's narrator gazes back into his own past, into his childhood: he is gazing into the well of his own being (*Poetics of Reverie* 114). Bachelard describes a "living childhood within us," a world or a state of being or memory that is "permanent [and] durable" (20). Eliade maintains that "through the paradox of rite, profane time and duration are suspended" (35). Mythical time is created through ritual and sacrifice and through the repetition and memorialization of those moments. Myth then constitutes the "abolition of time through ... the repetition of paradigmatic gestures" (35). The narrator's attempt to re-access his childhood through narrative is ultimately an attempt to mythologize that childhood. In a similar way, Lettie's sacrifice comes to encapsulate and preserve the narrator's childhood, even as she saves his life: the assimilation of her body back into the ocean creates a sacred time and establishes the ocean itself as the center of the narrator's myth of his childhood. In many ways, when Lettie enters the ocean, she takes the little boy's childhood with her.

That childhood resides in the ocean, to be accessed only when the narrator returns as his adult self to remember and re-narrate what he has forgotten, in an endless cycle of remembering, re-telling, and forgetting. The ocean becomes a repository of memory and knowledge: a memory-place accessible only to the past. The narrator's return to the farmyard becomes a reverie; an imaginative remembering in which his past is re-narrated as lived experience (Bachelard 22). Gaiman's narrator is a grown man, telling the reader a tale of his childhood: the story of Lettie Hempstock's ocean. At times he is an adult recalling the feelings, emotions, and actions of a child self who is present only as he narrates or re-lives his memories. But at other times, it is that remembered child self that speaks to the reader, as clearly as if the narrator had never grown up at all. Bachelard maintains that "one needs ... to live with the child which he has been" (20). In his *Poetics of Reverie*, he talks about a childhood that lasts through the self's existence; childhood "returns" (20). It is only by maintaining a sense of the presence of that childhood that adulthood can be animated out of a kind of emotional amnesia. In the "nucleus of childhood" the imagination and the memory are most intimately connected (100). Within that connection the constant, permanent world of childhood—and the child being itself—"binds the real with the imaginary," the remembered with the imagined (100). We "understand our attachment to the world" through our experience of childhood and the "lost childhood" must be re-imagined in order to be restored and re-experienced (126).

If, as Peter Hollindale maintains, children "construct childhood as they go along" and that they base that construction not merely on their own lived experience but on fictions, stories, and narratives other than their own, then childhood itself becomes a form of narration (14). In *The Ocean at the End of the Lane*, the little boy is constantly being forced to renegotiate and reassess his idea of what it means to be a child. The world of his childhood is invaded, altered, and expanded. His adult counterpart, the narrator, is engaged in a constant and evolving dialogue between experience and memory: a dialogue in which both elements are inherently unstable (Hollindale 71). At the text's conclusion, the little boy asks if Lettie will be the same when she comes back. Ginnie answers only that "people change as much as oceans" (224). Nothing is ever the same, even if we perceive it to be so.

There is a disjunction then between the lived experience of adulthood and the memory of childhood sensations. Past and present are temporally distinct and even distant but they are united in the act of narration and remembrance: the re-telling of stories "bring the past into the present" (Strauss 237). Gaiman's adult narrator tells the reader that he does not miss childhood but he misses the child's capacity to take pleasure in small things, even while greater things are cracking and falling away. As a child, he could not control the world or escape from the things that scared him but he was capable of taking joy in the things that made him happy: in the stories he read and the food he ate in the Hempstock farmhouse. The moral of Gaiman's memory-story is the undeniable fact that childhood is no protection from the world, from the knowledge that nothing is perfect, not even parents. Lettie Hempstock promises that she will keep him safe, that she will not let anything hurt him. But in a way, Lettie is a child too and the little boy *is* hurt, simply because he lets go of her hand. For all the narrator's memories of oceans and fleas and rips in the fabric of time, his story is, at its heart, the story of a lonely childhood: of a little boy whose special friend had to go very far away.

In the narrator's myth of his own past, his childhood cannot be represented or accessed except through the narrative of memory. The images of past and future which we use to construct our own narratives are in fact "present images" (Lynch 65); images which are continuously re-created and re-imagined as we return to them. If narration, or the act of telling a story is a "recurrent act of symbolic communication," a verbal ritual that involves a transaction between the teller and the listener, then narration is also a memorial process (Frye 105). In repeating and in re-telling, narration becomes memorialization. As we reach the conclusion of the tale, we realize, even as Gaiman's narrator does, that this particular retelling, this act of remembrance is part of a larger pattern of memory and memorial: a pattern that will continue in stages of forgetting and remembering, going, and returning. The narration is an act of remembrance—it is the adult narrator remembering himself. We free ourselves from the structures of time through recollection, through anamnesis (Eliade *Myth and Reality* 89). This is why the narrator equates the telling of his story with falling into the ocean all over again. His return to the farmhouse is a "return to origins" and an engagement with the possibility of rebirth (Eliade 30). He finds himself drawn back towards the center, towards remembrance. There is a moment when the narrator realizes where he is going "where [he] had been going all along" and we can see that his life has become a sequence of remembering and forgetting, a pattern of going and returning which has become mythical in its archetypically circular movement (3). Memory and imagination are intimately related, so much so that their functions can "overlap" (Warnock viii). Where does recollection end and imagination begin? Is every act of recollection not necessarily also an act of imagination? In order to narrate the story of a self, one must necessarily imagine that self at the center of a series of events, of memories. The attempts we make to turn memory into narrative ensure the continuity of identity (viii): in telling stories, in remembering what has happened we create a permanent narrative. Memory itself ebbs and flows like the tides of Lettie's ocean forming an "undulating core at the heart of our being" (Trigg xvi). In order to maintain a sense of self, and a sense of that self continuously existing in time, a connection between the past and the present must be maintained through a constant reworking or re-telling of a memory-narrative in the present. If, as Trigg writes, "imagination defines the experienced reality of memory," then the work of the imagination, the imaginative act itself is essential to the construction of the identity and the perception of the self in relation to time (xxv).

The memory-story at the heart of this text questions the extent to which children recognize a distinction between their selves as emotional and physical entities and the "objective reality" within which they operate (Piaget 1). The child self Gaiman's adult narrator remembers is selfish in the childlike sense of the word: unable to quite believe in a reality outside of his own existence. The narrator remembers closing the medicine cabinet in his bathroom and staring at himself in the mirror, wondering as he "wondered so often when [he] was that age" who he was and what exactly was looking out at the face in the mirror (67). His child self knows that the face in the mirror is not really him—because if something happened to his face, he would still be himself, on the inside—but he still wonders who he is and where his self resides. As the narrator remembers his child self looking in the mirror, the reader realizes the truth of Lettie Hempstock's words: that no one looks the same on the inside. The child self Gaiman's narrator remembers is superior neither to his environment nor to the characters he encounters: adults, other children, or monsters (Frye 33–34). At the heart of the mythic story he tells is the memory of how he was once an isolated, frightened child; a child caught in a conflict "between the inner and the outer world" (39). In the gap between his parents' perception of the world and his own experience, the little boy is lost. The powerlessness he experiences speaks to the child in us all and to the fundamentally mythic universality of childhood.

Myths then, are ultimately stories without ownership or stories that belong to us all. As Gaiman's narrator remembers, for his child self, "they weren't adult stories, and they weren't children's stories ... they just were" (71). Myths exist outside and transcend the boundaries and gaps between childhood and adulthood. To his child self, adult stories never made sense: instead of providing access into another world, they hinted at the existence of secrets, "mythic secrets" to adulthood (71). The little boy escapes into the children's stories which are his by right but ultimately, in this moment of intense loneliness, he finds no real comfort there. He envies the fictional children he encounters, the "cleanness of their lives," and is disappointed by the reality he perceives behind the myths that attempt to explain the nature of his world (90). If a story only matters, as Gaiman's narrator muses, "to the extent that the people in the story change," then in his own opinion, his story does not matter at all (233). Because people do not change. He was a seven-year-old boy when these events occurred and he is the same person at the end as he was at the beginning. Or was he? The memory of the self, the sense of a whole person "continuously existing through time" is essential to the development and the maintenance of a child's identity (Warnock 58). The ability to remember is closely linked to the ability to narrate, to see the self as existing in a continuum between past, present and future. As Locke writes, "it is the same self now as it was then," the same self existing continuously in time (Locke 226). Gaiman's narrator does not know what will happen now or where his home is precisely because he cannot or does not retain a continuous memory of his past. In the space between remembering and forgetting is knowing. It is in this space, in the moment before he leaves the farmhouse, that the narrator is truly himself, is truly aware of himself in time and in narrative. As he moves into forgetfulness, he loses himself and his way. In reflecting on the past, on what we have been, we determine, to a certain extent, what we will become (Warnock 62). The "lived relation" between memory, identity, and place is disrupted and diverted as the narrator moves away from the farmyard (Trigg xxv); away from remembrance and back into forgetfulness.

Works Cited

Bachelard, Gaston. *The Poetics of Reverie*. Translated by Daniel Russell. New York: Orion Press, 1969. Print.

_____. *The Poetics of Space*. Translated by M. Jolas. Boston: Beacon Press, 1994. Print.

Eliade, Mircea. *Myth and Reality*. Translated by Willard R. Trask. New York: Harper & Row, 1963. Print.

_____. *The Myth of the Eternal Return: Cosmos and History*. London: Routledge & Kegan Paul, 1955. Print.

Freud, Sigmund. *The Uncanny*. London: Penguin Classics, 2003.

Frye, Northrop. *Anatomy of Criticism: Four Essays*. Princeton: Princeton University Press, 1971. Print.

Gaiman, Neil. *The Ocean at the End of the Lane*. London: Headline, 2013. Print.

Hardy, Barbara. "Towards a Poetics of Fiction." *Novel* 2 (1968): 5–14. Print.

Hollindale, Peter. *Signs of Childness in Children's Books*. London: Thimble Press, 1997. Print.

Jenks, Chris. *Childhood*. London: Routledge, 2005. Print.

Knox, John. *Myth and Truth: An Essay on the Language of Faith*. Charlottesville: University of Virginia Press, 1964. Print.

Lesnik-Oberstein, Karen. *Children's Literature: Criticism and the Fictional Child*. Oxford: Clarendon, 1994. Print.

Locke, John. *An Essay Concerning Human Understanding*. Oxford: Oxford University Press, 2007. Print.

Lynch, Kevin. *What Time Is This Place?* Cambridge: MIT Press, 1972. Print.

Nikolajeva, Maria. *From Mythic to Linear: Time in Children's Literature*. London: Children's Literature Association and Scarecrow Press, 2000. Print.

Piaget, Jean. *The Child's Conception of the World*. London: Littlefield Adams, 1951. Print.

Stephens, John. *Language and Ideology in Children's Fiction*. Chicago: Longman, 1992. Print.

Strauss, Levi. *The Savage Mind*. Chicago: University of Chicago Press, 1966. Print.

Trigg, Dylan. *The Memory of Place: A Phenomenology of the Uncanny*. Athens: Ohio University Press, 2012. Print.

Warnock, Mary. *Memory*. London: Faber & Faber, 1987. Print.

Augustinian Memory and Place

ANDREW EICHEL

"When we are lucky the fantastique offers a road-map—a guide
to the territory of the imagination, for it is the function of
imaginative literature to show us the world we know, but from a
different direction."—Neil Gaiman, "Reflections on Myth"

Neil Gaiman's *The Ocean at the End of the Lane* is an adult's account of a childhood incident that defies explanation to such an extreme degree that it had been blocked, but not expunged, from the narrator's recollections.[1] Readers are granted access to a dark, fantastical realm mediated by the human faculty of recall, which helps reconstruct a compelling series of events and allows the main character to retrieve his fractured self from beyond forgotten boundaries of magic, fear, and necessity. Despite this process of disclosure, epistemological rifts cleave all layers of fantasy and reality, leaving the narrator stranded amidst a flux of information both newly-remembered and just-discovered—and at the center of this confusion is memory. Summarizing the importance of memory for Augustine of Hippo's spiritual autobiography *Confessions*, Todd Breyfogle suggests an ultimate purpose that mirrors the *telos* behind Gaiman's choice of theme in *Ocean*: "Augustine, in the ordering of memory, seeks an understanding of the meaning of his past and, consequently, of his present" (147). Through a confluence of memory and place, the two pillars of Augustine's memorial practice and the related, ancient discipline of memory augmentation known as *mnemotechnics*, Gaiman's protagonist gains a path to the lost truth of himself and thus begins to remember a past that had evaded full recollection for decades.

Several reviewers highlight *Ocean*'s appeal as the result of Gaiman tapping into the primal and chthonic mystery of memory in human consciousness. Michele Filgate calls it a "book about memory" (32), and critic Alex Hern describes it as "a book that ... plays so constantly with memory" ("*Ocean*"). Heidi MacDonald is more analytical, suggesting "the multiple levels of memory give Gaiman the chance to explore how the way we remember things makes them magic" (14). Examining how Gaiman explores the "magic" of memory through place reveals a striking proliferation of parallels between his formulations and the discourse of Augustine of Hippo in *Confessions*.

The overall influence of Augustine (AD 354–430) on the theological and philosophical developments of the Latin West is arguably more widespread than that of any other patristic father.[2] Born in North Africa to a Christian mother, Augustine was baptized in 387, ordained a priest in 391, and became bishop in 396. As a youth he was drawn to Manichaeism, a gnostic philosophy that preached a division of good and evil. He next formed a lasting passion for Neoplatonic philosophy in his 30s and later injected a strong current of its dualistic traditions into the doctrines of the early Church. In *Confessions*, a popular text among educated readers in the early and later Middle Ages and one that is still regularly read and studied, the bishop narrates the history of his intellectual and spiritual developments, confessing his life's story as a means of both worshipping God and locating access to the divine within human consciousness and memory. Augustine's fascination with memory earns the theme an entire section in *Confessions*. The bishop's choice to transition from the biographic timeline of his past, ending in Book IX with the death of his mother, Monica, to an extended philosophical meditation on memory in Book X is still a source of confusion. Scholars have reached no consensus on whether Augustine knew about or had access to the canonical texts in the *mnemotechnic* tradition; regardless, he is often cited in memory research because he shows interest in *memoria ex locis* ("memory from place") throughout the whole of his career and particularly in *Confessions*.[3]

According to the dictates of the ancient system of *mnemotechnics*, often translated as the "art of memory," compartmentalizing the mind into a familiar, physical structure and then using the features of that structure to organize memories can maximize the human faculty of memory.[4] Also known as the "method of loci," this materialistic systematization of memory is thought to originate in ancient Greek and Roman rhetorical texts and is associated with mental structures colloquially referred to as "memory palaces." The basic idea behind a "memory palace" is this: instead of letting memories slip into, and possibly out of, the mind at random, a person can imagine the internal makeup of their mind as taking the form of, for example, a childhood home; then, when the person wants to retain some bit of information, they picture it as residing within the structure of that childhood home. In this manner, groups of associated memories, organized however the mnemonic practitioner desires, can be deposited in specific rooms and thus will respond to recall more swiftly. This organizational scheme relies on the person's previous attachments to the physical structure which serves as the memorial template—the better they remember the details of their chosen "memory palace," the more memories can be inserted into its mental replica. In this age of digital technology, when entire libraries of texts can now be stored within molecular-sized silicon structures, it should not come as a surprise that this venerable, pseudo-mystic art has recently experienced a revival in popular culture. This boost in interest can be seen in references, to give just two examples, in the BBC's re-boot of *Sherlock Holmes*, starring Benedict Cumberbatch as a modern Holmes invested with his own memory palaces, and Joshua Foer's best-selling nonfiction book detailing the little-known modern world of memory enhancement competitions, *Moonwalking with Einstein: The Art and Science of Remembering Everything*. Although Gaiman makes no direct mention of *mnemotechnics* or memory palaces in *Ocean*, he consistently endows the most important sites of his main character's formative years with the capacity to assist in the recall of memory fragments. Without using *mnemotechnic* jargon, Gaiman imaginatively creates his own version of an "art of memory." The narrator's physical movements are thus movements through his memories, a narrativized interpretation of *memoria ex locis*, and each move the adult-narrator makes down the lane and towards the ocean is a retrieval of a past that had been taken from him.

At the start of his autobiography, Augustine laments about a fundamental paradoxical doctrine of Christianity, namely the juxtaposition of perfection with human fallibility, "How shall I call upon my God...? Surely when I call on him, I am calling on him to come into me. But what place is there in me where my God can enter into me?" (I.2). The fullest expression of Augustine's answer to this conundrum is in Book X, where he writes, "See how widely I have ranged, Lord, searching for you in my memory. I have not found you outside it. For I have found nothing coming from you which I have not stored in my memory since the time I first learnt of you" (X.35). One of the great realizations for the bishop is that God resides within man's memory—"What is inward is superior" (X.9). He has always been there as a truth and to gain access Augustine must understand memory's politics of placement, declaring, "I will therefore rise above that natural capacity in a step by step ascent.... I come to the fields and vast palaces of memory, where are the treasuries of innumerable images of all kinds of objects brought in by sense-perception. Hidden there is whatever we think about" (X.12). This passage is quoted often because it is a powerful support for asserting order and control over the internal workings of memory by visualizing the holdings of the mind as physical structures. Recollection thus becomes a dynamic activity because it is "as if going through the *motion* of memory would revive it" (Augustine *Saint Augustine's Memory* 9).[5] In other words, to retreat into one's memory palace is to relive the original experiences stored there.

Ocean relies on the same symbolic and physical association of memory and place to divulge the narrator's past experiences and enable him to retrieve a lost part of his identity, even if only momentarily before the recollections are again shifted to an Augustinian "abyss of human consciousness" (X.2). Gaiman does not hide or disguise the importance of location to this work—his title declares the story's focus on two specific places, the ocean and the lane. What's more, Gaiman establishes the world of the novel as a place where the hero is disassociated from his past memories—to some extent even his present experiences—and unable to connect with either until he reaches specific locations in his meandering journey. Once the narrator travels to those points of memorial intensity, the falsity of his previously-held memories is revealed and the remembrances triggered by the physical structures of the real world initiate the re-construction of a corrected version of a "memory palace" within the narrator's mind by substituting and re-arranging mental material.

After driving away from the funeral where he was "pretending to be an adult," the narrator finds himself passing familiar, if partially forgotten, locales from his youth (3). He follows a combination of "winding Sussex country roads" and turns taken "randomly" for some time before realizing he is "driving toward a house that had not existed for decades" (3). The narrator's recollection is sparse and he discloses, "I stared at the house, remembering less than I had expected.... I'd lived in that place, for a while, as a teenager. It didn't seem to be any part of who I was now" (4). Why should a lane or ocean, shortly to be introduced into the narrative with much more energy and detail, retain more significance than one's own home? The narrator hints, "The old house, the one I had lived in for seven years ... had been knocked down and was lost for good" (4–5). The "new house" is not saturated with the residue of memory or the imaginary worlds of the seven-year-old boy who thinks, "I loved the house, and the garden. I loved the rambling shabbiness of it. I loved that place as if it was a part of me, and perhaps, in some ways, it was" (58). The narrator makes the same observation towards the novel's end, albeit with less innocence. He states, "There was too much of my life bound up in those bricks and tiles, those drainpipes and walls" (169). Gaiman is not being subtle: in the fantasy world of *Ocean*, the external and internal are collapsed into *mnemotechnic* coordinates that are the echoes of the experiences and locations of their original formations.

Unsatisfied by hollow reminiscing, the narrator continues adrift down a country road until it "became the single-lane track I remembered from my childhood" (5). This apposition of the past in the present urges the protagonist to comment, "It felt like I had driven back in time. That lane was how I remembered it, when nothing else was" (5). A single-track frame of mind accompanies these memories and the narrator can throw aside his previous aimlessness. Where a childhood home had failed to surrender its cache of associated experiences and serve as a point of orientation, a hedge-lined lane that led only to neighbors succeeds. These sentences signal that the narrator has entered a landscape reverberating with the siren call of an "alternate pattern of events" that differs from what he remembered. In such close proximity to their origin, these competing sets of reference refuse to be silent, enervating the narrator's mind as they jostle for attention (168). The resulting confusion is made obvious when he muses, "I had been here, hadn't I, a long time ago?" (5). The rhetorical question highlights the gulf that separates the narrator's present understanding of his past from the events themselves. It also indicates that recollection as a process was already underway, accelerated by entering the confines of the lane. The ensuing remembrance of a kiss shared with a girl who had once lived on that lane is the most detailed glimpse of the narrator's fractured past yet, but the recall occurs only after he passes the former sweetheart's home. There is no such delay with the Hempstock abode—"I remembered it before I turned the corner and saw it, in all its dilapidated red-brick glory: the Hempstocks' farmhouse. It took me by surprise, although that was where the lane had always ended" (5). The environs—especially the ocean—are such a potent symbol in the narrator's memory that he has no need of an external trigger. The homestead is a part of his authentic memory structure, and one of his main tethers to the worlds of the past and present; as such it cannot be displaced in the same manner as other locations.

The "storehouse" of memory, even when organized, can still be difficult to navigate, according to Augustine, because "[s]ome memories pour out to crowd the mind and, when one is searching and asking for something quite different, leap forward into the centre as if saying 'Surely we are what you want?' Other memories come ... on demand with ease and without any confusion in their order" (X.12). Gaiman's narrator does not have a firm grasp on either his present or his past—his authentic memory palace is a broken relic that has sat vacant for too long, scattered about the landscapes of his childhood. The further he traverses the lane, the better his recall because the places he encounters elicit the correct memories, thereby replacing the false or incomplete fabrications. Augustine offers a description of this organizing principle when discussing sense-oriented versus inner knowledge: "by thinking we, as it were, gather together ideas which the memory contains in a dispersed and disordered way, and by concentrating our attention we arrange them in order as if ready to hand, stored in the very memory where previously they lay hidden, scattered, and neglected" (X.18). The physical retracing of the narrator's steps in this most important of places from his youth conjures parts of the layout for his true memory structure, but there are still errors to be addressed, remnants of that most unbelievable and tragic event of his childhood.

Some of the retrieved memories remain ravaged by *lacunae* deliberately put in place by the Hempstocks in order to protect themselves and the narrator. Fragments need to be reconciled with the whole, but *aporia*—blank spaces in what should be a seamless narrative—do not dishearten the protagonist, who, in a moment of clarity, seems to channel Augustine. He observes, "Childhood memories are sometimes covered and obscured beneath the things that come later, like childhood toys forgotten at the bottom of a crammed adult closet, but they are never lost for good" (5). Here again, Gaiman reinforces the imaginative links he has established between mental abstractions and physical structures while managing to reference some implications for temporality as well. Augustine, in Book X, includes an intricate discussion about forgetting that centers on the logical conundrum of memory somehow containing the very forgetfulness that shrouds whatever recollection is being sought. "What when the memory itself loses something?" he ponders. "This happens when we forget and attempt to recall. The only place to search is the memory itself. If something other than what we want is offered us, we reject it until the thing we are looking for turns up" (X.28). *Ocean*'s main character could not get what he wanted from the "new house" so he shuns it and continues to follow the lane, the key to his memories. He is searching with purpose, even if he cannot name what that purpose is or identify yet what he seeks. All roads lead to the end of the lane though—it is the boundary and the bond to the world that was snipped from the narrator's memory and it is just as central to the mind of his seven-year-old self.

During his nocturnal exodus from Ursula Monkton following the nightmarish near-drowning at the hands of his father, the protagonist's fear forces everything from his mind except that lane and its destination. The lane swells to encompass even time itself: "The future had suddenly become unknowable: anything could happen: the train of my life had jumped the rails and headed off across the fields and was coming with me down the lane, then" (80). This flight is a precursor to a pattern in the adult-habits of the narrator, who has returned to the end of the lane several times before, always at key moments in his life. He learns of these unrecalled visits from Old Mrs. Hempstock. In describing his current visit, the very purpose of which the narrator has already started to forget, compelled by the magic of the Hempstocks, the wizened lady says, "You wanted to get away from everyone and be on your own. So first of all you drove back to the place you'd lived as a boy, and when that didn't give you what you missed, you drove to the end of the lane and you came here, like you always do" (173). The narrator is understandably resistant to these revelations but the matriarch's testimony cannot be denied. As both a child and a man, the narrator has consistently viewed the lane as a guide and safe haven in times of great import and change.

While the lane is at the start of the narrator's remembrances, it is clear his memorial quest terminates at Lettie's ocean. In the prologue, after following the lane to the Hempstock farmhouse, the narrator exchanges brief pleasantries with Mrs. Hempstock. This conversation emphasizes that memory is by no means consistently stable for any character in the novel, even otherworldly females who wield mysterious control over memory, time, and space. Mrs. Hempstock recognizes the visitor but concedes, "I know you, but things get messy when you get to my age. Who are you, exactly?" (6). The ocean quickly dominates the narrator's thoughts though, and after turning down tea, he asks about the "duck pond," adding, "I knew Lettie had had a funny name for it. I remembered that. 'She called it the sea. Something like that'" (7). Mrs. Hempstock responds, "Do you remember the way?" (7). The narrator's internal response to this question is one of the strongest testaments of Gaiman's intentional yoking of memory to place in *Ocean*:

> If you'd asked me an hour before, I would have said no, I did not remember the way. I do not even think I would have remembered Lettie Hempstock's name. But standing in that hallway, it was all coming back to me. Memories were waiting at the edges of things, beckoning to me. Had you told me I was seven again, I might have believed you, for a moment [7].

Location is the only thing that has changed over the course of that hour. In *Ocean*'s reality, however, a change in place initiates a change in the status of mind and memory. "[W]inding Sussex country roads ... only half-remembered" lead to the "little country lane of ... childhood" and the end of that lane directs the narrator to the Hempstock farm, where one of its namesakes gives the directions to the pond: "You can get to it around the side of the house. Just follow the path" (3–7). Memories increase in detail and frequency at each new site. When the narrator is in that hallway, pleased for "remembering where I was, and what was coming next, and exulting in the knowledge," he is standing in his memory palace, or at least Gaiman's fictionalization of *memoria ex locis* (7). The narrator's last few steps to the ocean are crucial because he realizes something is happening with his memory. "I saw it and felt oddly proud of myself," he thinks when the pond is finally in view, "as if that one act of memory had blown away some of the cobwebs of the day" (7). The conditional "as if" is often a signpost for the truth in Gaiman's texts: looking at the pond leads to remembering more about Lettie, which in turn re-directs the narrator's focus to an entire network of re-arranged coordinates in his memory palace. This episode exhibits more Augustinian characteristics, for the bishop is adamant that, once memories are located and organized properly, "they easily come forward under the direction of the mind familiar with them" (X.18). For the narrator, "that one act of memory" is a signal that sets off a chain reaction of illumination within his mind. The gates are opened and more memories can flood in.

One of the most common metaphors for memory shared by *Confessions* and *Ocean* is that of a body of water, with both Augustine and Gaiman playing with the imagery in order to evoke the paradoxical reach of the human mind. "This power of memory is great, very great," Augustine writes, "It is a vast and infinite profundity. Who has plumbed its bottom?" (X.15). Augustinian memory's endless depths are accompanied by "most secret caverns" (X.17), "caves" (X.26), and "remote recesses" that serve to store even the most inconsequential of thoughts that "sink below the surface" (X.18). The totality of a person's experiences retained within "[m]emory's huge cavern, with its mysterious, secret, and indescribable nooks and crannies" cannot be fully grasped because some knowledge has been "swallowed up and buried in oblivion" (X.13; 12). *Ocean* uses similar imagery linking the ocean, mind, and reality, thereby shrinking the universe to fit into consciousness and expanding memory to equal the bounds of the cosmos. In one scene, the boy decides, "Oceans are bigger than seas. Your pond is just a pond," to which Lettie replies, "It's as big as it needs to be" (113). The child's struggle to understand the rationale of an "ocean running beneath the whole universe ... stretch[ing] from forever to forever and is still small enough to fit inside a bucket" resembles nothing so much as Augustine's struggle to understand how man's finite, mortal mind contains the infinite, a temporal godhead (144).

In Book X.26, the bishop acknowledges, "I fly here and there, and penetrate [memory and mind] as far as I can. But I never reach the end. So great is the power of memory, so great is the force of life in a human being whose life is mortal." Yet human recollection has its limits and Augustine determines,

"I will pass beyond even that power of mind which is called memory, desiring to reach you [God]" (X.26). The boundless structure of memory leads to the apparently greater, generative infinity of God. Augustine reiterates his perplexity in X.36: "You conferred this honor on my memory that you should dwell in it. But the question I have to consider is this, In what part of it do you dwell? ... Why do I ask in which area of memory you dwell, as if there are really places there?" Augustine accounts for this paradox by collapsing reality so that nowhere is the same as everywhere within memory—"There is no place, whether we go backwards and forwards; there can be no question of place. O truth, everywhere you preside over all" (X.37). There is no question because God inhabits indiscriminately, regardless of physical laws like space-time. Genesis 1:27 states, "God created mankind in his own image" and instilled within his creation the same paradox, identified by Augustine as "the power of memory, an awe-inspiring mystery, my God, a power of profound and infinite multiplicity.... It is characterized by diversity, by life of many forms, utterly immeasurable" (X.26). The bishop's language here draws attention to other parallels that render water an astute choice of metaphor for memory: the ocean, composed of trillions and trillions of individual water drops is also a realm characterized by a unification of multiplicities contained in an environment where directions mean less than they do on firm ground.

Gaiman tackles similar paradoxes as the bishop in depicting memory as a conduit to and extension of some type of collective unconscious. In fact, his formulation calls to mind the Neoplatonic "world soul," a concept from ancient Greek Platonism that Augustine encountered before his conversion and later transported into late antique Christianity. Although it is more likely that the young Augustine developed an appreciation for Platonic doctrines through readings of other Neoplatonists, Plato himself writes of the world soul in the dialogue *Timaeus*. The philosopher explains, "this world of ours was made in truth by god as a living being, endowed thanks to his providence with soul and intelligence ... the god made the world a single, visible, living being, containing within itself all living beings that are naturally akin to it" (19). Gaiman's titular ocean serves as the primary mnemonic coordinate for syncing the narrator with his childhood experiences, but later in the novel it is revealed that it also commands a similar capacity for accessing the memories of the entire universe. Looking at the water transports the narrator to his memory palace, but entering the ocean via the bucket allows him to achieve an *apotheosis* whereby he transcends the normal boundaries of human knowledge and experience and becomes mentally and physically united with all of reality for a brief, glorious moment. "I knew everything," he recognizes.

> Lettie Hempstock's ocean flowed inside me, and it filled the entire universe, from Egg to Rose.... I saw the world I had walked since my birth and I understood how fragile it was, that the reality I knew was a thin layer.... I saw that there were patterns and gates and paths beyond the real. I saw all these things and understood them and they filled me, just as the water of the ocean filled me. Everything whispered inside me. Everything spoke to everything, and I knew it all [143].

The narrator is immersed in the collective unconscious of all creation, a result similar to Augustine's communion with God, the Alpha and Omega to Gaiman's Egg and Rose.[6] "In filling all things, you fill them all with the whole of yourself," extols the bishop (I.3). The boy experiences an epiphany of neoplatonic unity "in the ocean which was the universe which was the soul which was all that mattered," while Augustine finds divinity in the memory that is of God who is the universe and all that matters (145). In the unity of God there is "no place" at all, the bishop claims; Lettie extols matching beliefs, warning that although the ocean will dissolve the boy's identity and memory,

> "you wouldn't die in here, nothing ever dies in here," she assures him, "but if you stayed here for too long, after a while just a little of you would exist everywhere, all spread out.... Never enough of you all together in one place, so there wouldn't be anything left that would think of itself as an 'I.' No point of view any longer, because you'd be an infinite sequence of views and points" [145].

This ocean offers knowledge of all as long as knowledge of self is sacrificed and the boy must choose to exchange his personalized memory palace for the oblivion of omniscience. Lettie explains that everyone used to know everything but "it's nothing special.... And you really do have to give it all up if you want to play" (146). The boy is then freed from the universe and given to himself again. This loss of transcendence leaves him devastated but to "play" is to live. Even the Hempstocks choose to coalesce their consciousness and memories around a singular point of identity, a place to call one's own.

Unlike the boy, however, the Hempstocks can retrieve some of that knowledge at will. They reveal their ability to manipulate memories as though they are physical objects to be cut from "the thinly painted scrim of reality" in a key scene (155). A "scrim," or cloth used for lining, is Gaiman's re-imagination of what is known colloquially as space-time "fabric." Gaiman extends the metaphor by granting the Hempstocks a power that is traditionally bestowed upon supernatural female triads in various world mythologies, including the Greek Fates and the Norse Norns. Lettie is the first to mention "[s]nip and cut" as a way to shield the boy, or "snippage" as Old Mrs. Hempstock prefers when she elaborates on the process (95). Ginnie produces the occult accouterments needed to re-shape consciousness, "a pair of scissors, black and old, a

long needle, and a spool of red thread," but the key item is the boy's damp
dressing gown (96). Since the clothing was worn during the bathroom scene,
and thus was a part of all the activities and thoughts that occurred therein,
the Hempstocks can utilize its material as a physical signifier for the relevant
memories. Then, those ineffable mental projections can be organized and nav-
igated, like a tailor's pattern or a treasure-hunter's map. By "snip-snip-snipping"
an "irregular section of fabric" from the gown and then hemming the void
with red thread, the Hempstock matriarch alters the parents' recollections of
that evening (96–7). The literal amalgamation of a physical object with memorial experience is reinforced when the eldest Hempstock returns the scrap to
the boy, advising, "Here is your evening.... You can keep it, if you wish. But if
I were you, I'd burn it" (100). Consigning the damp scrim to the fire does not,
however, obliterate the snipped events from the boy's memory: at the chapter's
end, he can still mention the "fragment of time that had, perhaps, been snipped
out of reality" (106). He asserts, "I *want* to remember.... Because it happened
to me. And I'm still me" (100). The typography reinforces that, by Gaiman's
estimations, when it comes to memory recall, desire is at least as important as
place.

Further examples of memory's resilience to tinkering emerge in the novel
briefly before and during the hunger bird attack (152). The narrator interjects
a meta-commentary into his past narrative, typographically indicated by italics
and parentheses:

> (*A ghost-memory rises, here: a phantom moment, a shaky reflection in the pool of
> remembrance. I know how it would have felt when the scavengers took my heart.... I
> know how that feels, as if it was truly a part of my life, of my death. And then
> the memory snips and rips, neatly, and—*) [157].

The implication is that although the hunger birds had killed the narrator, after
Lettie's sacrifice the Hempstocks interceded and relocated his memories. The
world of Gaiman's novel, therefore, shares Augustine's confidence, quoted
above from X.18, in the preservative capacity of memory even when the con-
tents of its "most secret caverns" are "hidden, scattered, and neglected" (X.17;
18). Memories in this state of dissolution "have to be thought out as if they
were quite new, drawn again from the same store" (X.18). Gaiman's narrator
is remembering but he is also re-experiencing his memories "as if they were
quite new." These snip-and-cut episodes attest to a pattern in *Ocean* of trans-
muting the memory fragments into concrete, localized structures, further proof
of Gaiman's use of an imaginative *mnemotechnics*—two types of memorial-
izing that are variations on the same theme.

In the epilogue, memory and place are still the dominant concerns because, despite the protagonist's recollections, his memory palace has not been completely restored: his mind is crowded with a jumble of false memories and true experiences. Old Mrs. Hempstock explains, "Different people remember things differently, and you'll not get any two people to remember anything the same, whether they were there or not. You stand two of you lot next to each other, and you could be continents away for all it means anything" (173). How can this apply to the narrator, an individual who is simply trying to reclaim his lost past? Gaiman has already provided an answer through a comment made by the eldest Hempstock, who tells the boy, "Nothing's ever the same.... Be it a second later or a hundred years. It's always churning and roiling. And people change as much as oceans" (164). Note another correlation between a body of water and human consciousness, that of incessant movement. Although the boy and the adult narrator are the same person, the events of his life have transformed him like waves on a beach shift the sand. "Place" changes from a location to a perspective, with an accompanying shift not in memories but in the value and interpretation of those memories. The memory palace the adult is wandering through over the course of the story is not his anymore. It belongs to the boy narrator, so there will be gaps and inconsistencies as he stumbles through the lost portions of his former self. The narrator denies the inevitability of change, however, when he professes that

> a story only matters, I suspect, to the extent that the people in the story change. But I was seven when all of these things happened, and I was the same person at the end of it that I was at the beginning, wasn't I? So was everything else. They must have been. People don't change.
> Some things changed, though [170].

Once again, Gaiman's use of a rhetorical tag question, "wasn't I?," clues readers in on the truth he is imparting to and through his character. The narrator *has* changed, verified, in one instance, though there are others, by the Hempstock woman's failure to register who he is on his return to the farmhouse. Whether or not the boy has gained enough of a perspective on his life to be objective about his own changes, there is a further clue that the Hempstocks understand this transformation.

When the boy first meets the trio, after the incident with the family car and the opal miner, Old Mrs. Hempstock calls him "a growing boy" and Ginnie calls him "the boy" (20). These basic descriptors, rather than his name, remain his primary identifiers until the final chapter, when Ginnie returns him to his parents. She announces, "Safe and sound, the soldier back from the wars. He had a lovely time at our Lettie's going-away party, but now it's time for this young man to get his rest" (168). This line is the only instance within the childhood portion of the narrative where the boy is referred to as anything but a child; after Ginnie Hempstock leaves, the mother lumps the boy in with his sister as "you children" (169). But readers should already know that the language of the Hempstocks is special and therefore worth paying attention to. Through the boy, readers learn those arcane ladies command the "first language ... the tongue of what is, and anything spoken in it becomes real, because nothing said in that language can be a lie. It is the most basic building brick of everything ... the language of shaping" (43). The language does not simply reveal the truth—it *is* that truth, just as, for Augustine, Jesus Christ is the Logos, or Word, of Truth (1 John 1:1). But what shaped the "growing boy" into a "young man" is the story he went through rather than any matriarchal pronouncement. This realization leads to the issue of audience and *Ocean*. Gaiman admits, "while my adult readers will happily read my children's books, I don't intend [*Ocean*] for children. It's a book that contains much more adult themes than you would find elsewhere" (Laforce). Readers get another confirmation of the novel's target audience from *Ocean*'s bookworm of a main character who confesses, "I liked myths. They weren't adult stories and they weren't children stories. They were better than that. They just *were*" (53). Regardless of the narrator's subjective interpretation of the events of his life, he has been changed and is no longer the boy he encounters in some of his memories. Considering Gaiman's blending of perspectives, temporalities, and even veracities, *Ocean* is like a myth itself.

Allusions and intertextuality are powerful components of Gaiman's style and most of his works display rich and eclectic knowledge of world systems of religion, philosophy, mythology, and cosmology.[7] Some critics have even noted Gaiman's borrowings from sources as diverse as Dante Alighieri's *The Divine Comedy* and Midrashic commentary.[8] Gaiman proclaims this style of re-appropriation and adaptation is the mark of a true story-teller for "we have the right, or the obligation, to tell old stories in our own ways, because they are *our* stories and they must be told" (68). Functioning as a narrative on the one hand and as philosophical commentary on the other, *Ocean* complements its fairytale packaging with devotion to ominous abstractions and intellectual themes. In taking up the topic of memory and its relationship to knowledge, Gaiman thrusts his readers into a literary and philosophical tradition that stretches back to *Confessions*, Augustine's record of seeking in his unfolding past a path to truth, specifically the truth of God. Part of what makes *The Ocean at the End of the Lane* a challenging yet rewarding read is Gaiman's overlaying of the minutiae of character and event with vast epistemological concerns that parse human consciousness. Combining an "ontological inquiry" into the implications of human knowledge and memory with a talent for creating worlds, Gaiman has written a novel that serves as an *mnemotechnic* coordinate to realms inside all readers (Slabbert 73). Unlike the all-consuming unity of Lettie's pond, however, Gaiman's *Ocean* establishes a grand palace of the imagination for children and adults alike to locate and explore.

Notes

1. For the sake of brevity, hereafter the abbreviation *Ocean* will be inserted in place of the novel's full title.

2. There are many introductions to Augustine and his work and more are published every year. Readers interested in Augustine's biographical details would do well to consult Peter Brown's magisterial *Augustine of Hippo: A Biography* (Berkeley: University of California Press, 2013). For an overview of the bishop's corpus and influence on Western society, James O'Donnell's *Augustine* is a reliable source (Boston: Twayne, 1985).

3. For a summary of the ongoing academic debates surround Augustine's knowledge of the scholarly canon associated with formal memory enhancement, see Dave Tell, "Beyond Mnemotechnics: Confession and Memory in Augustine" in *Philosophy and Rhetoric* 39.3 (2006), especially 233–36.

4. Memory studies has gained momentum over the last few decades and one of the most respected results of this increased scholarly attention is Mary J. Carruthers's *The Book of Memory: A Study of Memory in Medieval Culture* (Cambridge: Cambridge University Press, 1990). *The Art of Memory* (Chicago: Chicago University Press, 2001) by Francis A. Yates is considered a foundational study and worth consulting.

5. Emphasis in the original.

6. References to these famous Greek epithets for the Christian divinity can be found in Revelations 1:8, 21:6, and 22:13.

7. For a look at the wide range of research being done on these topics, see, for example, *Neil Gaiman and Philosophy*, eds. Tracy L. Bealer, Rachel Luria, and Wayne Yuen, Vol. 66, *Popular Culture and Philosophy* (Chicago: Carus, 2012).

8. See Davorin Dernovšek, "The Divine Sandman," *English Language Overseas Perspectives and Enquiries* 7 (2011): 45–62, and Cyril Camus, "The 'Outsider': Neil Gaiman and the Old Testament," *Shofar: An Interdisciplinary Journal of Jewish Studies* 29.2 (2011): 77–99.

Works Cited

Augustine of Hippo. *Confessions*. Trans. Henry Chadwick. Reissue. New York: Oxford University Press, 2008. Print.
_____. *Saint Augustine's Memory*. Trans. Garry Wills. New York: Viking Penguin, 2002. Print.
Breyfogle, Todd. "Memory and Imagination in Augustine's *Confessions*." *Literary Imagination, Ancient and Modern: Essays in Honor of David Grene*. Ed. Todd Breyfogle. Chicago: Chicago University Press, 1999. 139–54. Print.

The English Bible: King James Version, Volume 1 The Old Testament. Ed. Herbert Marks. New York: W.W. Norton, 2012. Print.

Filgate, Michele. "Locked in the Sweetshop: Seven Questions for Neil Gaiman." *Poets & Writers* 41.4 (July/August 2013): 30–35. Print.

Gaiman, Neil. *Adventures in the Dream Trade.* Framingham, MA: NESFA Press, 2007. Print.

_____. *The Ocean at the End of the Lane.* Hardcover. New York: HarperCollins, 2013. Print.

_____. "Reflection on Myth." *Columbia: A Journal of Literature and Art* 31 (1999): 75–84. Print.

Hern, Alex. "*The Ocean at the End of the Lane* by Neil Gaiman: A Half-Remembered Fairy Tale from Childhood." *The New Statesman* 27 June 2013. Web. 28 July 2014.

La Force, Thessaly, "Fantastical Read: Neil Gaiman on His New Novel *The Ocean at the End of the Lane.*" *Vogue* 21 June 2013. Web. 28 July 2014.

MacDonald, Heidi. "The Magic of Memory." *Publishers Weekly* 260.26 (2013): 14. Print.

Plato. *Timaeus and Critius.* Trans. Robin Waterfield. Oxford: Oxford University Press, 2008. Print.

Slabbert, Mathilda. "Inventions and Transformations: Imagining New Worlds in the Stories of Neil Gaiman." *Fairy Tales Reimagined: Essays on New Retellings.* Ed. Susan Redington Bobby. Jefferson, NC: McFarland, 2009. 68–84. Print.

Not at Home:
Examining the Uncanny

Yaeri Kim

The most disturbing scene in Neil Gaiman's *The Ocean at the End of the Lane* is not when the narrator is attacked by an otherworldly monster, chased on a stormy night, or even when sinister creatures come to devour him. It is when he suffers unexpected violence at the hands of his once-benevolent father, who nearly drowns him in a bathtub as punishment. This scene shatters not only the narrator's world but also the reader's perception of it. At the start of the novel, the narrator's father is portrayed as a caring if slightly clueless parent who prepares breakfast for his children, frequently engages in conversation with them, and buys comic books and a kitten for his lonely son. The narrator's home is an imperfect but reasonably comfortable and safe place where he can be "content" if not exactly happy, and where common problems and occasional unfortunate events do not threaten the family itself (13). The narrator adequately describes his emotional response to the bathroom scene as "the horror of something happening against established order of things" (72). It is the horror of finding everything "wrong" (72): "I was fully dressed. That was wrong. I had my sandals on. That was wrong. The bathwater was cold, so cold and so wrong" (72).

This sense of something being profoundly "wrong" marks this scene as not only frightening and troubling but also "uncanny"—the type of fear, as Sigmund Freud has famously defined, that is "nothing new or alien, but something which is familiar and old-established in the mind and which has become alienated" (Freud 241). The transformation of the familiar and reassuring—*heimlich*—into something unfamiliar and threatening—*unheimlich*—is exactly what happens in this scene: the father has become an inflictor of pain and threat to life; the bathroom, a space previously associated with comfortable memories and considered one of the narrator's "safe places," is transformed into a place of punishment and possible death; and the home has become the most dangerous place (Gaiman *Ocean* 71). However, this transformation is not contained in this single scene. On the contrary, the narrator experiences the disintegration of the familiar and known world and discovers its frighteningly unexpected aspects throughout the novel. The comforting pattern of everyday life is disrupted by the intrusion of strangers; the beliefs and assumptions about the home, the family, and the general ways of things are shattered; and the world becomes an uncertain place where no rules are absolute and "anything [can] happen" (80).

In his seminal work on the subject, "The Uncanny," Freud identifies the cause of the uncanny as the "return of [the] repressed" (249)—a formulation as developed and appropriated by later scholars as it is critiqued and revised. Accumulating a dizzying amount of fictional and empirical examples that can be considered uncanny, ranging from the literary themes of the double and mutilation to coincidences and superstitions of everyday life, Freud concludes that the uncanny feeling is produced "when infantile complexes which have been repressed are once more revived ... or when primitive beliefs which have been surmounted seem once more to be confirmed" (249). As Richard Gooding points out, this conceptualization implies that the ability to experience the uncanny, at least in the ways described by Freud, is not universal. Freud notes that the latter types of the uncanny cannot affect those who are completely immune to superstitions (248). Likewise, the uncanny effects produced by the revival of repressed complexes are not likely be experienced by young subjects who have not repressed their infantile fears and desires yet, and phenomena that invoke primitive beliefs will not generate uncanny feelings in a culture where such beliefs are accepted as valid explanations of reality. For this reason, Mladen Dolar sees the uncanny as a product of modernization, and Gooding regards the capability to experience and articulate uncanny feelings as an indication of psychological development. Freud himself suggests that children do not experience the uncanny in the same way that adults do, noting that the idea of a doll coming to life discomforts adults but does not scare children because it invokes "an infantile wish or ... belief" (233). Children, who have not repressed this wish yet, are more likely to find the idea delightful.

On the other hand, Ernst Jentsch, whose preceding theorization of the uncanny is arduously criticized in Freud's subsequent work, states that children are "particularly subject to the stirrings of the uncanny" due to their lack of "intellectual certainty" (13–15). Kerry M. Mallan echoes this view, suggesting that children may be more susceptible to uncanny effects than adults because of their limited ability to discern fiction from reality. Lucy Rollins points out that some things that adults find ordinary may strike children as uncanny. Focusing on Freud's lexical analysis of *heimlich*, which can be literally translated as "homely" or "homelike," and his discovery of the intersecting point of *heimlich* and *unheimlich*, where *heimlich* assumes an *unheimlich* meaning of "hidden" and "secret," she argues that home can be an uncanny place for children since it is "familiar" yet "full of secrets" (27–28).

The home, indeed, lies at the heart of the uncanny in *Ocean*. It is the place where the hideous monster masquerades as a pretty nanny and cooks meals that may have malicious magical power, the father turns into an adulterous husband and abusive parent, and the rules and patterns of everyday lives fall apart. Meanwhile, the magical world of the Hempstocks, the family of a grandmother, mother, and daughter living on the neighboring farm, becomes a source of protection and comfort. Their mysterious powers, otherworldly farm, and apparently ageless existence never bother the narrator, although they occasionally surprise him; on the contrary, their magic increasingly becomes the only aid which he can depend on. Even the malevolent monster that disturbs dreams and plants a magical worm in the narrator's foot seems less frightening than a real-life adult. Thus, the usual opposition of *das Heimliche* and *das Unheimliche* is inverted in *Ocean*: the commonsensical world of the everyday is portrayed as incomprehensible and unsettling, while fantastic creatures and events are often depicted as familiar and reassuring. Nevertheless, the uncanny in this novel is fundamentally the "class of the frightening which leads back to what is known of old and long familiar" (Freud 220). If Freud's examples are apparently unfamiliar yet "secretly familiar" (245), *Ocean* generates uncanny effects by making familiar aspects of everyday life unfamiliar. Either way, the uncanny is produced when "*heimlich* ... finally coincides with its opposite, *unheimlich*" (226).

The Ocean at the End of the Lane narrates a series of fantastic events during childhood as reminisced by the middle-aged narrator, centering on the mysterious Hempstocks—eleven-year-old Lettie, her mother Ginnie, and her grandmother Old Mrs. Hempstock. The Hempstocks, who possess supernatural powers and whose farm is a realm of magic, befriend the seven-year-old narrator and help him as he faces monstrous creatures from other realms as well as troubles at home. In the course of the narrative, the narrator encounters a gigantic and ragged monster, has his home infiltrated and disrupted by the same monster now disguised as a beautiful housekeeper, and is chased by ravenous "hunger birds" intent on devouring him. However, before all these things happen, the narrator's life is unsettled by the loss of his room.

Faced with financial difficulties, his parents decide to rent out his room, which results in the narrator sharing a room with his sister who teases him. Despite his subdued acceptance and claim that he was "not heartbroken" by the decision, the loss of his room is a traumatic event for the narrator, disrupting his life and damaging his sense of normalcy significantly (Gaiman *Ocean* 13). Moving to his sister's room is nothing less than "exile"—it not only uproots him from the only place where he feels familiar and comfortable but also disrupts the life he has built around it (13). He can no longer read books after bedtime, and despite his fear of darkness, now he has to close the door every other night since his sister prefers to sleep in darkness. However, the narrator's attachment to the room is deeper than a mere desire to have his own private space: the narrator perceives the room as a place that exists for himself, as suggested by the repeated mention of "a tiny little yellow washbasin ... just my size" that his parents installed in the room (13). The idea of other people "sleeping in *my* bedroom, using *my* little yellow basin that was just the right size for *me*" (14, my emphasis) strikes him as unnatural and causes a sense of uneasiness.

The unsettling changes, however, are not confined to the narrator's room. The whole house is now subject to the constant influx of strangers who rent the room. The narrator's vague "suspicion" about them takes a concrete form when the narrator's kitten Fluffy is run over by the taxi which brings the newest tenant, the opal miner. The incident is not only painful but deeply intrusive: the narrator comes home from school to discover his kitten gone and an utter stranger waiting for him in the kitchen. The narrator's pain is exacerbated by the opal miner's callous attitude and his attempt to replace the beloved kitten with another cat. Because of the presence of the opal miner and the new cat, the narrator cannot grieve for his kitten freely at his own home. "I wanted to cry for my kitten, but I could not do that if anyone else was there and watching me," the narrator explains. "I wanted to mourn. I wanted to bury my friend at the bottom of the garden, past the green-grass fairy ring, into the rhododendron bush cave, back past the heap of grass cuttings, where nobody ever went but me" (11). Instead, he is forced to accept the new cat the opal miner has brought. He does not dare to express his feelings to his parents, either, fearing that they may share the opal miner's view that "after all, if my kitten had been killed, it had also been replaced. The damage had been made up" (12).

The reader, having read the prologue, already knows that the renting business will not improve the family's financial situation enough to keep the large house. In five years, the family will move out and that the house will be demolished, much to the narrator's regret. However, the loss of the home has already begun at the beginning of the novel. The home has become a strange, porous, and unsafe place that allows strangers to interrupt the narrator's life and does not protect him. It has turned into an *unhomely* place.

Childhoods in Gaiman's works are more often than not disrupted. The eponymous protagonist of *Coraline* starts her adventure in a new and unfamiliar place to which she has recently moved; Helena's quest in the dream world in *MirrorMask* is initiated by her mother's sudden illness that uproots from the life she has known; and the Nobody Owens's life in *The Graveyard Book* begins with and is shaped by the massacre of his family and his adoption by the ghosts of the graveyard. The linking of the loss of the familiar scene of childhood and an uncanny experience in *Ocean* bears a particular similarity to "The Flints of Memory Lane," a ghost story first published in 1997 in *Dancing with the Dark* and then reprinted in 2006's *Fragile Things*.[1]

Like *Ocean*, "Flints" is told in first person by an unnamed male narrator, who recalls an extraordinary event that he experienced before reaching adulthood. Mundane events in his everyday life are also intermingled with the supernatural. His narrative is framed by a situation very similar to that of the narrator of *Ocean*: the destruction of the childhood home and the resulting displacement accompanied by a deep sense of loss. The narrator of "Flints" describes himself at the time of the event as a fifteen-year-old who has recently moved to a new house but is still missing his old home. His former house, an old Victorian manor to which he is deeply attached despite its reputation of being haunted, is sold and demolished, resulting in the family's relocation to a new house built in the place that used to be its garden. It is this newly-built modern house, not the reportedly haunted old manor, that becomes the setting of the ghost story. One night, returning home from his friend's house, the narrator sees a woman who is "dressed like a gypsy queen in a play, or a Moorish princess" staring at his house. The strange woman is depicted in "shades of yellow and black," similar to the way Ursula Monkton in *Ocean* is repeatedly described in the two-color scheme of pink and grey. The narrator asks her if she is looking for someone, but she does not reply. Instead, she just stares at him and smiles. The smile arouses an inexplicable and overwhelming fear in the narrator. He runs away, back to his friend's house, and calls his parents, only to be told that there is no one near the house.

The unsettling effect of this story is mainly created by its lack of explanation. Even the narrator himself laments his inability to make sense of this event. "I like things to be story-shaped," he states in the beginning, "Reality, however, is not story-shaped, and the eruptions of the odd into our lives are not story-shaped, either." After narrating the event, he expresses his wish for "anything that would give some sense of closure to the story, anything that would make it story-shaped," but there is none. And his inability to deduce any reason or meaning out of this event, to make this experience neatly "story-shaped," is the reason why "the yellow-black of her smile, and a shadow of the fear that followed," is so firmly embedded in his memory. Likewise, Gaiman's deliberate failure to produce a proper ghost narrative deprives the readers of the comfort of comprehension and leaves them in the state of uneasy suspension. This state of closely resembles real responses to uncanny events. However, the dissatisfactory closure of "Flints" also leaves a lingering suspicion that the strange woman on the dark street may not be the only uncanny presence in this story. The narrator is in the middle of changes beyond his control: as an adolescent, he is being involuntarily displaced from the familiar state of childhood in the same way he was displaced from his beloved childhood home. He is uncertain of himself and of his relationships, "skinny and gawky and wanting desperately to be cool" and dating a girl who is explicitly puzzled about "why she [is] going out with [him]." It is not just the strange woman who is inexplicable but life itself; what is not "story-shaped" is "reality" itself.

Unlike "Flints," *Ocean* provides sufficient, if not complete, explanations for the central supernatural event. The reader is informed of the origin and nature of the monster, its motives and desires, powers and limitations, and later its identity and name. Although many elements in the novel are ambiguous, with the hints that they are beyond explanation, the pieces of information that are revealed are enough for the narrator to make a "story-shaped" narrative out of the experience and for the readers to understand the story. Nonetheless, scattered around this story of an adventure completed, a monster defeated, and friendship proved are events that are far less fantastic and even less comprehensible. Although the narrator of *Ocean* is far younger than that of "Flints," what he experiences through the narrative is a similar process of transition, which begins with a relatively bearable changes in household to a frightening disillusionment about his family. By the end of the story, the world of *Ocean* is no more "story-shaped" than the strange event in "Flints."

Appropriately, it is losing his bedroom, which the narrator remembers as the first sign of disruption in his childhood, that eventually leads to all the uncanny events to come. The transformation of the bedroom into a room for rent lures the opal miner, whose suicide summons a monster from another realm. The monster, whose true name, Skarthach of the Keep, is not revealed until the moment of its demise, is intent on making people "happy" and wreaks havoc by giving money and unsettling dreams to people (42). Recently having befriended the Hempstocks, the narrator accompanies Lettie in her quest to banish the monster. Lettie successfully "bind[s]" the monster, but it leaves a gateway in the form of a hole in the narrator's foot and returns in the guise of Ursula Monkton, a young and pretty live-in housekeeper and nanny (42).

Despite her pleasing and familiar appearance, Ursula Monkton terrifies the narrator far more than she did in her monstrous form. Although he feels reasonably "scared" (28, 31, 42) by strange events following the appearance of the monster, he is not so scared that he is avoids joining Lettie to confront the monster (35). Neither does he refrain from fighting it with his bare hands when it attacks (41). Later, when he discovers that this encounter left him with a worm-filled hole in his sole, he is not even scared (48). He removes the worm calmly and methodically and afterwards curiously inspects it (48–49). Even the fact that a tiny part of the worm remains in his foot does not worry him (50).

Ursula Monkton the nanny, on the other hand, reduces the narrator to a state of utter terror and helplessness with her power to restrict his movement and her mundane threats: to lock him in his bedroom or the attic, to rob him of his books and tell lies about him to his parents. The narrator knows that she, being an adult, is capable of carrying out all these threats. Using the authority that her adulthood grants her, Ursula Monkton transforms the narrator's home into a hostile space where he has no ally and no freedom of movement. His parents trust her words more than his and are absent most of the time anyway, leaving him under her sole supervision; and his sister, who has never been his friend to begin with, is in love with the new pretty nanny. When he runs to the Hempstocks after the father's abusive behavior, the narrator fears that even Lettie is incapable of protecting him from Ursula because "Lettie was just a girl" despite all her mysterious power (86). "Ursula Monkton was an adult," he thinks. "It did not matter … that she was every monster, every witch, every nightmare made flesh. She was also an adult, and when adults fight children, adults always win" (86–7).

However, Ursula Monkton's greatest danger comes from her attractive adult body and the power it has over the narrator's father. It does not only exacerbates the relationship between the narrator and his father, who is attracted to Ursula and grows increasingly impatient with his son's seemingly unreasonable antagonism against her, but also threatens to disintegrate the family. After the narrator is sent to his room, Ursula visits him with his sister, who smugly teases him. Ursula commands, "We won't talk to him again until he's allowed to rejoin the family" (75). The narrator retorts by pointing out that she is not his "family," but the claim sounds empty (75). Ursula has in fact made herself the object of the father's affection to the point that an insult directed to her induces violent anger at his own son. At this point, the narrator is far more excluded from the "family" than Ursula is, with no one to trust or defend him.

His violent punishment distresses the narrator, but it is nothing compared to the shock and fear he experiences when he witnesses his father and Ursula engaged in a sexual activity. "I was no longer scared by what happened in the bathroom," the narrator states, because the possible implication of what he just witnessed is far scarier (78). He realizes that the bond between his mother and father may not be as "inviolate" as he assumed and that the family may be neither immutable nor indestructible (80). This overwhelms the narrator with uncertainty. He feels that "[t]he future had suddenly become unknowable: anything could happen: the train of my life had jumped the rails and headed off across the fields and was coming down the lane with me, then" (80).

Just as the narrator's room is transformed into a suspicious place that invites possibly harmful strangers, the home becomes an unsafe space that offers no protection from external dangers and generate threats from within. The family guarantees neither durability nor affection, and the everyday world itself has become a strange and incomprehensible place. Everything familiar is turned unfamiliar.

Against the intimidating uncertainty of the everyday world, the Hempstocks's magical world functions an emotional home that offers a sense of safety and certainty for the narrator. The Hempstocks, who have been living in the same place since the days of the Doomsday Book and seemingly do not age, represent immutability in an unstable world. The narrator finds their world comforting precisely because of its fairytale-like supernatural quality: as an avid reader of myths, the narrator knows how things work in the realm of myths and fairytales. As he confides in the earlier part of the novel, he is a child who finds "the existence and the nature of fairies easier to understand than that of lords," let alone that of financially struggling adults and unfaithful husbands (10).

More importantly, the rules are never violated in the Hempstocks' world. However powerful or dangerous they are, all the magical creatures as well as the Hempstocks themselves act within the boundary of an established set of rules. The monster that becomes Ursula Monkton gives only what people "want," she "would have given [people] wisdom, or peace, perfect peace" but what the opal miner asked for was money (42). Later, Lettie confirms, "She does what she does, according to her nature. She was asleep, she woke up, she's trying to give everyone what they want" (110). Similarly, the hunger birds can only appear when they are summoned and only "perform their function" (153).

Despite being always hungry, they devour only what does not belong to the world. Skarthach cannot stray from the boundary that Lettie has drawn with broken toys; the hunger birds cannot enter the circle drawn by Lettie or hurt anything that belongs to the Hempstocks. Likewise, everything can be clearly explained. The Hempstocks always have answers to the questions that the narrator asks, from the age of a silver coin (Old Mrs. Hempstock performs her version of carbon dating by examining the coin's electrons with her bare eyes) to why the boy is exempt from the monster's mission of making everyone happy (she used him as a gateway). Although in many cases the answer does not offer the narrator or the reader much understanding, it creates a sense of security that comes from knowing that there is a reason and meaning behind everything. The Hempstocks's world is story-shaped.

It is this certainty of the magical world that enables Lettie and the narrator to defeat Ursula Monkton. The narrator escapes his house by using Ursula Monkton's magical power of mind-reading against her, projecting the thought that he is in bed while he is actually running to the Hempstocks. Ursula follows him, but her supernatural nature prevents her from disobeying Lettie on the Hempstocks' land. In the end, Lettie defeats Ursula, now back in her monstrous form, by using magic and summoning the hunger birds, sending Ursula back into the realm of the fantastic. However, the strict rules of the magical world do not necessarily function in the narrator's favor. When the hunger birds demand him as their "lawful prey" on the grounds that he served Ursula as her gateway, even the Hempstocks cannot make them leave (158). It is only when the hunger birds accidentally injure Lettie that they are forced to apologize and to leave immediately.

The Hempstocks' world also highlights the flimsiness of the everyday world. For example, the narrator witnesses Old Mrs. Hempstock revising the past with "snipping and stitching," overwriting the events that led to his flight from home with a simpler and happier version in which he is simply invited to spend a night with the Hempstocks with his parents' permission (100). Later he sees the hunger birds eating away the world itself in order to pressure the Hempstocks into giving up the narrator to them, leaving "a perfect nothing" in place of what they devoured (155). "This was the void.... This was what lay beneath the thinly painted scrim of reality," the narrator realizes. "Soon enough, there would be no world. My mother, my father, my sister, my house, my school friends, my town, my grandparents, London, the Natural History Museum, France, television, books, ancient Egypt—because of me, all these things would be gone, and there would be nothing in their place" (155).

This realization prompts the narrator to leave the Hempstocks's protection and to submit himself to the hunger birds in order to stop them from destroying the world. This is the first truly mature and independent action that the narrator takes and it marks the end of his childish perception of the world where he is "the most important thing in creation" (156). It is also an act of acknowledgement that he belongs to this world of "reality," however unstable and treacherous it may be (155). Accordingly, it also leads to the narrator's banishment from the Hempstocks's world. In a desperate attempt to protect the narrator, Lettie throws herself over him, shielding him from the hunger birds' attack. The narrator is saved, but the rules are broken, and everyone involved in this violation must pay the price. Lettie suffers grievous injuries and is given to the "ocean" by the older Hempstocks without any guarantee of whether of when or if she will return. The hunger birds are forced to submit to Old Mrs. Hempstock's command and leave without harming the narrator. And the narrator is banished from the Hempstocks' world with his memory revised.

By the end of his recollection, he remembers a different version of the past: he hated Ursula Monkton without good reason, she left suddenly because she was discovered having an affair with his father, and Lettie has gone to Australia to live with her father. Now only the world of reality remains, uncanny in its uncertainty.

The Ocean at the End of the Lane, in a sense, is a story of losing home. In the course of the narrative, the narrator loses his room, his home as he knows it, and the emotional shelter which the Hempstock Farm has become, along with his memories about this place and his friend Lettie. Through this process, the everyday world reveals itself as an unfamiliar and unknowable place, where the narrator can never be at home. The prologue and epilogue depict the narrator as a middle-aged man who has not found, and perhaps never will find, his place in the world. He is only "sometimes" satisfied with the artwork he produces, he is struggling to recover from his divorce and is not particularly close to his grown-up children, and he is still in the process of "grow[ing] a new heart" in place of the one which was eaten by the hunger birds decades ago (175). He feels lost in this world: when the Old Ms. Hempstock urges him to return home, he replies, "I don't know where that is, anymore" (176).

The loss of home and the resulting state of being lost without home, Anthony Vidler argues, is what Freud's concept of *das Unheimliche* is, which he translates as "unhomeliness" (7). He explains that the uncanny is invoked not by mere unfamiliarity but by "the fundamental propensity of the familiar ... suddenly to become defamiliarized, derealized," and therefore is inseparably linked to nostalgia and homesickness (7). Here Freud's idea of *das Unheimliche* can be connected to Martin Heidegger's, as George Steiner and Kathy Justice Gentile point out. In *Being and Time* Heidegger defines being *unheimlich* as "not-being-at-home" in the world, the opposite to the usual state of being obliviously familiar to the world (189). Steiner translates the term as "homeless" or "unhoused," defining it as the feeling of "emptiness" that one feels when "the familiarity of the everyday life shatters" (99). The uncanny, then, signals the moment when the world ceases to be one's home, when the home as one's place in the world is lost.

However, according to Heidegger, the uncanny signals a moment of ontological revelation, when the comforting façade of the everyday world is stripped and one is forced to confront the true face underneath. He argues that "being-at-home" in the world is a convenient illusion, "being absorbed in the world" (80) in its superficial appearance and indulging oneself in "tranquilized self-assurance" (189). Only when the uncanny destroys it and disclose "the uncanniness of everyday familiar world" (393) can one see one's true condition in the world. Thus, "uncanniness is the basic kind of Being-in-the-world" (322) "not-being-at-home" in the world is nothing less than the recognition of the true relationship between the self and the world.

If so, the growing-up should be not a process of finding one's permanent place in this world, which is merely an illusion but that of losing one's place in the world again and again, facing the fearful possibilities hidden under the comforting and familiar reality. This is the alternative story of growing-up that *The Ocean at the End of the Lane* tells: a story of realizing and accepting the uncanniness of the world, of finding oneself not at home in the world yet to be still able to live in it.

Note

1. The similarities between *The Ocean at the End of the Lane* and "The Flints of Memory Lane" may be due in part to their semi-biographical nature. While *Ocean* is a novel, Gaiman has commented that it is heavily inspired by his childhood experiences in many ways (Campbell). He also describes the writing process of the novel as "plunder[ing] the landscape of [his] childhood" and "reshap[ing] those places into a story" in the acknowledgement of the book (Gaiman *Ocean* 180).

Works Cited

Campbell, Hayley. "The Ocean at the End of the Lane." *The Art of Neil Gaiman*. New York: Harper Design, 2014. 244–46. Print.

Dolar, Mladen. "'I Shall Be with You on Your Wedding-Night': Lacan and the Uncanny." *October* 58 (1991): 5–23. Print.

Freud, Sigmund. "The Uncanny." Trans. James Strachey. *The Standard Edition of the Complete Psychological Works of Sigmund Freud.* Vol. XVII. London: Hogarth Press, 1955. 219–256. Print.

Gaiman, Neil. *Coraline.* New York: HarperCollins, 2002. Print.

_____. "The Flints of Memory Lane." *Fragile Things: Short Fictions and Wonders.* New York: HarperCollins, 2005. n.p. Kindle.

_____. *The Graveyard Book.* New York: HarperCollins, 2008. Print.

_____. *The Ocean at the End of the Lane.* New York: HarperCollins, 2013. Print.

Gentile, Kathy Justice. "Anxious Supernaturalism: An Analytic of the Uncanny." *Gothic Studies* 2.1 (2000): 23–38. Print.

Gooding, Richard. "'Something Very Old and Very Slow': *Coraline,* Uncanniness, and Narrative Form." *Children's Literature Association Quarterly* 33.4 (2008): 390–407. Print.

Heidegger, Martin. *Being and Time.* Trans. John Macquarrie and Edward Robinson. New York: Harper & Row, 1962. Print.

Jentsch, Ernst. "On the Psychology of the Uncanny (1906)." Trans. Roy Sellars. *Angelaki* 2 (1995): 7–16. Print.

Mallan, Kerry M. "Uncanny Encounters: Home and Belonging in Canadian Picture Books." *Canadian Children's Literature* 115 (2004): 17–31. QUT ePrints. Web. 2 Aug. 2014.

MirrorMask. Dir. Dave McKean. Sony Pictures Home Entertainment, 2006. DVD.

Rollin, Lucy. "The Mysterious and the Uncanny in *Nancy Drew* and *Harriet the Spy.*" *Psychoanalytic Responses to Children's Literature.* Ed. Lucy Rollin and Mark I. West. Jefferson, NC: McFarland, 1999. 23–29. Print.

Steiner, George. *Martin Heidegger.* Chicago: University of Chicago Press, 1989.

Vidler, Anthony. *The Architectural Uncanny: Essays in the Modern Unhomely.* Cambridge: MIT Press, 1994. Print.

"The essence of grandmotherliness": Ideal Motherhood and Threatening Female Sexuality

Courtney M. Landis

After a moment of danger in Neil Gaiman's 2013 novel *The Ocean at the End of the Lane*, the narrator (a seven-year-old boy) is ushered into the bath with a warm cup of soup at the Hempstock farm. Soaking in front of the fire, the narrator confides, "I felt safe. It was as if the essence of grandmotherliness had been condensed into that one place, that one time" (Gaiman 92). The Hempstocks offer food and protection, existing as an exemplified idea of maternity. An incarnation of the threefold goddess, the Hempstock women contain an intense, god-like power that is crucial to the survival of the narrator. The antithesis of their motherly care is Ursula Monkton, a creature from another plane of existence masquerading as a woman in order to secure a home in the human world. Ursula adopts a sexualized performance of femininity, utilizing a pretty appearance and seductive behavior to gain a position of power within the narrator's home. As the Hempstocks and Ursula battle over the narrator's life, the novel positions the reader to carefully consider these different depictions of femininity and female power. Based on the number of powerful women and the significance of female agency within the story, it would be easy to categorize *Ocean* as a feminist novel. However, readers must closely examine the portrayal of the Hempstocks as completely desexualized paragons of domesticity and maternity. This ideal recalls Freud's Madonna-whore dichotomy when placed in comparison to the destructive and "evil" sexuality of Ursula (Freud 165).

The threefold goddess is described by Robert Graves, a poet and mythological scholar who identifies cross-cultural examples of a singular, powerful goddess appearing in triad form: "The moon's three phases of new, full, and old recalled the matriarch's three phases of maiden, nymph (nubile woman) and crone.... Her devotees never quite forgot that there were not three goddesses, but one goddess" (Graves 14). Gaiman often incorporates representations of the threefold goddess, such as the Fates in *Sandman*, the Lillim in *Stardust*, and the Japanese *onmyoji* in *The Dream Hunters*. Aaron Drucker points out the appearance of the Fates in the form of Crone, Mother, and Daughter in *Sandman* 58:14–17, and notes that as these would be "instantly recognizable" to the reader as "the Triple Goddess in tripartite role," Lyta Hall identifies them as *Macbeth*'s Weird Sisters (Drucker 90). These Fates feature less than the Hempstock women in *Ocean*: Lyta has a glimpse of her future and that of her child, but no answers, and she continues her quest alone (Gaiman *Sandman* 58:15–16). The Hempstocks take an active role of protection, and speak plainly and lovingly to the narrator of *Ocean*. While both representations (the Fates of *Sandman* and the Hempstocks) rely heavily on the trope of the threefold goddess, Gaiman allows more depth of character for the Hempstocks, building their individual characters while the Hempstocks control most of the action of the novel.

Coralline Dupuy similarly contrasts the role of the *onmyoji* as representative of powerful female figures in Gaiman's use of folklore with the Fates of *The Sandman*, and identifies them as another representation of the threefold goddess: "The three witches in *Dream Hunters* are repeating characters (or a three-in-one character) from Gaiman's work ... the fact that the triad is female is particularly important.... The three women echo the Fates as well as specific members of the Endless" (Dupuy 133). However, this representation of the goddess seems particularly grotesque, as Dupuy describes them as "the visual embodiment of the frightening, dark side of the picture" (134). In *The Ocean at the End of the Lane*, the Hempstocks as the threefold goddess differ from Gaiman's other representations in appearance and temperament, in addition to serving as the "heroes" of the novel.

As neatly as the Hempstocks fit into the traditional format of the threefold goddess, Gaiman subverts the trope by slightly altering the ways that the Hempstock women create this trinity. The maiden is traditionally framed as either a babe at the mother's breast or as a young woman maturing sexually in preparation for her future/simultaneous role as mother. Lettie, the youngest Hempstock, is initially described as "much older than me" by the seven-year-old narrator, but this idea is somewhat humorously followed up with "at least eleven" though we learn that she has been eleven for a long time (19, 30). Physically, "Her red-brown hair was worn relatively short, for a girl, and her nose was snub. She was freckled. She wore a red skirt—girls didn't wear jeans much back then, not in those parts. She had a soft Sussex accent and sharp gray-blue eyes" (19). Assuming the narrator has correctly identified her as being "at least eleven," Lettie's form is prepubescent, lacking the prominent secondary sex characteristics (budding breasts or hips) that often identify the maiden as being young and fertile as well as virginal. However, neither is she a babe in arms. At eleven (even if it is an immortal kind of eleven), Lettie has agency of her own, collecting the narrator from the scene of the suicide, attempting to bind the flea, and spearheading the efforts to remove the flea from the narrator's world before finally sacrificing her life. The narrator may be the protagonist, the teller of this story and the lens with which the reader tries to understand it, but Lettie is the hero.

Like Lettie, Gaiman's depiction of Ginnie Hempstock as the mother is similarly changed from the archetype. When the narrator sees her for the first time, she is "stocky" with "red-brown hair [that] was streaked with gray, and cut short. She had apple cheeks, a dark green skirt that went to her knees, and Wellington boots" (20). Later, protected in her arms after the attack of the hunger birds, the narrator holds onto Ginnie: "She smelled like a farm and like a kitchen, like animals and like food" (160). Mrs. Hempstock is maternal— she is not initially introduced as a mother, but the narrator assumes that she is Lettie's mother because "She seemed like she was somebody's mother"— but her body does not exhibit her reproductive capabilities; rather, it displays a touch of age, and is clothed in utilitarian rather than divine raiment (21).

Old Mrs. Hempstock, called "Gran" and "Mother," is perhaps the most in line with the conventions of the threefold goddess. She is "an old woman, much older than my parents, with long gray hair, like cobwebs, and a thin face" (19). When the narrator asks her how old she is, she casually replies, "Old enough ... I remember when the moon was made" (33). The narrator accepts her description with a fully childlike and unquestioning trust, and he is not wrong. At the end of the novel, the narrator enters the ocean in the bucket and he sees the end of everything: "the next Big Bang.... I knew that Old Mrs. Hempstock would be here for that one, as she had been for the last" (143). In a glorious display of power, it is Old Mrs. Hempstock that coaxes Lettie's ocean into the bucket, but her efforts exhaust her so much that she has to take a "lie-down" that lasts for "a few minutes or a hundred years" and is only interrupted by the attack on Lettie (143, 151). Surrounded and exhausted, the narrator and the two younger Hempstocks are powerless against the hunger birds when a voice comes from the heavens. Astonished, the narrator says:

The voice sounded like Old Mrs. Hempstock. Like her, I knew, and yet so unlike. If Old Mrs. Hempstock had been an empress, she might have talked like that, her voice more stilted and formal and yet more musical than the old-lady voice I knew.... It was Old Mrs. Hempstock, I suppose. But it wasn't. It was Lettie's gran in the same way that.... I mean.... She shone silver. Her hair was still long, still white, but now she stood as tall and as straight as a teenager. My eyes had become used to the darkness, and I could not look at her face to see if it was the face I was familiar with: it was too bright. Magnesium-flare bright. Fireworks Night bright. Midday-sun-reflecting-off-a-silver-coin bright [158–159].

Old Mrs. Hempstock removes the hunger birds, chastises them, and restores the world to rightful order. There is no denying that Old Mrs. Hempstock is old, wrinkled, and occasionally needs a rest, embodying literal characteristics of the crone as old woman. However, Old Mrs. Hempstock equally displays the depths of her power; simultaneously, she is aged and tired while luminous and awesome.

While Gaiman subverts some of the problematic considerations of reducing the mother/maiden/crone to their reproductive stages, he does establish the Hempstocks collectively as an idealized maternal figure, a characteristic dramatically highlighted against the maternal performances of the narrator's mother and Ursula. The narrator's mother has little to no presence in the novel, appearing significantly less than the father. Her first dialogue does not appear until the third chapter, when she informs the narrator that he has won the Premium Bonds (a symptom of the flea causing a sudden influx of money), and that, to his chagrin, she is going to stow his £25 in his post office account (25–26). His mother does not appear again for another three chapters, and does so only to tell him that she has found a job, and thus is hiring Ursula (51–52). At no point does the narrator explicitly blame his mother for Ursula's presence; in fact, before learning that a nanny was hired, he says that he did not mind her having a job: "I would be fine on my own" (52). However, the mother's absence allows Ursula to dominate the narrator and his father. Ursula herself links her power over the father's actions to his attraction to/affair with Ursula, events that could only happen in the mother's absence.

The Hempstocks, in contrast with the narrator's mother, physically and emotionally care for the narrator. They protect him from evil and provide a home, albeit a temporary one. At the beginning of the book, Lettie collects the narrator from the crime scene, neatly guiding him away from the traumatic sight of the dead opal miner and into their home, where her family serves him warm milk and breakfast (18–20). Upon his second visit to the house, Old Mrs. Hempstock gives him honey and cream, and Ginnie Hempstock chides maternally, "Mother! ... Giving the boy honey. You'll rot his teeth" (34). When the narrator runs away, the Hempstocks put him directly into a hot bath, mend his clothes, feed him dinner, and set him up to spend the night (91). After choking on a coin, the narrator wants to confide in someone, but is not sure who: "I knew enough about adults to know that if I did tell them what had happened, I would not be believed. Adults rarely seemed to believe me when I told the truth anyway. Why would they believe me about something so unlikely?" (28). Still, he promptly tells Lettie, who tells Old Mrs. Hempstock (29, 32). Neither expresses any doubt whatsoever about his story. Rather, Lettie fetches Ginnie, while Old Mrs. Hempstock consults with the narrator about where to place her vases of flowers in the kitchen, and when "we placed the vases where I suggested, [I] felt wonderfully important" (33). The narrator's own family or mother never make him feel important: he has to give up his bedroom for lodgers (14), and the narrator is often certain that his parents "never noticed" significant events like the appearance of the new kitten (171). The three Hempstock women create the maternal ideal: they feed him, clothe him, comfort him, and (most importantly) make him feel validated and important.

The Hempstocks offer the narrator not only a home, but protection. After the narrator's father nearly drowns him, the narrator sneaks out of the house and flees to the Hempstock's farm, and only escapes Ursula once he stumbles onto Hempstock land and Lettie finds him (88). When Ursula grabs the narrator in an attempt to return home via the gate she lodged in his heart, the narrator screams for help: "'Mummy!' I shouted. 'Daddy!' Then, 'Lettie, make her put me down.' My parents were not there. Lettie was" (126). Lettie and the other Hempstock women save and protect the narrator: his parents are never the force coming to his rescue. At the end of the book, when the narrator rushes at the hunger birds to sacrifice himself, the Hempstocks rewrite reality. "She ... sacrificed herself for me," the narrator says, and Ginnie responds, "After a fashion, dear.... You screamed so piteously as you died. She couldn't abide that. She had to do something" (174). Once Old Mrs. Hempstock has removed the hunger birds, she reassures the narrator that he is "safe as houses," and he is: the hunger birds have left him in peace for the rest of his life thus far (161). Were it not for the Hempstocks, the narrator would have been dead long since. Not only does Lettie protect, feed, and house the narrator, she gives the ultimate sacrifice and trades her life for his. Furthermore, if it were not for the Hempstocks, the memory of his own death would be hanging over him forever; a case of fuzzy memory implies that the same memory-stitching that removed the memory of the attempted drowning allows the narrator to forget his death. Not only do the Hempstocks preserve the narrator's life, they preserve his ability to cope and peace of mind. Finally, Old Mrs. Hempstock's choice of the words "safe as houses" is a significant indicator both of a maternal ideal and of a divine representation of motherhood. In *A Madwoman in the Attic*, Sandra Gilbert and Susan Gubar point out that houses are traditionally associated with the female: "The female womb has certainly, always and everywhere, been a child's first and most satisfying house, a source of food and dark security, and therefore a mythic paradise imaged over and over again" (88). Just as the Hempstock women are inextricably linked with their farm, so is the security they provide the narrator and the people around him.

As they seek to protect and feed the narrator, the Hempstocks embody a sense of Virginia Woolf's "Angel in the House," a womanly ideal who is "intensely sympathetic. She was immensely charming. She was utterly unselfish. She excelled in the difficult arts of family life. She sacrificed herself daily" (Woolf 5). The Hempstocks have more personality than the milquetoast mothers and sickly children of Louisa May Alcott and Coventry Patmore, but still subscribe to some of the key elements of the Angel in the House: sympathy, unselfishness, sacrifice. Gilbert and Gubar point out that the "angel in the house" trope has religious roots: "there is a clear line of literary descent from divine Virgin to domestic angel" (Gilbert and Gubar 20). The Hempstocks manage to be a manifestation of the two ideas together, being actually divine while still maternal and homey, almost literally angels in the house.

Of all the manifestations of an idealized maternity within *Ocean*, perhaps the most visible and sensuous example is food. In almost every scene in which the narrator interacts with the Hempstocks, he receives something delectable to eat or drink (and usually both). In the prologue, as the now middle-aged narrator stumbles back onto the farm at the end of the lane, he wanders into the barn and meets again Old Mrs. Hempstock. She asks who he is, and when she asks if he is "Lettie's friend? From the top of the lane?" he responds, saying, "You gave me milk. It was warm, from the cows" (6). The memory of the Hempstocks is linked, almost instinctively, to the comfort of warm milk. After that first cup of milk the day he meets the Hempstocks, Lettie asks if he has eaten and promptly leads him to the house for breakfast of "warm porridge from the stovetop, with a lump of homemade blackberry jam, my favorite, in the middle of the porridge, then she poured cream on it. I ... was as happy as I have ever been about anything. It tasted perfect" (20). The narrator's first interactions with the Hempstocks are built upon food, and again the next time the narrator sees Lettie she asks, "Have you had breakfast?" (29). When Lettie leads him back to the Hempstock house for food, the narrator describes the kitchen, particularly the fireplace: "There was a hearth in that kitchen, and there were ashes still smoldering in the hearth, from the night before. That kitchen was a friendly place" (31). More than any other space in their house, the narrator tends to associate the Hempstocks with cooking, the kitchen, and the hearth; all symbols traditionally linked with the threefold goddess and feminine deities. A few pages later, Old Mrs. Hempstock offers him honeycomb and cream (34), and yet again when the narrator flees his home to the Hempstocks in the middle of the night, he is soothed with soup, "rich, and warming"; for dinner, custard "creamier and richer than anything I had ever tasted at school or at home" (92–93). In the morning, there is more porridge with honeycomb and cream and toast and jam. "I wish I could purr, too. I would have purred then," the narrator states (110). After emerging from Lettie's ocean in a bucket, he is brought back to the farm and fed warm shepherd's pie and spotted dick with custard (146–148). He tells the reader:

> I ate it with joy. I do not miss childhood, but I miss the way I took pleasure in small things, even as greater things crumbled. I could not control the world I was in, could not walk away from things or people or moments that hurt, but I found joy in the things that made me happy ... perhaps I was going to die that night and perhaps I would never go home again, but it was a good dinner, and I had faith in Lettie Hempstock [149].

Repeatedly, the narrator links the joys of childhood with food, specifically the food that comes from the Hempstocks. After Lettie's death and return to the Ocean, food disappears from the narrative along with her until the epilogue, when Old Mrs. Hempstock brings the narrator "a perfect cup of builder's tea" and a tomato and cheese sandwich: "It was good, really good. Freshly baked" (173). The Hempstock's food is linked to the comfort and security that the Hempstocks provide, and thus disappears when the narrator is in a position of danger or sadness away from the Hempstocks; after the harrowing experiences of finding a dead body and fleeing his home, the narrator is soothed by food. After the narrator relives the heartbreak of Lettie's death, he is again comforted by food—and not just any food, but real food that "taste[s] like something" (173).

The real food that tastes like food is described in sharp contrast to the burned or possibly poisonous food that the narrator's family and Ursula attempt to feed him. In the second chapter, the narrator's father makes breakfast, but burns the toast as he "usually" does (15). As they walk down the lane, the narrator holds his charred toast sadly camouflaged with peanut butter, but "did not eat it.... I hid my piece of burnt toast behind my back.... I wished my family would buy normal sliced white bread, the kind that went into toasters, like every other family I knew" (15–16). After seeing the dead man, he takes a bite of the toast:

> It was burnt and cold. At home, my father ate all the most burnt pieces of toast. "Yum!" he'd say, and "Charcoal! Good for you!" and "Burnt toast! My favorite!" and he'd eat it all up. When I was much older he confessed to me that he had not ever liked burnt toast, had only eaten it to prevent it from going to waste, and, for a fraction of a moment, my entire childhood felt like a lie: it was as if one of the pillars of belief that my world had been built upon had crumbled into dry sand [18].

By providing terrible food and pretending that everything was okay, the father shakes the narrator's faith in his perception of childhood, just as the father will betray the narrator's perception of the father and mother as "inviolate unit" by kissing Ursula (80). At this point in the novel the reader knows nothing of this future deception (nor does the narrator, necessarily, if he is remembering the story as it is related to us), but the meal of burnt toast immediately establishes the father and the father's food as untrustworthy. Upon the narrator's introduction to Ursula, she brings him a plate of peanut butter sandwiches. He refuses: "I was starving. I wondered whether the sandwiches were dangerous or not. I did not know. I was scared that I would eat one and it would turn into worms in my stomach, and that they would wriggle through me, colonizing my body, until they pushed out of my skin" (55). Ursula serves dinner that evening, a "thick vegetable soup, then roast chicken and new potatoes with frozen peas." These are all foods that the narrator loves, but he notes, "I did not eat any of it.... I sat there hungrily" (62). The food looks perfect; the narrator's father scolds him for not eating, and the rest of the family devours the meal happily (61). Still, for no rational reason, the narrator is convinced that the food is as good as poison and is somehow inherently bad. The following day, the narrator's mother is gone, and Ursula prepares meatloaf for dinner. "I would not eat it. I was determined not to eat anything she had made or cooked or touched. My father was not amused.... 'I won't eat anything she made,' I told him. 'I don't like her.'" When his father angrily presses for a reason, the narrator confesses, "Because she's not human.... She's a monster.... She's a *flea*" (68–70). The father is enraged, and this anger is what leads to the waterboarding punishment in the bathtub before the narrator flees to the Hempstock farm (72). Between one of Ursula's poison-meals and the next, the narrator's father has entirely turned against him and destroyed the safety of his home.

Whether the descriptions are concerning the toothsome meals of the Hempstocks or the poisoned meals of Ursula, Gaiman heavily stresses the importance of food in *The Ocean at the End of the Lane*, even considering alone just how much space this relatively short book devotes to long depictions of food. On the tour for the release of *Ocean*, Gaiman touches on the significance of the food imagery in the book:

> I had two Jewish grandmas, with competing chicken soup recipes. I would go into their kitchens, and it was that sense that this thing was made especially for you, and you were loved. Children can take pleasure in small things, like "I'm sorry your best friend at school said you stink … do you want to get an ice cream?" And you go and get the ice cream, and things are OK. At a certain point as an adult you cross a line…. "I'm sorry you're battling erectile dysfunction—let's go get an ice cream?" doesn't really work anymore. So things are really dark and dangerous [in *Ocean*], but the food is great [qtd. in Schnelbach].

For Gaiman, food (specifically warm, homemade, and uncomplicated food such as a chicken soup) is linked with grandmotherliness, the same quality that defines the Hempstocks' kitchen. However, this sense of love from food is a gift available only during childhood; beyond the threshold of adulthood, problems become less easily answered ("don't really work anymore" [Gaiman]). In the flashback timeline of the novel, the narrator is still in a place where his problems can be solved by food, and by a warm kitchen. The narrator's father, on the other hand, has crossed that line and is in a position to experience the kinds of "adult" problems Gaiman describes, beyond the automatic comfort of a warm meal. Interestingly, Gaiman chooses sexual dysfunction as the example of an adult problem, in a similar vein as the narrator's father's affair with Ursula if not exactly the same.

Ursula, while apparently not an actual woman (or even human), performs an idea of femininity ranging from her appearance to her domestic work in an attempt to ingratiate herself with the narrator's family. When the narrator sees Ursula (in human form) for the first time, he tells the reader, "The woman was very pretty. She had shortish honey-blonde hair, huge gray-blue eyes, and pale lipstick. She seemed tall, even for an adult," and she wears a "gray and pink skirt" (53–54). At no point in the novel is the appearance of any of the Hempstocks qualified as pretty or ugly, while Ursula is immediately labeled as pretty. His sister is charmed by Ursula, telling their mother, "When I grow up I want to be Ursula," and telling the narrator, "I like her so much…. She's my friend" while showing off the purse and half-crown Ursula had given her. When the narrator tells his sister he does not like Ursula, she only responds with, "I like her. She's pretty" (62). After the mother leaves, Ursula brings the children a plate of sandwiches with "a sweet smile beneath the pale lipstick" (55). As a beautiful, blonde, cooking caretaker, Ursula embodies Judith Butler's idea of gender as "the *appearance of substance* ... a constructed identity, a performative accomplishment which the mundane social audience, including the actors themselves, come to believe and to perform in the mode of belief" (Butler 520). Through this performance, Ursula succeeds in winning the belief of the narrator's family by giving them exactly what they want—except the narrator. At dinner with both of his parents at home, the narrator "sat there hungrily, while Ursula laughed at all my father's jokes. It seemed to me he was making special jokes, just for her" (62).

Later, the mother leaves, and the narrator overhears Ursula ask his father, "'So, is your wife away every evening?'" The father explains that the mother is away frequently doing charity work: raising money for Africa, to drill wells and provide contraception. Ursula responds, "I already know all about *that*" and laughs, a "high, tinkling laugh, which sounded true and real, and had no flapping rags in it" (64). Spending time alone with the father, making light-hearted jokes about being familiar with contraception (and thus sex out of wedlock, as an unmarried woman)—Ursula's flirtation could not be more obvious. The next day, the father shows Ursula around the garden giving her flowers and "standing too close" to her. As Ursula and the father walk back into the house with the sister, the unseen narrator notices that "my father's free hand, the one not holding my sister, went down and rested, casually, proprietarily, on the swell of Ursula's midi-skirted bottom. I would react differently to that now. At the time, I do not believe I thought anything of it at all. I was seven" (66–68). The narrator may not have thought anything of his father's behavior towards Ursula at the time, but the incident stands out in his brain clearly enough to be recollected as an adult.

After the bathtub scene as the narrator sneaks out of the house, he sees a light on in the drawing room, "where we children never went, the oak-paneled room kept only for best and for special occasions." Through a crack in the curtains, he sees his father and Ursula, but

> I was not sure what I was looking at. My father had Ursula Monkton pressed up against the side of the big fireplace in the far wall. He had his back to me. She did too, her hands pressed against the high, high mantelpiece. He was hugging her from behind. Her midi skirt was hiked up around her waist. I did not know exactly what they were doing.... As I ran, I thought of my father, his arms around the housekeeper-who-wasn't, kissing her neck, and then I saw his face through the chilly bathwater as he held me under, and now I was no longer scared by what had happened in the bathroom; now I was scared by what it meant that my father was kissing the neck of Ursula, that his hands had lifted her midi skirt above her waist. My parents were a unit, inviolate. The future had suddenly become unknowable [79–90].

The narrator repeats over and over that he does not know what he was looking at, that he did not understand what his father was doing hugging Ursula, but he does understand what this means for his family. Ursula is giving the father exactly what he wants (her body), while simultaneously contributing to the destruction of the narrator's family unit.

As the narrator predicts, soon after he escapes Ursula comes after him, and as she floats through the air "Her pink blouse was open and unbuttoned. She wore a white bra. Her midi skirt flapped in the wind, revealing her calves" (83). Ursula's partial nudity is almost certainly a product of her affair with the father, but the parts of her body exposed are significant to the narrator. Taunting him, Ursula tells the narrator, "Your daddy likes me now. He'll do whatever I say [...] and every night I'll kiss him and kiss him" (84). Ursula describes all the ways she can control and torment the narrator, and even as Lettie drives her off, she smiles: "She was power incarnate, standing in the crackling air. She was the storm, she was the lightning, she was the adult world with all its power and all its secrets and all its foolish casual cruelty. She winked at me" (86). Later, as Lettie attempts to send the nanny home, Ursula says, "I'm not going anywhere," and the narrator notes "she sounded petulant, like a very small child who wanted something. 'I've only just got here. I have a house, now. I have pets—his father is just the *sweetest* thing'" (117). Ursula's affair with the narrator's father may have been giving the father what he wanted, but since Ursula taunts the narrator with her ability to "kiss [the father] and kiss him" she is obviously aware of her ability to use her sexuality as a weapon.

During this encounter, Ursula is naked, and the narrator points out that "she was the first adult woman who was not my mother that I had seen naked, and I glanced at her curiously. But the room was more interesting to me than she was" (117). Fresh from intercourse with the narrator's father, out in the elements, and, significantly, mostly clothed excepted for the gaping blouse exposing her bra, Ursula is "the adult world." Utterly naked and in the sanctuary of her own room, Ursula suddenly becomes comparable to a petulant, small child. The emphasis on the exposed breasts and bra become more significant and frightening to the narrator than complete nakedness. Earlier, after fleeing his home, the narrator is ushered into a bath in the Hempstocks' kitchen, and says, "I knew that *naked* was wrong, but the Hempstocks seemed indifferent to my nakedness" (92). This unexplained contempt for *naked* extends to Ursula, the first adult woman he has seen naked, and while her nakedness is supposedly dismissed as less interesting than the room she is in a few lines later, it is still conspicuously noticed and pointed out to the reader.

The Hempstocks, in contrast, are utterly desexualized. While subverting the traditionally sexually-focused triple presentation of the threefold goddess, Gaiman represents each woman in the least sexualized form allowed by the mythology: the maiden is eternally prepubescent; the mother is in her late 30s with visible signs of age; the crone is elderly. While the two older Hempstocks both go by "Mrs.," which indicates their married status, there are no husbands or men at all on the Hempstock farm. In his examination of the origins of the White Goddess, Graves points out that "the Great Goddess was regarded as immortal, changeless, and omnipotent; and the concept of fatherhood had not been introduced into religious thought. She took lovers, but for pleasure, not to provide her children with a father. Men feared, adored, and obeyed the matriarch" (13). The Hempstocks have clearly established themselves as matriarchs, and in harmony with the original tradition have no use for patriarchs. Near the end of the book, the narrator asks Ginnie Hempstock whether Lettie is *really* her daughter, and she replies, "More or less.... The men Hempstocks, my brothers, they went out into the world, and they had babies who've had babies. There are Hempstock women out there in your world, and I'll wager each of them is a wonder in her own way. But only Gran and me and Lettie are the pure thing" (167). At this, the narrator questions Mrs. Hempstock if she or her daughter had a daddy. "No, love," she responds. "We never went in for that sort of thing. You only need men if you want to breed more men" (167). The night he sleeps at the farm, the narrator asks again:

> "Aren't there any men?" "Men!" hooted Old Mrs. Hempstock. "I dunno what blessed good a man would be! Nothing a man could do around this farm that I can't do twice as fast and five times as well." Lettie said, "We've had men here, sometimes. They come and they go. Right now, it's just us." Her mother nodded. "They went off to seek their fate and fortune, mostly, the male Hempstocks. There's never any keeping them here when the call comes. They get a distant look in their eyes and then we've lost them, good and proper" [94].

The narrator does not ask any more questions on the subject. What exactly makes the Hempstock women of the farm at the end of the lane so much more "pure" than the Hempstock women who were born out of unions with Hempstock men is never explained. Within the Hempstock mythology, women exist entirely apart from men to the point of asexual reproduction that are "the pure thing," and that while the men might leave to explore the world, the women stay at home, farm, and cook forever. The Hempstocks do not exhibit any bitterness about the lack or presence of men at the farm; aside from Old Mrs. Hempstock's assertion that she does just as much work as a man (which is doubtless true), there is no wistfulness that the men might stay, or gloating at their absence. For the Hempstocks, the inconstant presence of men on the farm is simple as a law of nature.

In telling the story from the perspective of a seven-year-old, Gaiman places the reader in a position to value maternity over sexuality: he repeats when confronted with Ursula's sexuality that this is something beyond his childish comprehension: "at the time, I do not believe I thought anything of it at all" and "I did not know what they were doing" (68, 79). In the meantime, he is constantly praising the maternity of the Hempstocks through their food and home (the "essence of grandmotherliness" [92]), while discounting any of Ursula's attempts to be maternal (the peanut butter sandwiches, the seemingly delicious meals of roast chicken and meatloaf, all uneaten). Ursula performs as a maternal figure in many more ways than the narrator's actual mother does: cooking meals, staying at home to watch and discipline the children, engaging sexually with the father. Still, all of these actions are painted as not only incorrect but actually *unnatural* as the narrator refuses to eat Ursula's food and is unsettled by her relations with his father. The Hempstocks and Ursula are both supernatural (or unnatural) and from another world: the Hempstocks' immortality since coming to England from "the old country" (1, 22); Ursula claiming that she is "the lady of this place" and has been here "for such a long time. Since before the little people sacrificed each other on the rocks" (41). Arguably, the Hempstocks are just as inhuman as Ursula. But nothing is wrong with *their* food.

At the end of the novel, the narrator's world is restored to normalcy with Ursula's banishment: yes, the Hempstocks have removed the supernatural evil from this world, but it is significant that evil took the form of a woman aberrant from the maternal femininity valued by the narrator. The world is returned to normalcy when the slut is dead. By establishing conflict in *The Ocean at the End of the Lane* between the Hempstock women as representations of the Threefold Goddess and Ursula, Gaiman places women in the key positions of power (both as antagonist and protagonists) within the novel. However, by glorifying the maternal and desexualized aspects of the Hempstocks while condemning the actions of the un-maternal mother and the maternal but sexualized Ursula, Gaiman engages in a rework of Freud's Madonna-whore dichotomy that only allows female sexuality to exist as the unnatural threat.

Works Cited

Butler, Judith. "Performative Acts and Gender Constitution: An Essay in Phenomenology and Feminist Theory." *Theatre Journal* 40.4 (1988): 519–31. *JSTOR*. Web. 15 July 2014.

Drucker, Aaron. "Empowering Voice and Refiguring Retribution; Neil Gaiman's Anti-Feminism Feminist Parable in *The Sandman*." *Feminism in the Worlds of Neil Gaiman: Essays on the Comics, Poetry, and Prose*. Ed. Tara Prescott and Aaron Drucker. Jefferson, NC: McFarland, 2012. 81–101. Print.

Dupuy, Coralline. "Outfoxed: Feminine Folklore and Agency in *The Dream Hunters*." *Feminism in the Worlds of Neil Gaiman: Essays on the Comics, Poetry, and Prose*. Ed. Tara Prescott and Aaron Drucker. Jefferson, NC: McFarland, 2012. 131–147. Print.

Freud, Sigmund. *The Standard Edition of the Complete Psychological Works of Sigmund Freud, Volume XI*. London: Hogarth Press, 1957. Print.

Gaiman, Neil. *The Ocean at the End of the Lane*. New York: HarperCollins, 2013. Print.

_____, with Mark Hempel, et al. (a, i). "The Kindly Ones." *The Sandman* #57–69 (Feb. 1994–July 1995). New York: DC Comics. Print.

Gilbert, Sandra M., and Susan Gubar. *The Madwoman in the Attic: The Woman Writer in the Nineteenth-Century Literary Imagination*, 2d ed. New Haven: Yale University Press, 1984. Print.

Graves, Rupert. *The Greek Myths: Combined Edition*. London: Penguin, 1992. Print.

Schnelbach, Leah. "An 'Accidental' Novel? Neil Gaiman Talks About *The Ocean at the End of the Lane*." TOR.com. 20 June 2013. Web. 1 Mar. 2014.

Woolf, Virginia. *Killing the Angel in the House: Seven Essays*. London: Penguin, 1995. Print.

Remixing Time and Space

MERIDETH GARCIA

"In everything there is a trace, the experience of a return
to something else, of being returned to another past, present,
future, a different type of temporality that's even older than
the past and that is beyond the future."—Jacques Derrida

Neil Gaiman's characters have a penchant for stumbling over the boundaries of time and space. Coraline steps through a door into another world. Morpheus journeys to hell in an attempt to correct his cruel failure to grasp human perceptions of time. The Doctor answers a distress call thousands of years too late. Across Gaiman's work, the extraordinary lurks around every corner, only occasionally showing the seams where it joins with the ordinary; magic and memory leave their traces everywhere, in material, often mundane, objects that hold the power to connect people across time and space in both intended and unintended ways.

On February 4, 2013, Gaiman embarked on a collaborative composing experiment on Twitter, *A Calendar of Tales by Neil Gaiman and You*. He tweeted out twelve questions, one for each month of the year, over the course of twelve hours, and fans responded. From thousands of Twitter replies hashtagged with the particular month's question they were responding to, Gaiman selected his favorite answer to each question and wrote a short story inspired by it (Gaiman "*A Calendar of Tales* Update"). In a short video reflecting on the process, Gaiman describes the result: "thousands upon thousands of people just got to throw their feelings and their thoughts out into the world. What came out of it was 12 hours of art, and it felt like a kind of art we don't yet have a name for" (Ayame-Kenoshi). Over the next two weeks, he posted on his blog about the selection process for the tweeted responses and the creation of voice recordings for each story (Gaiman "*A Calendar of Tales* Update").

On February 19, 2013, he announced that the stories were complete and that he was now looking for fans to create and submit illustrations inspired by his stories ("Now up!"). Gaiman selected his favorite illustration for each month for inclusion in a limited print edition from over 9,000 submissions ("Project Focus"). The online version includes several illustrations for each tale, the flexible format allowing Gaiman to recognize a broader range of artistic interpretation. They cascade down the screen like leaves falling from a tree, evoking a sense of connection and motion at the same time. While the art, the coding required to convey it appropriately, the response and selection processes, and the work of moving across all of these domains to coordinate the final project are all worthy of further investigation, this essay focuses on the notion of simultaneous connection and motion in *A Calendar of Tales*. Gaiman reaches in to his substantial body of work while also reaching out to collaborate with fans, and in doing so forges a link between the two that suggests new narrative possibilities for understanding the construction of narrative time and space.

Like Tristan Thorn crossing The Wall or Richard Mayhew descending into London Below, Gaiman reached through the thin space of Twitter's boundary between fan and creator. This project connected the imaginations of Gaiman and thousands of fans in instantaneous and asynchronous ways that were specifically facilitated by Twitter and the practice of linking. The resulting work bears traces of both the theme of boundary-crossing that permeates his longer-form projects and his particularly powerful use of tweets as objects that index relationships that exist outside the visible space-time of the tweetstream. The collaborative process and the creative product facilitated by social media create the conditions for a new narrative chronotope, a new way of thinking about how we experience time and space when we enter digital worlds. This chronotope, the "Link," differs from previously identified chronotopes in how it organizes relationships between characters who do not share space and time in traditional ways. Gaiman's *A Calendar of Tales* project draws attention to the traces of an invisible world of potential relationships in both its content and in the method of its creation.

Narrative chronotopes use space to assist the reader in understanding the characters' experience of time. In his essay "Forms of Time and of the Chronotope in the Novel," Bakhtin identifies several different ways that narratives treat time, including mythological, adventure, historical, and agricultural time. Each is associated with different spatial images that serve as metaphors for the way time is represented in a concrete form that influences the characters of the story. For example, adventure time relies on the figure of the road as an organizing feature, while historical time utilizes the figure of the castle. The reader is led to think about the hero of an adventure story as traveling from one encounter to another in a chronological fashion that builds the experiences into a linear progression toward a final destination. A popular, and seemingly self-aware, example of this kind of chronotopic narrative organization appears in the Cartoon Network animated series *Adventure Time*, where Jake and Finn travel the Land of Ooo having encounters that mark their growth as characters (their progression through time) in terms of their progress through space. A character experiencing historical time, on the other hand, wanders through different rooms of the chronotope that Bakhtin calls the Castle, learning in bits and pieces how the puzzle of the story fits together. In the recent BBC television series *Sherlock*, Holmes demonstrates the Castle chronotope when he accesses his mind palace to understand the connection between bits of information collected at different times and places that might be brought to bear on the case of "The Hounds of Baskerville." The essential elements of the chronotope are established in its name: the passage of time takes concrete shape in the story in a way that supports the characters' movement through space toward their narrative goal. According to Bakhtin, chronotopes

> are the organizing centers for the fundamental narrative events of the novel. The chronotope is the place where the knots of narrative are tied and untied. It can be said without qualification that to them belongs the meaning that shapes the narrative [250].

He is careful to maintain that chronotopes do not necessarily exclude each other and may overlap, and that a "chronotope can include within it an unlimited number of minor chronotopes; in fact, as we have already said, any motif may have a special chronotope of its own" (252). Bakhtin concludes that "every entry into the sphere of meaning is accomplished only through the gates of the chronotope," and, in fact, the introduction of new storytelling media has generated new gateways in the representation of time and space (258).

For example, several scholars have identified new chronotopes that account for the changes that moving visuals introduced to storytelling. To explain how filmmakers use images and motion to construct narrative time, scholars have proposed the Rise and Fall chronotope (Alexander), the Database chronotope (Manovich), and the notion of Crystalline Time (Deleuze) to explain how filmmakers use images to evoke different experiences of time. Yet this attention to the way characters, and often audiences, are situated in particular experiences of time and space is still bounded by the "real" or run time of the film, from start to finish. Most films aim for an experience of total immersion and suspension of disbelief for a captive audience, with little opportunity to wander from the world of the film into another time and place.

The Link chronotope is an attempt to account for the way that texts created with a digital sensibility encourage just that kind of wandering, in both their narratives and their audiences.

The collaborative potential of composing on and for digital platforms offers new possibilities for understanding how time and space function when more than one storyteller is in play. Social media spaces such as Twitter shape time differently because the story (the tweetstream) is being built by multiple storytellers (users) who are interacting (or joining the conversation, as Twitter advertises it) from varying positions of synchronicity. It is possible in just a few moments to scroll through an index of a person's entire day, either as they live tweet or hours after they have tweeted, experiencing their tweetstream as a compressed representation of adventure time. This multiplicity of access creates alternate and parallel experiences of time as it is indexed by the user and received by the reader. In this sense, a reader's access to a user's tweetstream narrative can take place in at least four ways: synchronously, asynchronously, synchronically, or diachronically along what looks (on screen) like a traditional linear progression.

A synchronous reading would take place in "real" time, with the user and the reader sharing both the time and the digital space of the tweetstream. In an asynchronous reading, the reader and the user share the space, but not at the same time. Synchronically, a reader would move through the user's tweets in the order they were posted. Diachronically, a reader moves backward and forward through the tweetstream from whatever tweet caught their interest as a starting point. The use of retweets, mentions, hashtags and links expand the story outside of linear time and sometimes beyond the digital space of Twitter.[1] The 140 character constraint forces users to construct the space-time of the story in concentrated ways that link out to experiences and conversations happening elsewhere in time and space. The practice of creating short-links, running a hypertext link through a program like Bitly that will generate a less character-consuming link made of random letters and numbers, further obscures the context of those conversations by replacing named links that might bear a relationship to the content indexed with a string of characters that purposefully avoid meaning for the sake of brevity. For example, Bitly shortens this link to *A Calendar of Tales*: http://ayame-kenoshi.deviantart.com/journal/Neil-Gaiman-Presents-A-Calendar-of-Tales-355276614 to: http://bit.ly/1kolCmS. The first link clearly advertises what the website is about, but it is too long to adhere to the character constraint on Twitter. The second link fits the space, but obscures the content. Because Twitter opens the tweetstream to users who are both known and unknown to the original author, it introduces an uncertainty of the characters in (at least) two ways: What is the relationship between the characters (people) who are interacting and what is the relationship between the characters (text) and the larger conversation that is happening outside of the tweetstream? These two respective aspects of the figure of the Link can be described as "linking out" and "linking in."

Linking Out

With over two million followers and more than sixty-nine thousand tweets, Gaiman's Twitter presence is impressive. He "is always on Twitter, engaging with fans directly" (Penny), and "while you can credit the fanboys [and fangirls!] for making this author of the comic-book series *The Sandman* and fantasy best sellers like *Stardust* and *American Gods* popular, it's his everyguy tweets that keep followers around" (Morrison). He frequently appears on lists of writers to follow (*The Telegraph*, Peek, Morrison). He uses Twitter for both personal and professional communication, connecting with family, friends, and fans, and promoting his appearances and favorite causes. This variety allows Gaiman to construct an identity on Twitter that indexes a range of relationships with varying levels of in-person and virtual investment. His Twitter followers might encounter a *Doctor Who* joke, find out about a last minute ticket to one of his readings, eavesdrop on expressions of affection for his daughter, or learn about his work on behalf of Syrian refugees. Each of these tweets performs the function of *linking out* to relationships that are only comprehensible to people who have the necessary context from outside. For example, Gaiman's "Occupy Gallifrey" *Doctor Who* joke resonates differently when the reader knows that Gaiman has written episodes for *Doctor Who*, that he supports causes that promote social justice, and that he complains of not having enough time to write (see fig. 1). The joke links to each of these three ideas and connects most effectively with the reader who has accessed those stories about Gaiman in other times and places. Each person he retweets or mentions suddenly has access, in the form of that *Link*, to a claim on a relationship, even if it is only a momentary one. This *Link* creates the impression of intimacy in the form of special knowledge ("I know enough about Gaiman to understand what he is referring to") or conversational status ("Gaiman read and retweeted *me*!").

His Twitter followers feel recognized when he responds to or retweets them, as evidenced by the many who blog and tweet about it. One fan even wrote a song called "Neil Gaiman Tweeted Me" and then blogged (and made

Top: **Figure 1. Gaiman's "Occupy Gallifrey" tweet.** *Bottom:* **Figure 2. Panel from** *Debs & Errol,* **"Home Alone," by Errol Elumir (2013). The full comics can be found at www.debsanderrol.com.**

a comic) about the experience of Gaiman retweeting a link to the song (see fig. 2). Gaiman is likewise attached to his interactions with friends and fans on Twitter. He recently gave interviews to *The Guardian* and CNET warning fans of his upcoming "Twitter sabbatical" and inviting them to follow his blog, saying, "If you are used to hanging out with me on Tumblr or Twitter or Facebook, you are very welcome here. Same me, only with more than 140 characters. It'll be fun. Or it'll be like watching someone giving up smoking" (Gaiman "Where Did I Go?"). He describes interacting with fans on Twitter as "hanging out," implying that giving up that interaction might be as difficult as quitting smoking, framing his tweets as participation in a casual, perhaps addictive, relationship built between his online persona and responsive fans, 140 characters at a time. That (textual) character constraint, which keeps the interaction brief and the (personal) character development incremental, encourages practices that make Twitter a highly specialized space-time for collaboration. Users follow, mention, retweet, hashtag, and hyperlink to build narratives together, pulling from the same tweetstream from different times and places, at different paces. Twitter relies on users to participate in this way, each user creating alternate and parallel narratives that grow out of their particular points of entry (in time and space) to the conversation. An exchange that takes place first thing in the morning might be retweeted by someone who only catches up on Twitter in the evening, and that action presents the possibility of new narratives, dislocated in time from the original, but connected to it through the Link.

In a series of reflective videos on the making of *A Calendar of Tales*, Gaiman describes the importance of making connections with readers and collaborators, and it becomes clearer that what we are seeing on the surface— the tweet, the hashtag, the link—is actually indexing another existence, another relationship, often sustained in a different time and place (Ayame-Kenoshi). It surfaces as a trace of something that exists elsewhere. It might be obvious that a tweet directed at a specific person with whom he has a specific connection, for example a tweet to his wife Amanda Palmer (see fig. 3), is only a glimpse into a much larger and more complex relationship, but what do we make of something as innocuous as a quick response to and retweet of an unknown fan? (see fig. 4) Does it also index a larger (less visible) relationship? Gaiman does not know @mgarcia in person, but there is a world of relational activity on her side of the Link. She has the full run of *The Sandman* comics in individual issues and graphic novels, has heard him speak on both a book tour and as a substitute for Wil Wheaton at w00tstock, and is currently writing an essay theorizing the role of Twitter in shaping his collaborative fiction project. This invisible relationality motivates her academic interest in his work, and the trace of that relationship, validated here in a simple retweet, contributes to Gaiman's construction of himself on Twitter as a character who is reachable through characters, a figure of the accessible author who *Links* with his readership through both casual and carefully crafted tweets.

Top: Figure 3. Gaiman's 4th of July tweet to his wife, Amanda Palmer. *Bottom:* Figure 4. Gaiman's retweet of @mgarcia.

Gaiman conceives of his fan audience as made up of "people who have read something you wrote and it touched them, or it changed their life, or it opened a door or a window and showed them a world they might not otherwise have seen, and it's important to them" (Penny). In this sense, the relationship indexed by a passing tweet may seem one-sided, but when Gaiman posted on his blog about the experience of receiving a flood of responses to his tweeted *A Calendar of Tales* questions, he noted that he "didn't expect this bit of the project to feel like art, but watching the amount of connection it has made between people, I think perhaps it was. I felt like my heart was being broken and healed, all at the same time" (Gaiman "VERY Late Blog"). His attention to fans on Twitter coupled with this expression of reciprocity, mixed in with tweets that trace his in-person relationships and causes, make the boundary between creator and fan seem more permeable. In a series of short videos made to describe and promote *A Calendar of Tales*, Gaiman explains that he has "been trying to figure out for years a way to collaborate with readers" and describes the act of reading as passing through "a door to another world, to another person's head" (Ayame-Kenoshi). This conception of reading as an activity that enables people to cross thresholds and connect to others in both expected and unexpected ways is evident in his use of Twitter as a collaborative tool to connect to his fans and in the way he shapes time and space in his fiction to perform the Link between characters.

Linking In

Online responses to the *Calendar* project—in articles, blogs, and advertisements—have focused on the novelty of the collaborative process and the complexity of the web design that underpin the final product, but little has been said about the stories themselves. As a multimedia text produced for online publication that utilized online platforms to support collaboration and distribution, the narrative of *A Calendar of Tales* is in a unique position to help us consider the representation of time and space generated by online practices. That being said, *A Calendar of Tales* is not so much a break from or new stage in Gaiman's writing, but—like the tweets that point to larger relationships with varying levels of visibility—an index that is linking in to themes in his longer-form works. Examining the text of these short narratives for the traces of relationship to other people and other texts provides a useful lens for thinking about how digital practices are remixing time and space through the Link chronotope to shape the ways we create and read narratives in the digital age.

As a structuring genre, the calendar has two classical Bakhtinian chronotopes immediately available to it: the journey and the cycle.[2] Gaiman takes up both of these chronotopes at various times in the *Tales*, notably in "January Tale" and "December Tale" which bookend *Calendar* with stories of coextensive younger and older versions of their respective main characters. However, Gaiman complicates the closed narrative system of the line or the circle with characters who stray from the path, make mistakes that have no ready solution, and receive messages they have no hope of comprehending. Objects take on powerful roles, both representing and replacing people, places, and memories. Gaiman's usual themes of multiplicity and magic lurking around ever corner are evident, and the thin spaces between worlds are bridged by material talismans that connect characters to other stories in just the way links and hashtags on Twitter can take the reader out of one world of thought and into another in an instant. Like tweets that constrain the text and direct themselves to both specific and broad audiences, many of the material objects in *A Calendar of Tales* narratives carry cryptic messages that may or may not make sense to their recipients. Sometimes they make better sense to the reader than the character; sometimes the character knows more than the narrative makes available to the reader. The materiality of tweets, sent out to an audience that cannot be fully imagined and picked up by both intended and unknown recipients, is reenacted by objects in *A Calendar of Tales* that carry traces of other characters, other stories, across time and space. Though these objects, and their efficacy as "connectors," vary, their persistent presence in the *Tales* signals a shift in the time-space of the story. As readers who click on links to enter and exit worlds, we understand that when these characters encounter these objects, they are traveling through the Link, moving through time and space in non-traditional ways. Though almost all of the *Tales* offer constructions of time that play with the connection between time and space, three tales in particular pay specific attention to the role of objects in mediating connections between worlds.

"September Tale" offers a ring as a memento of a specific character—the mother—and as a symbol of the relationship between mother and child, but also as a potential connector between the world of the living and the world of the dead. Bruno Marafigo's illustration (included as one of the "alternates" in the online version, but not the main one chosen for the PDF) functions also as a linking in to Gaiman's work by visually referencing Merv Pumpkin-head, a character from the *Sandman* series (see fig. 5). The lost ring is imbued with the power to do "small magics," and its return to the owner by means of a stranger, the belly of a fish, and an animated scarecrow all point to the ways that the mediating object is moved through space and time by other agents. The complete journey is invisible to both the reader and the narrator, and while the narrator goes to great lengths to dispose of the ring, crushing it within an old car and shipping it Romania, and later moving to Brazil and living under an assumed name, the intent behind the returning ring is unclear. In spite of these precautions, the narrator wonders, "how she's going to give it back to me next time." This object performs a rhizomatic linking out between the mother and child, branching through other bodies to leave and return to its owner(s). The story works as a "linking in" to Gaiman's themes of magic in the family, which appears in *Good Omens* and *The Ocean at the End of the Lane*, and the idea of invisible networks of travel and communication, as is evident in *Neverwhere*. The ring possesses an almost ephemeral quality, slipping away from the owner without notice and returning by means

Figure 5. "September Tale" by Bruno Marafigo, from Gaiman's *A Calendar of Tales*.

of other characters and is akin to virtual mediating objects (links, hashtags, retweets) that are posted and reposted, appearing and reappearing according to networks that operate through distributed agents whose identities and motives are often unknown. One of the chief characteristics of the Link chronotope is the notion of waiting woven into the material of the object, and the narrator's closing line about "next time" captures the power of the object to both contain and evoke that sense of anticipation.

While "September Tale" suggests that "some things aren't meant to be kept," and a corresponding patient resignation to the appearance and disappearance of linking objects, "February Tale" focuses on the vulnerability of objects to interference by other characters and gestures toward the anxiety of archiving in the digital age. The narrator watches three generations of women search for a lost pendant, ultimately returning it to the granddaughter fifty years after its disappearance, claiming to have found it only the year before. The narrator reveals to the reader, but not to the little girl, the fact that the grandmother is her little sister and that the loss of the pendant was the result of "the joke I had played on her" (see fig. 6).[3] The grandmother left the pendant under a particular rock for safe-keeping, and when she returned, it was

Figure 6. "February Tale" by Kenneth Rodriguez, from Gaiman's *A Calendar of Tales*.

gone. She imagined that she had simply forgotten which rock she used to anchor her mediating object, but in fact, another character had apparently intervened and removed the Link. Without access to the object that links her to the time and place of her home, which the granddaughter does not know the location of, she is left stranded and wandering, searching for the Link that will reconnect her. In response to the narrator's question, "Is she still alive?" the granddaughter answers, "Yes. Sort of," leaving even the grandmother's status as living or dead uncertain. The disappearance of the linking object can be thought of as a kind of dis-or re-location in the archive. Presumably, the two characters Linked by the object both still exist somewhere in space and time, but the disappearance or deletion of the Link prevents the desired connection. The linking out unexpectedly led to interference that disturbed the time and place of the Link.

Perhaps the most Twitter-like of traces can be found in "May Tale." Gaiman asked: "What is the weirdest gift you've ever been given in May?" and @StarlingV responded, "An anonymous Mother's Day gift. Think about that for a moment." This answer feels ready to support any number of sinister or sad narratives about lost children or lost memories. Instead, the unnamed narrator receives a series of deliveries, messages and objects which appear and disappear without context or explanation, from an unknown source. Every month brings a new surprise: postcards from the Emerald City of Oz, a package containing *Action Comics* #1 and lost masterpieces by Shakespeare and Austen, a Christmas card from the North Pole, chocolates that are marked as "evidence," a feeling that "two of the goldfish appeared to have been taken and replaced by identical substitutes," and a ransom note for an uncle that the narrator does not have (see fig. 7). These objects perform the function of linking in to Gaiman's longstanding involvement with comics, as both a creator and a fan; his reinterpretation of Shakespeare in *Sandman* #19, "A Midsummer Night's Dream"; and his growing experience as a children's book author, alluding to *The Day I Swapped My Dad for Two Goldfish*.[4] Almost every Link offered

Figure 7. "May Tale" by Christian L. Frey, from Gaiman's *A Calendar of Tales*.

here is accompanied by a "note," a short bit of text meant to locate the object in a meaningful context, but faced with this dizzying array of apparently mis-delivered items, the narrator fails to understand the Link being offered. The moment of imbrication fails to materialize. Like a boosted post that does not belong on your timeline or a broken hypertext link that leads to nowhere, the time, place, and audience fail to achieve the moment of overlap. In the linking out sense, the narrator functions as a recipient node for objects that pass through her existence without offering any meaning. In spite of this lack of understanding, the narrator attempts to engage with two of the Links, fol-lowing the directions on the ransom note to carry a pink carnation, eat only salads, and look for the books to read in a moment of down time in spite of "having little interest in comics, Shakespeare or Jane Austen." By the time the narrator had thought of a use for these items, they were lost in the odd space-time of the story, like so many tweets buried in the rush of information. The failure to connect feels like a missed opportunity; the objects (presumably) carry on to their next destination in search of a more receptive point of con-tact, and the narrative concludes with, "WE APOLOGIZE OF THE INCONVEN-IENTS," a poignant and haunting expression of sorrow and misunderstanding.

That rush of information, produced by so many characters "throw[ing] their feelings and their thoughts out into the world," hoping for someone to respond, to understand, to Link with them across time and space, corresponds closely to the kinds of layered worlds that Gaiman has produced in works like *The Sandman, Neverwhere,* and *American Gods.* Like his characters who move between worlds, Gaiman constructs himself on Twitter as someone who crosses time and space, whose existence is made up of and sustained by text and by those who read and respond. Gaiman routinely uses Twitter to connect with others at multiple levels of intimacy, a practice which holds out the tan-talizing prospect that the Link made of tweets could materialize in another time and place as a virtual or in-person relationship. When he used Twitter to collaborate with fans, he/we/they created a work that indexes both the theme of crossing into other worlds and the practice of crossing time and space digitally to connect with others. Twitter supports interactions that are instantaneous yet asynchronous, that are directed to specific yet undefined audiences, and that inhabit both a material and a virtual existence. The Link is forged on one side, given textual, material existence on a virtual platform, and left waiting for the click on the other.

Gaiman's narratives are filled with these material links, in the form of objects bearing traces of other times and places, other intentions, other stories, waiting—sometimes patiently and sometimes urgently—to be part of the conversation. For the space of the *Calendar* project, Twitter served as a structuring landscape where links indexed, rather than enacted, a collaboration between artists, between Gaiman and *You*. By attributing authorship to the unspecified *You*, Gaiman effectively untethers authorship from time and space, collapsing the hierarchical distinction—perhaps only momentarily—between fan creator and author, and leaving the reader to interpret whether that *You* is singular, plural, directed at the reader, or perhaps at another figure in the crowd. Gaiman has invited fans to continue to "make good art" out of his work and has made his text and his voice recordings of the *Tales* available as source material, so the *You* in *Gaiman & You* is ongoing, continuously held open to new construction and interpretation, to new relational possibilities. In this way, to recognize the *You* as the trace of an invitation, as a chronotopic Link that exists both in and outside of a specific time and space, is to experience the moment of connection and to participate in a complex world of relationality that, as Derrida says, is "even older than the past and that is beyond the future." Gaiman's fiction remixes time and space in ways that reflect both his thematic concern with characters crossing boundaries between fictional worlds and his Twitter practices that express, in 140 characters or less, the collaborative potential of forging even the smallest and most constrained of creative Links for those brave enough to cross the threshold.

Notes

1. There are subtle differences between a reply, a retweet, and a mention on Twitter, mostly having to do with where the user is notified that their Twitter handle has been tweeted by someone else. A reply begins a thread that other users can follow in order to catch up on the conversation if the tweets are public or if they are following both users. A retweet (RT) is simply a copy of the original user's tweet, unchanged, with the original user's handle at the beginning of the tweet. The original user is notified that their tweet has been retweeted in their notifications. A modified tweet (MT) is a tweet that has been retweeted, but altered, usually to accommodate the character limit, but sometimes to comment on the content of the tweet being boosted. If the retweeter changes the RT designation to MT, then the original tweeter is not always notified that they have been retweeted.

2. Other works organized around a calendar take up both linear and cyclical chronotopes. For example, in Edmund Spenser's *The Shepheardes Calendar*, Colin Clout travels through the year, passing through seasons which parallel the stages of life, positioning Colin as a character on a journey (life) with a finite end (death) while positioning nature as an endless cycle of birth, death, and rebirth.

3. The story does not actually reveal the gender of the narrator, but Kenneth Rodriguez's illustration constructs her as female.

4. Sandman #19 won a World Fantasy Award in the short fiction category in 1991.

Works Cited

Alexander, Lily. "Storytelling in Time and Space: Studies in the Chronotope and Narrative Logic on Screen." *Journal of Narrative Theory* 37.1 (Winter 2007): 27–64. PDF.

Ayame-Kenoshi. "Episode 2: Neil Gaiman Presents 'A Calendar of Tales.'" *DeviantArt*, 19 Feb. 2013. Web. 6 Aug. 2014.

Bakhtin, M. M. "Forms of Time and of the Chronotope in the Novel." *The Dialogic Imagination: Four Essays*. Ed. Michael Holquist. Austin: University of Texas Press, 1981. 84–258. Print.

Burton, Bonnie. "Sorry Neil Gaiman Fans, He's Taking a Twitter Break." *CNET*. 1 Jan. 2014. Web. 7 Aug. 2014.

Deleuze, Gilles. *Cinema II: The Time-Image*. Minneapolis: University of Minnesota Press, 1989. Print.

Derrida, Jacques. "What Comes Before the Question?" Online video. *YouTube*, 26 Dec. 2007. Web. 6 Aug. 2014.

Elumir, Errol. *Debs & Errol:* "Home Alone." *Thoughts from the Test Chamber*. 30 Mar. 2013. Web. 7 Aug. 2014.

Gaiman, Neil. "A Calendar of Tales Update, and Two Covers." *Neil Gaiman's Journal*. 17 Feb. 2013. Web. 24 Aug. 2014.

_____. "Now Up! Read a Calendar of Tales. And Make ART." *Neil Gaiman's Journal*. 19 Feb. 2013. Web. 24 Aug. 2014.

_____. "A VERY Late Blog, About Trying to Make Art with a Lot of People, Including You..." *Neil Gaiman's Journal*. 4 Feb. 2013. Web. 7 Aug. 2014.

_____. "Where Did I Go? What Did I Do? Nothing. OR, Why I'm Coming Back to the Blog Once More." *Neil Gaiman's Journal*. 31 Dec. 2013. Web. 7 Aug. 2014.

Gaiman, Neil and You. *A Calendar of Tales*. 23 May 2013. PDF.

"The Hounds of Baskerville." *Sherlock*. BBC. BBC America. 13 May 2012. Television.

Lea, Richard. "Neil Gaiman Prepares for Social Media 'Sabbatical.'" *The Guardian*. 14 June 2013. Web. 7 Aug. 2014.

Manovich, Lev. "Database as Symbolic Form." *Convergence: The International Journal of Research into New Media Technologies* 5 (1999): 80. Print.

Morrison, Tim. "The 140 Best Twitter Feeds of 2011." *Time*. 28 Mar. 2011. Web. 7 Aug. 2014.

Peek, Lauren. "Top 20 Authors to Follow on Twitter." *Social Media Delivered*. 18 Feb. 2013. Web. 7 Aug. 2014.

Penny, Laurie. "Neil Gaiman Interview: 'It was much, much more fun being absolutely unknown.'" *New Statesman*. 13 Nov. 2013. Web. 7 Aug. 2014.

"Project Focus: A Calendar of Tales." YCN. n.d. Web. 24 Aug. 2014.

"Top Ten Most Prolific Authors on Twitter." *The Telegraph*. 27 Mar. 2013. Web. 7 Aug. 2014.

Whitney, Manda. "Neil Gaiman Tweeted Me...and Normal People Don't Care." *Thoughts from the Test Chamber*. 30 Mar. 2014. Web. 7 Aug. 2014.

Sandman: Overture (2014)

Aperture for a Storyteller: An Interview with JH Williams III

John Bultena

JH Williams III is a *New York Times* bestselling comic book artist and writer. He has worked on *Promethea, Batwoman, Batman*, and hundreds of other comics. He is illustrating *Sandman: Overture*, written by Neil Gaiman. He has worked with Alan Moore, Grant Morrison, Greg Rucka, and Warren Ellis, among others. For his efforts, he has won multiple Eisner, Harvey, and GLAAD Media awards.

On Saturday, March 8, 2014, John Bultena sat down with JH Williams III to discuss the wildly anticipated new iteration of the *Sandman* series. This interview took place one afternoon in the living room of Williams III's home in Central California. At the time of the interview *Sandman: Overture #2* was completed and at press, to be released in just over two weeks. As of February 2015, Williams III continues to work on *Overture*.

Since Vertigo is a part of DC, you working for Vertigo makes sense, but how did you get involved with Sandman? How did you make the connection with Neil Gaiman?

It is kind of a silly story, but I have always had a list of writers that I wanted to work with if I ever had the opportunity. I'm sure that every artist that works in the industry has that list of people they would love to work with, and as overly ambitious as I can be, I've gone to only picking the absolute best cream of the crop people, whether I deserved to work with them or not, and Neil was on that list.

Wendy [JH Williams III's wife] and I were coming out of our hotel in San Diego at Comic Con, and Neil was there at the front of the hotel. He was either getting in or had just gotten out of a cab, standing near with the door open, having a conversation with some other people. I was telling Wendy, "Hey, that's Neil Gaiman," and I was like maybe we should go say hello, and she said, "We should go up and introduce ourselves," but then he was in the middle of a conversation with people. So I said, "Naaah, let's just keep going." So we walked about thirty feet maybe and I stopped and I was like no, I need to at least go shake his hand. Ultimately it was sort of a rude gesture, here I am, interrupting his conversation with these other people just to say hello and shake his hand. I said, "I'm so and so, I worked with Alan Moore on *Promethea*," and he was replied, "Oh! I love *Promethea*!" At that point I said, "If you ever want to work together, I would love to do something with you." He never forgot that and the cool thing about it is I've always thought that it was pretty rude of us to approach him the way we did, it was not the most professional behavior. But when Neil first contacted me to do the new *Sandman* project, he talked about that first meeting and remembered how much enthusiasm I seemed to have for what he does, so it was very gracious of him not to view it the same way I did. I thought I was being a completely rude person, and he stated, "No, not at all." He never really forgot that, and was already familiar with my work and enjoyed what he had seen so far. He kept it in the back of his mind I guess and the right thing came along.

And you were actively doing Promethea at the time?

I don't remember if I was still on *Promethea* at the time, or had just shortly come off of it. So he had actually remembered that meeting a good few years before the subject of *Overture* ever got broached.

So how did the subject get broached for working on Overture?

Essentially I just woke up one morning to an email from Karen Berger, who was in charge of Vertigo at the time, a long letter spelling out they've got this big plan for *Sandman* and Neil wants to work with me, would I want to do it? I woke up to that and had a big freak out moment. At first, Wendy and I were like, "We have to do it, we have to do it," but the timing was a bit awkward because I was still working on *Batwoman*, with a lot still to do on that, and there were plans after *Batwoman* that would have to get delayed to do *Sandman*, but it was one of those things where you can't say no, we'll figure it out. That's how it kind of got set up, while still doing work on *Batwoman*. It was kind of a weird situation because I loved working on *Batwoman* so much, but then there was this other opportunity that is equally as grand, that you can't say no to. There could be worse positions to be in, in terms of going from one great project to another great project and having to choose between one or the other. I can't complain.

What were some of your initial concerns about working on **Sandman**? *Not necessarily hesitations.*

[It was] a tricky thing for me because *Sandman,* for a wide variety of reasons, became this huge legacy project that was highly revered and adored by a lot of people and so I wanted to make sure that I could do a new story justice. While at the same time I wanted to do something that honored the original material, my own personal feelings about the material needed to be creatively valid choices. I also wanted to feel like I was bringing something new to the equation that wasn't just doing what everyone else before me had done. So that kind of was daunting in a lot of ways. There were, however, many issues of the original series that ran a long time, all very creative material, and here I am having to follow that. How can I bring something new to that table and feel like it's still *Sandman*?

One thing that has been going under-noticed with the first issue of **Overture** *is how much of it is scripted by Neil, versus how much of it is interpreted and presented by you? How much freedom are you getting under Neil to work with the subject matter?*

A lot of freedom. We've had conversations numerous times on the phone, where I said, "I have got such and such visual idea" for whatever scene he's talking about in the script, and he said, "It's you, do what you do." He obviously liked what I did enough before, that he felt he can trust in what I do to bring that to the table in terms of his story, so there's a lot of creative freedom there. I think he trusts that I'm going to bring my own sensibility into the equation, but not in a way that is going to be detrimental or intrusive or destructive in any way to the intent of what he is writing. Which is key for me. That is how I approach any project that I do.

You mentioned before the interview that Neil asked you for a list of things you are interested in drawing. Can you talk about the list of things you shared with Neil?

I don't know if this is something he has done with other artists he has worked with on *Sandman* in the past, but I can imagine it likely that he has asked that same question of other people. So before he started writing, he knows the story he wants to tell, he already knows what needs to happen and where it's going, but I think he's interested in hearing things that the artist is interested in, in terms of the visual textures that can be applied to where he wants to take the story, the visual nuances and stuff like that. He asked me for a list of things I was interested in, things I'm influenced by, or would like to draw. I sat down one day and started making a list, whatever was coming to the top of my head, things that I just knew would be cool to draw, or subjects I liked. The list was as random as going from my love of Jim Steranko to drawing insects. It was that kind of list, a very randomized sort of thing and he likes picking and pulling things from that to apply to different scenes, and it's almost like a sharing of imaginations between each other.

It's almost like, "What do you want for Christmas little boy?" [Laughter] Neil Gaiman is the Santa Claus and gives you the story to draw that you want …

Exactly. Basically by saying something like "I think drawing insects is cool," Neil is like, "I'm going to make a scene that has insects because Jim likes to draw insects," so he comes up with this cool thing. Neil figures out how to take elements from the list and make them story appropriate for where he wants to take things. The only other person that actually did that with me was Alan Moore, Greg Rucka may have as well. Alan did that on *Promethea*. We had many early conversations about that sort of stuff, and all of that ended up working its way into *Promethea* in one form or another.

It sounds like one of the major tenets of working with Neil Gaiman, as an artist, is that he wants to maintain a level of enthusiasm from you and get the best from you he can. Are you still enthusiastic about this project?

Oh yeah, oh yeah. There's definitely moments of artistic struggle as I'm working on pages. I felt like issue two had difficult to handle sections and sometimes that can make it hard to maintain a certain level of energy. But then the next chapter comes, I've set issue two down, I've finished it, the next chapter of the story comes and I read what's in there and it sort of re-energizes me all over again because there is always a "Aww that's so cool!" moment. There is always enthusiasm, but sometimes it can be hard when it actually gets down to making that enthusiasm live tangibly on paper. If that makes sense. [Laughter]

*You worked on **Promethea** with Alan Moore and are now working with Gaiman on **Sandman**. There's a lot of similarities between these two works. They are both about these godlike beings that are manifestations of imagination, dream, art, etc. I am curious what are the similarities, not just storywise, but as a storyteller in these two works? In regards to the creative process.*

Everything I do comes from what the story is dictating to me it needs, regardless of what I'm working on. I can't help but come at it from that point of view. *Promethea* and *Sandman* are very, very similar in that regard for my own personal storytelling process on how I come up with images. I look at what's written, try to get to its heart, the subtext of it, and observe that and try to reflect it in some way interestingly. How successful that is, it's not up to me to decide, but that's my ultimate goal.

I was also interested in regards to the two pieces, the notion of reading **Promethea.** *I've heard you describe it as meditative, with mantras in it.*

I don't think I've ever seen another comic that does this. *Promethea* is all about metaphysics and has ritualistic magic to some degree, and is a grimoire in a lot of ways about that subject, or introduction to that subject... I've never seen a comic that does this, where you've got the title of the comic on the cover, it reads *Promethea*, you open it and when you get to the title page it reads *Promethea* again and then the chapter title. It does that every issue so when you look at the series as a whole reading in book form, it's basically chanting the word *Promethea*, the name *Promethea*. That becomes some sort of ritualistic component. That one aspect alone seems like a very purposeful choice to make. Because most comics, you open up an issue of say *Amazing Spider-Man*, or *X-Men*, or even *Sandman*, it doesn't repeat the series title multiple times. I've never seen a comic do that before. That one idea alone is, like you said, almost like a chanted mantra, that repetitive aspect feeds into what you were saying.

Where **Promethea** *is a meditation to obtain a certain state of mind,* **Sandman** *would be a dream. It flows, the establishment of the ritual isn't as important.*

I would say that's pretty true. In a lot of ways, when you read a *Sandman* story, even the way it's sort of written, does feel like it has more of a dream logic to it. Some stuff isn't so spelled out for you. Much like when someone dreams themselves, the dream will do these strange, bizarre twists in it, the dreamer themselves don't know why that dream was like that, but there's some sort of weird puzzling logic to it. So when you read *Sandman*, it definitely feels like the way the story plot moves and functions, that things will diverge in ways that you might not anticipate, in terms of logical plot progression. Where in *Promethea*, as surrealistic as it gets, it always feels like there is a very clear direct momentum, that it's all headed towards somewhere. You might not know where yet, but you know that there is definitely something on the horizon, feeling maybe more orchestrated, I guess, is the proper way to put it. And with dreams, dreams don't feel orchestrated, they sort of are fluid and kind of...

Unfold.

Right. Unfold and diverge, and morph. Where *Promethea*, even though it's surrealistic and it has a lot of transformational imagery, it still feels very like it's on a linear progressive path.

Both works have the title character presented in different forms. Promethea appears in different forms throughout history. In* Overture, *there is a four page spread, with forty Sandmen. What's interesting is whereas in* Pro-methea, *each one of those Prometheas is established with an identity, an attitude, a history, time, and place; the Sandmen, which are Dream, are not so much established.

Exactly, they're all aspects of the same person, viewed through different lenses and different dimensional perspectives, and different worlds. Where, like you said, in *Promethea*, yes, they're all Promethea, they're all aspects of this entity, but they're all very distinct and they all have a time place in history. There is a very linear pattern to their existence, where in *Overture*, there isn't a linear mode and pattern to all these various versions of Dream.

With Dream's multiple incarnations it lends itself to the idea that you dream yourself, but it is not yourself.

Yes.

And you don't know why you're that person, but you are that person.

Right.

That was another interesting aspect of* Sandman *so far.

Yeah, I can definitely see that in there, and ... yeah. [Laughter]

The dream versus meditative ideas are different in these narratives but they're both definitely trying to hit some level of artistic expression. This question might be overboard, but how do these demonstrate the strength of comic books?

[Laughter] It's surprisingly a simple answer.

Because the things that happen, in *Promethea* and *Sandman*, in terms of visual narrative, basically prove the theory that there are things comics can do that no other medium can, in terms of how they disseminate information to the reader. It does a lot of different things that just cannot be repeated in film or prose, even though you can probably convey the same ideas in terms of content, but the way it does it through visual calisthenics, can only be done in comics. There's things that they do that play with the form of the printed visual page. Because it's a real synthesis ... comics are this interesting thing because they are this flow of narrative images in conjunction with words to build a story. The images need to feel like there's a flow to them, but at the same time, they're still images. It's not like film, where it's being presented to you and it feels like you're watching people move around and stuff. You have to imagine a lot with comics. And prose completely relies on your mind inside, where comics sort of can move inside and out of that. I think *Promethea* and *Sandman* are prime examples of how that is true. There's many other comics in history that have proven that, but it's something that a lot of regular, this sounds terrible, but a lot of other comics don't necessarily think about in terms of how far it can be pushed, the idea that it doesn't have to be just panel one, panel two, panel three; it can be panel one, panel three connecting into panel two, that sort of weaving in and out idea. This is really commented on a lot in *Promethea* and in *Sandman*.

How would you, in a film or prose, depict the Mobius strip scene from **Promethea?**

[Laughter] You would, I think, have to deconstruct it. I think you'd have to almost do it in a literal sense, like it does in the comic, where you see the entire Mobius strip. You would literally have to basically transport that image into super high res special effects and have the characters move along this Mobius strip as they're having a conversation and stay there and not try to do close ups of the characters as they speak and move on film, it's literally a film of the entire visible Mobius strip and the actors are moving around it. In a way, you'd almost be sort of going against the convention of standard film, in that way. That's the only way I can see it.

What about prose?

I don't think it's possible, really. I mean other than just saying they're walking along the Mobius strip and this is what they're saying as they go across the bend, they're curving around the other side of the Mobius strip. You really have to be relying on the reader to fully understand what a Mobius strip is.

This is one of the major questions I have, stemming from Scott McCloud's **Understanding Comics.** *He writes about how comics are fascinating because they demand so much of the reader at the same time as the creator whereas film and prose don't as much. The Mobius strip demands the reader to understand that you can start anywhere and it always works no matter where you begin.*

There is no taking that exact idea for film. You'd just see the scene linearly, doing one shot as the characters move through. It still cannot do what you just suggested like you can with the comic. On film or in prose, that conversation can't start wherever you want it to as the person viewing the film still has to start it where it starts and end it where it ends before you cut to the next scene. Where in the comic, you're right, you can start the conversation anywhere on that Mobius strip and follow it from that point and you can't do that in film.

Because of the invested power of the reader in comics you get to choose when it ends and the only way I could see that working in the film is like putting an art installation at the museum or in a gallery, you couldn't just put it on television, you couldn't put it on DVD unless they hit repeat on it, so it would be kind of awkward to do that and I think you're right about the prose, I'm not sure how that would work either. That's one thing I find fascinating about the format and fascinating about your work—you are really good at manipulating time. Have you had any trouble manipulating time or trying to create time in Sandman*? By the way, how does time even work in* Sandman*? [Laughter]*

So far, all of the ideas about time in *Sandman* have all been very literal, in terms of how time can be viewed in the context of the story's movement itself. So there hasn't really been any opportunity, drawing wise, to make readers feel like time moves differently in *Sandman*. I've been telling the story as it needs to be told. I'm trying to be as visually interesting as possible, and I suppose some of the unorthodox things I do in *Sandman* force the reader to slow down quite a bit more than they normally would so that can kind of manipulate their sense of time. That's more of just forcing them to focus on all the tapestry, really, it's not really purposefully trying to make them lose sense of time, or trying to make them feel like the images are moving differently in time than they are. I haven't been able to have that opportunity in *Sandman* to do that concretely. I've had that elsewhere, but not so much here.

But time, it is interesting that you ask that question because time is definitely a topic or a concept being talked about within the parameters of the story, sort of around the edges of the story because it's very circular in ways, even though its taking place prior to the beginning of the *Sandman* main series, it is also showing parts that seem to be taking place after the *Sandman* series, so it's very, very circular at the moment.

There's a key scene in issue two indicating to the reader why we're seeing what we're seeing, and the why of *when* we're seeing it. Where Daniel is reaching behind that piece of furniture down in the asylum basement. He pulls out that strange pocket watch, that when he's touching it, it seems to become fluidlike, and then he lets it go and it keeps kind of being wobbly and melty in a way and then it shrinks and vanishes. His dialogue there, he's talking about time and Mad Hettie is as well. She's complaining about that stupid watch, she can never make it work and it's broken. Daniel is basically telling her time kind of just flies sometimes. When he's letting it go, by that one line alone, he's kind of insinuating that, I'm letting this watch go, time goes ... and it's very much an alien looking watch when you look at the digits and details ... they're all not what we would recognize. I think he's probably sending that watch, because it has some sort of power, into the past while saying sometimes time flies. What's interesting about the context is that we're seeing that scene next to scenes of Dream, of Morpheus, in 1915, well before Daniel even existed in the main series story. There is no coincidence that we're seeing these things together, that's how it's becoming circular. We're seeing events that took place before the beginning and after the end of the main series.

Sandman: Overture *at this point, represents, in many people's opinion, this state of the art of comics, in regards to not just the sense of the quality of the art, writing, and production quality. There's special editions of the issues already, it is available as same-day digital release, it feels like there's going to be newer editions in the future too. Not to mention the promotion for the book in television commercials and even ads on the sides of phone booths. What do you think that tells us about the state of the art and industry?*

It says good and negative things. As far as the state of the art and the production quality, ultimately, that all boils down to what a publisher wants to put their dollars into. These production values have been around for a very, very long time. It's just whether a publisher wants to spend money on doing that particular thing for that particular project. But printing technologies have improved dramatically for the artwork to become more and more complex. I guess for hurdles to be leapt over for the visuals. It's inevitable in any creative field other than, say, prose. If you write a book, you write a book, but certainly the design of that book can have an impact on how a reader feels about that book as they hold it, that might not necessarily impact how they feel about that story. But with film, or comics, or even animation, the level of technology progression can dramatically affect how that product is received as story content itself, if that makes any sense at all.

Now in terms of the promotional aspects of how *Sandman* is being treated and what that says about the industry, is all great for *Sandman*, but is not great for everyone else at times. Again it all boils down to dollars. They're deciding what they think has merit and what doesn't have merit. There could be comics out there, even under the same publisher that might have as equal creative power as *Sandman*, but doesn't get the recognition, because it doesn't get the company support. The reason why this particular project has so many dollars behind it, in terms of putting commercials on TV and so forth, is because it's a legacy project. *Sandman* has already proven itself to be a million dollar project, being published all around the world in multiple languages. They know that over time this is a big deal. The sad thing about a large publisher is they tend to think a lot like a corporation in that the dollar is the bottom line. So they're only going to put their money behind something that they know already makes money. Which is kind of a sad thing in terms of creativity for the industry as a whole. I don't like that things are thought about that way.

I would love to see a time where muscle is behind other unproven projects. But something like *Sandman*, now that's already a proven commodity, that's the word, commodity. The current approach is sort of like "oh, we'll financially back something once it's already made itself successful." It's kind of like … well you're not really helping it achieve that goal if you're just sort of releasing it on the side over here, maybe some people will see it and some won't. [Laughter] It's kind of weird.

I think that's an interesting term, "proven commodity." That's where the real money is, proven commodities, not a matter of trying something new that might blow everyone's mind.

Exactly. What's so frustrating about it on a creative level is that someone could come along to develop a new idea, new movie, new comics concept, or whatever, and it's brilliant. Even if it ends up being made, it doesn't mean it's going to get the support, the full financial might of a company behind it. Therefore getting it in front of more people. It's kind of a weird situation, I think it's been that way for a long time.

I've asked you in both personal and professional settings to describe what you do, and the number one word that comes out of your mouth is "storyteller." Not "artist," "writer," or "creator," but "storyteller." You stated this even before being the lead writer on **Batwoman**. *How did you come to the conclusion of describing yourself as a "storyteller"?*

Well I think part of it is that comics is the chosen medium that I'm working in, and comics is storytelling even though the workload is divided up into different categories. So you have writers, artists, colorists, and so forth, every one of us is a component of the authorship in some degree. With comics, the writer couldn't do what they do without the artist and the artist couldn't do what they do without the writer or the colorist or the letterer and it's all circular. We're all storytellers. Everything that every one of us does affects the final outcome of how that story is perceived and as someone who works on the art side of it, pretty much is the lead person, sort of. I'm the first thing that people see when they pick up a comic book. They don't know what the story is yet, they might have an idea or have their own assumptions based on a few images they've seen, or a synopsis they've read, but when it comes down to it, the visuals are the first thing that they see. The art is very relied upon, needing to be good at telling a story. It's sort of like, the art isn't just there, it needs to play an interactive role in what the writer is trying to get after, and the writer plays an interactive role with that artist in terms of making their vision clear to that artist in order for it to be conveyed, it's not just "oh let's throw a bunch of cool images down on the page and hope that it makes sense."

It's almost like comics in a way are very similar to the idea of storyboards for film. Storyboards for film spell out visually what the script or the screenplay is saying. The storyboard artist breaks it down into visuals that the director then looks at and goes "okay, that's the shot, or hey I'm not happy with that shot, lets change that." It's similar in nature to that. That's why I say I'm a storyteller, but my storytelling mainly deals in presenting visuals that you can comprehend, in terms of a narrative structure.

The thing about you is that you stand at this fascinating crux in comic books. You've worked with Grant Morrison, Alan Moore, Neil Gaiman, Warren Ellis, Greg Rucka, Alejandro Jodorowsky. You stand at a crux where all of these people intersect with you. These are all great writers, not always in terms of sales, but in terms of quality and the messages they try to convey because all of them try to give the reader something to think about and take away from it afterwards. Being at this unique point in the industry and as a storyteller, what have you taken away from being at this crux, what lessons have you learned about storytelling? Inversely, what do you think they have taken away from you?

I'll answer the second part first because that's the easiest. I have no idea what they have taken away from me, I could not even begin to imagine. But I've taken away a lot from them, because I understood going in that I was working with these certain individuals that are very thoughtful. We'll start with Alan Moore because he was the first person of that caliber I got the opportunity to work with.

At this point he had *V for Vendetta*, *Watchmen*, *From Hell*, it just goes on and on. So, when *Promethea* came to me, in some ways I almost feel like, the terms of the quality of my images hadn't matured enough to match Alan's capability. The thing is that I'm one of those types of people that embrace a challenge and am willing to meet that challenge whether I can be successful at the challenge or I succumb under its pressure. I'm willing to go there, I'm willing to go over the cliff to try to do something, and I think I grew in my time with Alan. I knew I would learn a lot from him, there was no question. I didn't even really need to think about it. It wasn't even something I had to consciously tell myself, "oh I'm going to learn from this guy." I just knew it was going to be there because of who he was and what he's done. Once you get that opportunity to actually be around that for a while and you're working with somebody like that, it's impossible for you not to take away something from that, it allows you to grow beyond where you were when you started because … I mean this sounds weird, but he is a genius level thinker. It's hard to explain to somebody unless you actually have a conversation with him, of what he's like, but he is a super brain and you can't help but be in awe of it while at the same time hoping that when the project is done, somehow some of that has resonated inside of you and you have grown because you understand that the person you are working with understood a hell of a lot more than you did. And that was pretty cool. I feel like I've tried to come at every project, since then, with a similar sort of mindset.

Now the thing I think these writers may have taken from me is, but don't know for certain, like with Alan, I think they see my eagerness to try to face any challenge that they wanted to throw at me, and I was of the mind "bring it on!" I think that can be appreciated, that I was willing to try something, even though it might not work as well as it could have, we at least attempted it. There's a lot of people that might not be willing to do that. And so I always come at it from that kind of point of view. When I worked with Greg Rucka, we'd have conversations about on how to visually present something. And I'm always trying to find that unusual angle and I think maybe these guys want to work with me because they can see that and it maybe makes them feel more comfortable in terms of trying to present bigger and bigger ideas, maybe. I've never wanted to ask them this. That might be kind of silly to say, but I don't know what they're taking away from it, other than they obviously appreciate what I'm bringing to the table.

What did you take away from Moore? What insights to the way to be a storyteller did you gain from him?

I guess the biggest insight I took away about being a storyteller from him was when I write something for myself, when I'm writing for other artists, is to know what the hell I'm trying to say and to make that as clear as I possibly can. That is one thing, when you look at an Alan Moore story, as far out and bizarre as he can get sometimes, you never come away from it feeling like, wait, I didn't understand what the point was. He makes damn sure you understand what the point was, and I definitely learned to make sure that, even if it means to hold the reader's hand on occasion to get the point across, ultimately the goal is to make certain that your point isn't misconstrued in a bad way. Try to do that as best you can. I always strive for that. I learned that from him.

It seems like this notion of a purposefulness to writing. Not just "I'm going to write this story about a person who dresses like a bat and goes out and kicks butt," but "let's write a story that really tries to give an end goal."

Right. What is the story saying? What is the point of telling a story if it doesn't have something to say? Even if it's something that is still a fun piece and meant to be a light entertainment, it's a waste of time if it doesn't have anything to say. Dwayne McDuffie, a writer I really didn't get to work with, has one of the best quotes that I ever read. He says as a writer, "In all entertainment we must educate." Paraphrased, but that is a great motto to have in any story you're going to try to develop. What is your point? What are you trying to say? How are you trying to affect the viewer or the reader? For example this *Little Nemo* story I am doing. I didn't want to do something that just was an opportunity to do a bunch of trippy shit [Laughter]. I wanted to do something that maybe had some poignancy to it. As a creator or writer, I don't have any interest in working on something that isn't going to have some form of meaning to it. Working with the writers I have, and being a fan of all of them, well before ever getting to work with these guys their purposeful storytelling really impacted me a lot. By the time I got to collaborate with them, I already understood that whole idea ... do something that matters to someone.

What about Grant Morrison? What did you take away from him as a storyteller?

There is definitely meaningful content in Grant's work, but I think the thing I took away from him was his level of enthusiasm. There's always this pop and sizzle in his stories, you know what I mean?

No I don't, please go ahead.... [Laughter] Pop and sizzle?

Yeah, it just sort of crackles with weird far-outness. It doesn't come across as just being far out and weird, there's an intention. There's this kind of energy in there that's kind of wild. I like that. So what I took away from that is that when I try to do my own stuff, how can I infuse it with that weird little element that you might not be expecting that kind of pops and you think, "Wow, that's weird!" How that makes you think a little bit.

***Do you have a contemporary example of that, maybe from* Overture *or* Batwoman?**

Yeah, the first thing that comes to mind is, there is this villain in *Batwoman* called The Hook. He eventually gets defeated and he has this big giant metal hook and there is just two elements surrounding it that are just so bizarre. He's based on an urban legend of this murderous guy who runs around killing people and he has a hook for a hand. But when we developed his origin, we decided to make the hook actually an interdimensional alien sentient thing. That's something you wouldn't expect, it's sort of like a bizarre out of left field sort of thing. When he gets defeated the hook is ripped off his body and cast into the ocean. The sentient machine that the hook actually is, isn't dead, it's not defeated and it floats to the bottom of the ocean, and attaches itself to a crab and it walks away controlling the crab. That is the sort of thing that I'm talking about. "What? That is so weird," but it's just kind of a cool thing that you wouldn't expect to see, but when you see you're thinking, "Aww that's so fun," you know? [Chuckles]

What did you take from Warren Ellis?

Ellis has a great grasp on the darker, seedier intentions of humanity's spirit sometimes. But what's fascinating about his stories is that he can be really cynical and very dark, but at the exact same time, you always feel that there's a sense of humanity in there, which is hard to do. I don't know how he does that. Because I've read tons of dark, cynical stories and they're usually just dark and cynical and you can see some sort of commentary about mankind in it, but you still don't feel like there's any relatable humanity. Ellis always seems to have that. So when I worked on *Desolation Jones*, you had these moments, where here is this guy, Desolation Jones, who does some seriously messed up stuff, but you can't help caring about him and relate to him as a human being, and that he's gotten through some sort of intense bad experience himself that's made him the way he is. You care even though that character's outlook is very cynical. Ellis is really good at that. I don't know if I've taken anything away from it that benefits myself as a creator, but it's definitely something that I noticed right way and latched onto and liked a lot. If I ever get the opportunity to tell a really dark story, like he tends to do, I would hope that no matter what, people would see the humanity in the characters.

What did you take away from Greg Rucka?

Rucka, I think, is a really great craftsman in terms of setting up a dynamic action oriented mystery. His sense of pacing is really amazing, and it's something to learn from. He's really good at the big surprise bang that you might not have seen coming, or you did see it coming, but you're still excited for it anyway. I think he's really good at that. And he's very good at humanizing characters, very grounded.

Yeah, I saw a lot of that in Batwoman: Elegy, *there was a lot of humanity to the characters, despite the grim nature of the whole situation.*

And how fantastical it got. He introduces this whole idea of this religious cult, of what we called a "were-beast" cult because they all could transform into various forms of hybrid human animal people, which is like this far out crazy thing, but he manages to set it in with all these other elements around it that are so grounded, that you have to accept what you're seeing, instead of "oh that's just ridiculous."

And all of his characters always have this real great sense of humanity and familial qualities in them, strong supporting cast and stuff like that. So, I think there's lessons to be learned from everyone I've worked with.

What have you taken from Neil Gaiman in regards to storytelling right now? I mean you've been active in scripts, you've gotten through two issues, what does he bring to the table as a storyteller that you feel is influencing you as a storyteller?

We'll use a comparison in order to make this point clear. Let's backtrack to Alan [Moore] a little bit. Alan knows very much where things are going, and he is very concrete about leading you there and feeling very orchestrated in doing so. Neil's stories feel, like we had mentioned before about them being dreams, that there's sort of this fluidity to it all and I kind of feel like I have no idea where we're going necessarily, in terms of the story, but it's certainly a lot of fun to float there. The story is figuring itself out as it's going. Neil probably very much knows every little nuanced detail of what he wants to do. But I don't know that plan as concretely. His story so far for *Overture* feels like it's discovering how to get there itself. Alan's stories feel like they know how they're getting there from page one. I could be completely wrong about that, in terms of what's going on in these writers' heads. So, for what I'm learning from Neil, is to try to loosen up a little bit in expectations, trying not to preconceive where the story is going to go when you turn the page. Most stories, the reader isn't just completely in the moment of what they're reading, they might have an idea of where the next plot point is going to go. And to me, Neil's stuff sort of feels like you're *not* going to know where the plot is going to go, but you're not going to care because you're having fun where you are, it's a journey. [Laughter]

That is a really fascinating dichotomy. So it's been quite a few years since the original **Sandman** *comics have come out. How do you view this current rendition of* **Sandman** *that you're doing in regards to the twenty-first century?*

It's hard to say. This kind of goes back to the circular nature we're seeing in terms of the story itself, and how the story feels. It feels circular and cyclical in a way because it's a prequel to the original series, it's a prequel to the very first issue of *Sandman*, but at the same time parts of the story take place after the main series ended. So, the series, as it stands per today's time, feels like its straddling both those things, its straddling nostalgia and something brand new. It feels that way to me when looking at the material in the story itself, because it's very self-referential, its referring to all kinds of things that happened in the main series even though this is technically supposed to be a prequel. It's very fascinating from that point and I think it's creating this interesting existence in the past but existing in the now, but not necessarily coming across like a nostalgic trip.

You've worked with people at different times over the last twenty years or so and that means that you've had different technologies to communicate with and everything, can you kind of give us an insight into the workflow of the situation with Neil along with how do you work with Dave Stewart, the colorist, and Todd Klein, the letterer, or Shelly Bond, your editor? What kind of workflow situation are you engaged in?

We had touched on earlier about Neil asking for that list of things that piqued my curiosity and interest. That's his sort of introductory creative communication. As he works he builds some things off of that, off of his own notions and writes the script. Then I get the script and see what the script and the story are doing. Then I will have ideas in terms of my own and how I can represent that visually. On issue one, I decided since I hadn't really worked with Neil before, that it might be a good idea to take the issue and interject my notes into the written script, asking, "What do you think of this idea for this scene?" or how this could function as a two page spread instead of two individual pages, that sort of thing. I really kind of went in and pre-thought out a lot of stuff, which I very rarely do, and sent that along. He loved seeing all of that and there were some things he was like, "Oh we have to see that!" He was excited over it, but he didn't try to go in and overthink my thoughts. He was kind of like, "Oh this is what Jim wants to do with it, sounds cool." He didn't have a lot of questions of where my mindset was at. But with issue two and with issue three, I'm not doing that same process. I'm going in with stating some vague things of what I'm thinking about how the overall issue should feel visually, and how it should flow, but I'm not being very detailed with that, I'm figuring things out as I go, which is pretty much how I would normally do things anyway. But, with issue three's script, with the western influence stuff, I basically said we should try to reach for this sort of feeling, this sort of goal for it, and that prompts a response from Neil, and he responds, "Oh yeah, that sounds really cool, what about this, or look at this," sort of that kind of back and forth.

Issue three sounds like one that's very open and the ideas flow both ways, which is fantastic.

Yeah, exactly, but at the same time it's not like we're talking on the phone or exchanging emails every day, it's sort of like I know what he does and I trust what he does, he knows what I do and he trusts what I do and we'll share some ideas in between.

The creative process with Dave Stewart.... Dave Stewart has got to be the finest colorist the industry has. He is super open to working closely, collaboratively, because he's one of those guys who understands that as the colorist, he's sort of following after the artistic vision that has already been set, it's already been put down. First, you have stuff coming through the script, what the writer is trying to convey or wants to see for something particular, and the artist is following that and then the artist really solidifies everything into a visual narrative, therefore the color at that point, it sort of has to make sure it falls in line with that, but still feel like they're being creative too.

When I draw pages, I think design oriented and atmospherically, stuff like that. So I cannot help but think about the color as I'm developing the art. I'll provide Dave with a set of notes based on what I'm thinking and if he has questions about that he'll ask me about it. There's stuff where I'm like, "hmmm I was thinking this, but I'm not quite sure, what are your thoughts Dave?" and we'll talk about my notes over the phone and I'll ask him questions, "what do you think about that idea?" Either he'll say, "Oh, that's cool or this other thing might be cool, this is how we can build upon it." On occasion, I'll have something where I kind of know what I'm seeing in my head, but I'm not quite sure, and I'll ask Dave, "What do you think?" and then he'll go, "Yeah, let's try it." So, it's really collaborative and once I get the colors from him that is sort of a draft stage and we'll make little tweaks here and there like if something really didn't work like I was thinking it would or the palette just for some reason isn't quite working. Most of the feedback I give him at that stage is usually, "If you look over here, part of this guy's leg is colored blue and it should be red or whatever" [Laughter], things involving detail continuity.

With Todd, usually a letterer does their own placements of where the lettering is or that's dictated to them by an editor, sometimes the writer. I need to put so much thought into what I'm doing with the layouts and the design, I have to take that all into consideration ahead of time so I have a really good idea where those placements need to be. It's something I trained myself a long time ago to do, and so I provide those placements for Todd. Most of the time it works out, sometimes something will have to get adjusted, or didn't fit quite the way I thought it would, or he'll adjust the placement either in a way that I agree with because its a better choice or I disagree with and we'll talk about it and make adjustments from there. His work gets proofread in terms of the actual text by Neil and Shelly [Bond], the editor. I don't bother to try and proofread it because I didn't write it. [Laughter] I am more concerned about making sure the placement works the way it needs to work and flows with the page.

It sounds like you have a lot of oversight with the process. A lot of communication falls on to you and you have to consider the creative team's needs.

Yeah, I try to do that. I try to put a lot of thought into what I'm doing and therefore, I have to communicate. I have to think about those things, if I don't think about these things, how can I expect everything to match up? I know there's a lot of artists out there that draw the story, that's it, they don't have anything more to say about it. There's a lot of guys that operate that way, but I can't, I have to think it all the way through. It's probably a bit of a control issue.

For someone who does comics the way I do them with such a design-oriented process and goal in mind, if you don't think about those things, you're headed for disaster. It's going to feel just so disjointed. Fortunately, I work with people who really understand that, they understand that mode of thinking. They get why I work the way I do.

Can you tell us more about the role of editorial from Shelly Bond on **Overture***?*

She's been really great. This sounds bad, but a lot of the time, editors that I've worked with in the past can be almost not there. Shelly is very hands on, she's very detail oriented. My relationship with her might be different than it is with other people she works with, primarily because she has to trust in what I do. Because I don't do thumbnails with my work, even though it is design oriented. I don't turn in a bunch of thumbnails and expect feedback and redrawing, so they have to trust in what I do. Fortunately, I think I've really proven myself over the years and so they were okay with that situation even though that's not necessarily ordinary. So Shelly, she's there to make sure I have everything I need, she's there to make sure that communication is running smoothly between Neil and I, if I can't reach him and I need something, or vice versa. Very rarely we've needed her to kind of step in on anything in that way, but she's there a lot being extremely supportive of the project, being enthusiastic, making sure everyone is copacetic and having a good time as much as they can. At the same time she's also there to make sure that the work is getting done, which can make things kind of difficult sometimes. Sometimes with the balloon placements once the lettering is done, if there's suggestions from Neil to move something, what makes her cool is, instead of her just arbitrarily moving things around and I don't see it until it's printed, we go over it. And either I agree with what she's saying or I don't agree with it. If not, then we work it out and find a middle ground. She's been really great at that. I can't say the same for some other editors, unfortunately.

Many comic book professionals have been active in social media circles, Twitter, Tumblr, Facebook. What role do you think that is playing with you as a creator? Is it helping or hindering you as a creator? What do you think the attraction to social media is for comic book professionals?

I don't know if it's really done anything for me creatively, but the thing that's always happened with this industry, and I think that is why there have always been so many comic book conventions honestly, where creators get together and where fans get together, is because we work in this industry, where most of us, even with other professionals, we don't see each other. We're in our offices or home studios, and doing what we do, it can be very isolated. So, what conventions provided was a sense of community and relating to other people that are like yourself or interested in the same things you're interested in. I think something like Twitter and these other social media concepts have provided an extension for that same mentality. So it allows a comic creator who lives in New York to chat in a light way with someone who lives on the West Coast rather spontaneously than say a planned phone call or email exchange. A lot of times with email exchanges you're not going back and forth quickly, where on Twitter you can. It is a little more conversational and communal. Comic book people, a lot of us who work in the industry, grew up reading comics and were fans of comics and we were fans of people who are working today. Twitter is just another way to feel communal with those people. That aspect has always kind of been there and that's why there have been so many comic book conventions, in comparison, let's say, to other industry conventions.

One of the comic industry highlights on Twitter in the last year was when Jim Steranko got on Twitter. He has been around for over half a century and is one of these guys who people will go out of their way to talk to at a convention, because he is this personality and just a fascinating and creative guy. But when he got on Twitter, it was insane in just how accessible it made him. The stuff that he would convey to people that you would have never heard in your life, and here it was on Twitter.

Yeah, he basically used it the same way, because I've never gone to a convention where he's done a comic, been on a panel, or gotten a chance to really talk to him that much. I've heard that he likes to tell stories, that there's been panels where he sort of just goes off and starts talking about things he's done or whatever. When he went on Twitter, he sort of kind of did the same thing, you know, "I was an escape artist, this is what I did."

I even suggested to him to do an autobiography. He said "Yeah, as a graphic novel, and you should illustrate it Williams." I told him, "That would be amazing. [Laughter] If you want to do that, I will do it." I think comic book professionals like to see, and be able to understand that people enjoy their work. While fans like to see that individuals, such as Steranko and others, and myself, are human beings. But at the same time, it's kind of a weird situation in some ways. You may run into fans who hold your work, or Steranko's work, or others' to such high regard, almost loftiness, and that can be a bit daunting, giving you a weird feeling, but then at the same time they want to see that you're human as well. So Twitter has kind of provided this interesting platform to exchange ideas.

That's about the upside, what about the downside then? Do you find anything detrimental about it for the industry or for comic book professionals? I mean, aside from there possibly being a time sink?

Fortunately, I've been really smart and have not allowed Twitter to get in the way of me doing my work. I'll go days where I'm not on there.

It's a good way to get distracted, absolutely, so that's kind of a bad thing. I think a lot of the social networks, the computer and the internet in general, are ideal for distraction and that's not a good thing. The other thing with Twitter is its format, because you can only use so many characters, and a lot of times people think that a limitation on characters means efficiency in exchange of information, but it also can be limiting in terms of making sure that information is clearly understood. People can get in overheated arguments on there. I've seen it happen, where people can lose their minds on there. A lot of times it's because they don't fully understand each other. You can only communicate in small bites on there. In a way, it's not a real conversation, it is not sitting in front of someone like you and I are and actually talking about stuff and making your perspectives clear, and so I think that is bad, you've seen some devolved conversations occur on there. [Laughter]

That's a very kind way to put it. [Laughter]

That is kind of a bad thing, but I guess that is the nature, the evolution of digital social media communication. It is not always going to be smooth.

Warming Up the Strings

Tara Prescott

"An aperture ... a disclosure, discovery, revelation.... An opening
of negotiations with another person ... a first hint *of* something....
An orchestral piece ... forming the opening or introduction
to an opera ... often containing ... themes from the body
of work."—"overture," *Oxford English Dictionary*

Twenty-five years ago, Neil Gaiman launched the first issue of what
would become the most innovative and beloved of comics: *Sandman*. When
the long-running series came to its inevitable conclusion a decade ago, fans
were devastated. Teased by the release of several spin-offs and reissued volumes
in collectible bindings, fans continued to bear their fiery torches, dreaming of
Gaiman's return to the Dreaming.[1] And a curious thing happened over the
resulting decades: Neil Gaiman's original *Sandman* became its own myth. Just
as he revisited fairy tales in *Fragile Things* and completely rewrote ancient
deities in *American Gods* and *Anansi Boys*, Gaiman is once again drawing upon
older stories and reinventing them for a new era—but this time, his source
material is his own story.

To quote R.E.M. riffing off Cole Porter, Gaiman has started to "Begin
the Begin." He had been planning a return to the series, perhaps to commem-
orate its twentieth anniversary, but the stars were not in alignment just yet.
He needed the right time, and the right talent, and the right commitment
from the publisher, to bring the new tale alive. Artist JH Williams III reveals
the most obvious hurdle to anyone taking on this task: "I wanted to do something that honored the original material.... I also wanted to feel like I was
bringing something new to the equation that wasn't just doing what everyone
else before me had done.... How can I bring something new to that table and
feel like it's still *Sandman*?" (Bultena). Williams III's trepidation about return-

216

ing to the beloved series was shared by readers as well. "As exciting as the project is, it also feels rather dangerous for writer, reader, character and publisher. You know what they say about going home again," writes reviewer J. Caleb Mozzocco. But what many early reviewers did not note is that Gaiman is not really "going home" with *Overture*. He has kept some of the original architecture, but this construction, like the MC Escher-looking dollhouse of horrors on the cover of issue #2, is a different beast altogether.

The first issue was released in October of 2013, with "the Floating Word" by Neil Gaiman, "lines, paint," "scratches and blobs" by JH Williams III, "hues" by "Maestro of Color" Dave Stewart, "fonts" by "Typography Lord" Todd Klein, "assistant edits" by "Cheering" Assistant Editor Sara Miller, and edits by "Editor Extraordinaire" and "Head Honcho" Shelley Bond (as they are playfully credited in issues #2 and #3). Even with agonizing delays that reduced the publication schedule to only three issues in a year, *Sandman: Overture* is already bearing the marks of a new classic. But what exactly it is, and how it fits in the Gaiman oeuvre, has yet to be determined. The title indicates that this is the large orchestral piece at the start of the composition, or given the name of the first *Sandman* story arc, a prelude to *Preludes*; it is perhaps the enthusiastic efforts to win our affection, and readers have been told that this story arc will reveal the events leading up to Dream's capture in the first *Sandman* issue, "The Sleep of the Just." *Overture* makes several major diversions from the "rules" of the original series—in terms of how time operates, where in the universe the story takes place, and most shockingly, Dream's new ability to co-inhabit and interact with multiple incarnations of himself at the same time.[2] Williams III addresses the time issue in particular, stating, "So far, all of the ideas about time in *Sandman* have all been very literal, in terms of how time can be viewed in the context of the story itself ... time in *Overture* is very circular in ways, even though it is taking place prior to the beginning of the *Sandman* main series, it is also showing parts that seem to be taking place after" (Bultena). The aberrant movement of time, highlighted by the Dalí-melting-pocket-watch in issue #2, helps explain the dozens of co-existing versions of Dream that form the climax of the first issue.

Some readers will consider *Overture* part of the original canon, others will look at it as a standalone story arc, but it is clearly a hybrid text. Readers may feel ownership of the way that "their" *Sandman* works—after all, the basic characters and mythology have been virtually unchanged since the series finished. It is time for Gaiman to shake things up. Close analysis of the first issue shows that the author has put us on notice that what we think we know about *Sandman* is all going to change (and which consequently calls the entire arc of the original story into question). Along with the Williams III's exquisite artwork, Gaiman is enthusiastically pushing the technological, artistic, creative, and narrative boundaries of the series. He is daring to pull apart a revered late twentieth-century comic that has attained canonical status and reinvent it for the twenty-first century.

Sandman: *A History of Reinvention*

In the DC universe, the Sandman character began in the 1930s as a super-hero in a green suit, fedora, and gas mask. In the 1980s, DC began re-imagining several of the minor characters in its catalog. It was "a damn good season to dream of doing something ambitious and substantial in the world of comics. Indeed, comic books were enjoying more hip credibility than at any time since the 1960s," notes Mikal Gilmore (the same can be said of the 2010s, an auspicious time for *Sandman*'s return). Gaiman pitched an idea for the Sandman title, and after the success of *Black Orchid*, Karen Berger suggested Gaiman pursue that idea for his new monthly comic. Gaiman developed the look and feel of the new *Sandman* with Sam Keith and Mike Dringenberg, and the "dark magus" they created "bore little resemblance" to the "war-era crime fighter" who preceded him (Gilmore).[3] And just as the original *Sandman* "bore little resemblance" to the title that prefigured it, the new *Overture* actually bears little resemblance to the title that came before it—the original *Sandman* itself. Unending transformation is in fact a hallmark of this series.

From the very beginning, *Sandman* has been conspicuously collaborative, with room for multiple artists to add their distinctive touch. The flavor of the main characters and storylines changed significantly depending on the artist. Although *Overture* has one primary artist for the whole story, its use of variant covers retains the kaleidoscopic feeling of the original, with room for multiple artists to add their distinctive versions of the characters and world. Each issue of *Overture* offers alternate covers by Williams III and original series artist Dave McKean, giving more opportunities for creative expansion and play.[4]

The multiplicity of covers adds to the fragmented, serial nature of the text. On the one hand, the new series follows in the footsteps of the original in terms of its proclivity for lush, artistic covers—originally a gamble, as they were often ambiguous and did not sell the hero the way most traditional super-hero covers did. In fact, many *Sandman* covers did not show the Sandman at all and deemphasized the title, putting the luscious art at the forefront. McKean's covers in particular broke with comics tradition. Fueled by a Joseph

Cornell Wunderkammer aesthetic, they included collages and photographs and objects rather than an easily recognizable—and easily read—cartoon cover. The celebrated covers were later published as a collection of their own, *Dustcovers: The Collected Sandman Covers*. But even as *Overture* gives us the innovative, beautiful covers that we are used to, it also makes a break from the past by introducing Williams III, an artist who never worked on the original series.

Although a cynic might argue that releasing multiple covers is a blatant attempt to sell more issues, there is more at work here. By providing multiple points of access into each issue's world as interpreted through different artists' eyes, they are a subtle reminder that the character of Dream and the universe(s) he inhabits are not fixed: the look, feel, and rules by which they operate change from artist to artist and issue to issue. Yet even as fans are accustomed to new artists changing the look of characters, they are not used to Gaiman himself changing the rules he first established.

Overture consciously forces the reader to view it as a construction rather than a seamless, transparent story. This is mostly evident from Williams III's art, which embeds messages in the shapes of the panels and in the panel frames, as well as the self-referential moments in Gaiman's text. In an unusual move, Vertigo is also releasing special editions that show the issues between stages, so that readers can see Williams III's original work before final inking and colors.[5] This is another example of how *Overture* asks the reader to think about its own construction, to be able to take it apart and enjoy it in pieces. The special editions, which are released after the regular issues, are offering the type of retrospective that is usually done long after the story itself is complete. Again, this is a move that facilitates a kind of on-the-ground investigation of the series as it unfolds. This destabilizes the reader by shifting the time but also the emphasis of the excitement—we expect *Overture* to be a celebration of the original series, when in fact, it is making a fresh break.

Serialization as a Dreamlike, Fractured Experience

Readers of Gaiman's original series were fortunate to experience the first issues as they arrived in the mail or in the weekly pull at the local comic book store. They felt the uncertainty of reading the story issue by issue, with time to re-read and digest before knowing what the next installment would bring. Fans who came to *Sandman* via its trade paperbacks know a different experience, a far more common one in today's era of binge-watching entire series on Netflix.[6] Reading the story all at once helps a reader to make stronger connections and see the story as a whole, though missing out on the longing and conjecture that comes with reading a story in serial format. In some ways, serialization encourages more reader participation, as there is more room for insertions, guesses, and predictions, which are precluded by a complete and collected story.

By releasing *Overture* in the same serial format as the original series, Gaiman is not only reflecting on the earlier format but also reminding us that it can be changed. Collecting issues into a bound edition fixes characters and storylines in many ways; cover to cover, the story is contained and complete. The quality and colors may change (as they notably did with the *Absolute Sandman* releases), but the story is over, the characters will not change next month. By their very nature, serialized stories have a broken-up nature; they are fragmented in time and place. For Gaiman to choose to release a story in 2013 in serialized format is to return to the original methods of delivery, but also to shake things up. You thought you knew the story of Snow White, and then "Snow, Glass, Apples" came along. You thought you knew what Easter was, and then you met her in *American Gods*. And you thought you knew how the *Sandman* universe worked, and then a Dream died and showed up to chat with thirty different versions of himself.

The fragmented nature of serialized comics is further split and differentiated by the use of technology and platforms that did not exist twenty-five years ago. The hotly anticipated first issue of *Overture* was available in several formats and could be read online or as a digital download on computers, laptops, e-readers, and cellphones, in addition to the individual paper issues (and will eventually, no doubt, come in trade paperback and collected editions. But by then, the feeling of having the story ripped out from underneath you will be gone). Each of these formats has its strengths and drawbacks, and each offers a slightly different and individualized experience.

Even something as basic as the ads in the paper issues, which Gaiman of course does not control, add to the reader's interrupted experience and hearkens back to the popularization of serialized novels in the Victorian era—also the setting for Dream's appearance in the London office in issue #1. The idea of serialization is essential to comic books, but it has been lost in recent years as more and more readers reach for the published collections. The original generation of *Sandman* readers had that experience and could see characters develop over time. And in some way, Gaiman is bringing that experience back by choosing to release *Overture* in serial format. He is effectively introducing the serial to a generation of readers who have not had that experience. It is one of the features of *Overture* that makes the comic paradoxically both modern and Dickensian.

For some readers, *Overture*'s ads detract from the experience, while for others, they serve as welcome introductions to outside works connected to *Overture*, broadening the reading experience. The first three issues and special editions include ads for video games, the trade paperback re-releases of other Gaiman comics, other comics by Williams III, new spinoff comics featuring characters from the original *Sandman* series, other new Vertigo releases, television and film adaptations of comics, comic websites and conventions, and the odd junk food item. For some readers, these ads are a disruptive annoyance. "DC sure went bananas with the ads in this thing," writes Mozzocco in regards to the first issue. Yet comics are very much a product of their time and oddly enough, the advertisements that accompany them offer context, snapshots into their creation and reader reception. They may be annoying or innocuous, disruptive or informative, but they are also part of comics' serialization heritage. As material culture, they reveal what Vertigo expects its target readership to be, as well as its faith in Gaiman's ability to draw an audience. Whereas early issues of *Sandman* included ads for Atari Lynx, and the Essential Vertigo reprints in the 90s featured ads for PlayStation, *Conspiracy Theory* on Pay-Per-View and *The Best of Judas Priest* at Circuit City, *Overture*'s ads are now promoting major conventions dedicated to the study and celebration of comics. From the funny pages to graphic novels and sequential art, comics have come a long way from being "just" superhero stories for kids. The ads are a testament to comics' serialized history in addition to being silent commentary on the mainstreaming of comics in 2013.

Initially slated for six issues to be released bi-monthly, *Overture*'s publishing delays, although not intentional, have also shaped the experience of reading it. "A lot of potential readership might already be inclined to trade-wait," Mozzocco adds, acknowledging the drawbacks to reading a story meted out slowly over many more months than anticipated. Yet even this frustrating format does not stop fans from buying. "At a mere 20 pages (ah, but what beautiful pages!), one can't help but feel that *Sandman: Overture* might have been better served released as one volume than in bi-monthly installments. But the novelty of seeing Neil Gaiman play in his most famous and beloved sandbox is just too delicious to complain about," writes Michael Cecchini. *Overture*'s extensive delays, particularly between the releases of the first three issues, have also affected the serial reading experience. And yet for many readers, the experience of reading the story in real time as it is released is part of the joy, an anticipation that builds and sustains in an era of instant gratification. "Had *Sandman: Overture* stuck to its originally intended shipping schedule, the series would be almost finished now instead of just reaching the halfway point," writes Jesse Schedeen in his review for issue #3. "But if this comic isn't worth waiting months and months for, what is?" he asks.

On the one hand, releasing *Overture* in a serialized format rather than as a book (as Gaiman did with *Endless Nights* and *The Dream Hunters*) is a nostalgic return to its roots. On the other hand, its simultaneous release on the web and in multiple formats furthers its break from its own tradition. Depending on the platform and device, the reader's experience differs widely. For example, reading the PDF online with a laptop, a reader has to double click to get close enough to see detail. You cannot take in the page all at once while also being able to read text at the same time, the way you can with paper. The nature of online versions forces the reader to prioritize reading the text or reading the art. In some spreads, such as the triangle zigzagging in issue #3, the issue has a guided "click through" zoom option which actually determines the order that the panels are read—it basically teaches the reader how to read the comic (which can be positive or negative, depending on your point of view). Gaiman himself commented on the drawbacks of the medium, tweeting, "Seeing some people unsatisfied with Kindle/screen versions of *Sandman: Overture*. The paper version's special & definitely recommended by me" (Gaiman neilhimself).

Other drawbacks to the online version include the difficulty of telling where the gutters are. For example, the two-page Corinthian eye-mouth spread appears as a single image online, so it lacks the shock value in relation to the preceding pages, which are comparably sized online. However, Williams III's art on-screen literally glows—the striking gorgeous hues of his artwork, backlit by a high definition screen, are mesmerizing on screen. They come alive entirely differently than they do in print.

This experience is heavily impacted by screen size, of course, and reading *Overture* on an iPhone seems like a travesty. But the experience of paging through *Overture* on a crowded subway or spontaneously escaping into the Dreaming on a cross-country flight offers something different and desirable that could not be achieved with the paper format alone. The experimentation is what matters—multiple formats, multiple relationships to the original text—and a reminder that comics are a fluid, malleable format, hardly stuck in time, adapting to newly emerging technologies even while constantly reinventing them itself. Fans may believe that Dream and *Sandman* cannot radically change, that the myth is in place and they like it the way it is. Gaiman, however, is taking every opportunity to reinvent his own myth, not merely by adapting it to twenty-first century technology but by destabilizing the anticipated limits of the *Sandman* mythos itself.

Metamorphosizing Morpheus: Issue #1

As Morpheus's name implies, he is a character who can change into anything else—he is impossible to pin down. And the slipperiness of the serialized *Overture* fits the slipperiness of this figure. A reader's first glimpse of *Sandman: Overture* registers that this comic is entering very new territory. Williams III's Cover A shows Morpheus, the god of dreams, walking through a field of burning flowers. The cover draws upon the Greek mythology of the Lotus Eaters, the people who spend so much time asleep in dreams that they are rarely awake in real life. To readers familiar with the original *Sandman* series, this echoes what happens to some people during Dream's imprisonment: they sleep nearly every hour of the day. In Homer's *Odyssey*, the god of sleep, Hypnos, has a son named Morpheus who "became fascinated with the way a little corner of man's mind remained awake in sleep, making new pictures." Morpheus "went to Persephone and said, 'I need a flower that makes sleep. It must be purple and black. But there should be one petal streaked with fire-red, the petal to make dreams'" (Evslin 11). In *Overture* #1, the fire-red petals echo in the flower/Dream that later bursts into flames.

In turning the first page of *Overture*, the reader gets another surprise: these flowers are not used to aid dreamers but, in fact, are the dreamers themselves. These wild creations, so gorgeously imagined by Williams III, are Georgia O'Keefe's labial poppies, *Little Shop of Horrors'* Audrey II, and the *Odyssey's* Lotus Eaters all rolled into one. They are "a race of huge carnivorous plants, with limited mobility but beautiful minds" (1). And one of them, introduced on the first page, is the protagonist, the curiously-christened Quorian.

Quorian is the first non-mammal in the history of *Sandman* to encounter Dream in the Dreaming. Throughout the series, Dream assumes shapes that are suitable to the dreamers, appearing as an Elizabethan poet to William Shakespeare, a sleek black tomcat in "A Dream of a Thousand Cats," and a pale ghostly fox in the Japanese folktale within *The Dream Hunters*. Given the creativity of the series, it is surprising to meet Quorian and Plant Dream and yet the reader wonders why this type of incarnation has not happened before. Why shouldn't plants have capabilities beyond what mere humans can know or assume? Given Quorian's prominence on the cover and in the first few pages of the issue, it is surprising that he disappears from the rest of the narrative. In fact, readers who are unfamiliar with the *Sandman* universe may see Quorian as one of the main characters, and it adds to their disorientation when both he and his black and white dried-sunflower friend disappear.

The first *Sandman* issue, "The Sleep of the Just," began in the home of the man who had been trying to capture Death but accidentally caught Dream instead; although supernatural forces were at work, the story was firmly rooted in the world of men, of humanity, of a world almost analogous to our own. And though the story jumped to gods and immortality, it was still anchored in our world, or in their world of dreams connected to sleeping women and men. But the first issue of *Overture* takes a sudden departure by situating itself in an extraterrestrial world that readers of the series have never seen. The solar system, which appears on McKean's Cover B as a series of balls that Dream juggles, looks like our own ... but not. The "small" planet belonging to "a star system containing six other planets" has a moon that looks like ours ... and then another one. It has continents like ours, ice caps, even "a race of human-oids" that look a bit like they have stepped out of *Planet of the Apes*, and, like many people today, "believe that their planet was alone in the universe." So far, so good. But in the three interconnected circle panels on the first page, linked almost as if they are magic rings or a Venn diagram, the story starts moving off Earth into speculative fiction: a race of "small, mindless, insect-like creatures who swarmed when the mood took them, taking on shapes capable of making art or exploring the solar system, until they fragmented back into tiny flying cells interested only in egg-laying and food." Suddenly, as foreign as these alien insects *look*, their base nature and self-interest start to sound awfully human again. The largest and final circle introduces the race of car-nivorous plants, and at their center, the dreaming Quorian. Issue #1 is firmly situated in outer space, in the fantastic, and yet in an uncanny move, it is also deeply familiar. Both Gaiman's text and Williams III's art invite readers to critically think about their own world in a new way through the lens of some-thing initially foreign.

The fractured nature of the storyline, which jumps radically from scene to scene, can disorient readers, but Williams III and Gaiman counter this feel-ing by introducing patterns and motifs to ground us again. There are visual patterns—recognizable characters from the original series, repeating geomet-ric shapes that bookend each issue (issue #1 uses three interlocking circles, issue #2 uses nested and then inverted pentagons, and issue #3 uses nested tri-angles). The patterns remind the reader that each issue is a self-contained fragment of a larger story, which is itself a fragment of an even larger mythol-ogy.

In Quorian's dreams, the reader discovers the wonderfully-playful version of Dream, with nearly-indistinguishable eyeslits and crisp black dried leaves. In comparison with all of the other Dream incarnations to be revealed in the gatefold at the end of the issue, this Plant Dream is notably missing a key feature: his ruby. Readers of the original *Sandman* series know that Dream's ruby and helm, featured on Cover A, were stolen from him at the start of the series. Does this mean that Plant Dream exists at the same time that Dream is trapped in the bubble at the very start of the series? Plant Dream announces, "something is very wrong," and Quorian speaks for the reader when he responds, "I do not understand" (2).

"Something is hurting. Something is waking up. Something is damaged," Dream states, which describes another incarnation of himself, trapped in the first issue of *Preludes and Nocturnes*. But as of the first three issues of *Overture*, readers do not yet know where to place this story in time. On the next page, Death comes for Plant Dream, who erupts into fire across a constellated sky, picking up visual echoes of the planets from the cover and first page, as well as textual echoes of the "gas giants" referenced on the first page. In all of the conflagration and excitement, the pages also announce that this is Chapter One.

The very next two-page spread rips the readers out of Quorian's planet and plunges them into World War I London. These luscious, horrific pages— each panel appearing as a tooth in the Corinthian's mouth-eye—are absolutely stunning. Readers unfamiliar with *Sandman* have not yet been formally introduced to the Corinthian, but the art instantly expresses the horror that surrounds him. At first glance, the image follows the emotional detachment of medical illustration, but that is marred by the jagged incisors and lone string of saliva connecting the top and bottom teeth. These are, to quote David Sedaris, "what we in France call 'good-time teeth'" (7). They are jagged, they are scary, and they are clearly beyond the reach of modern orthodontia. Just next to the upper right bicuspid, a carefully inserted round eyeglass frame helps orient the reader: we are seeing these scenes from the Corinthian's point of view, even as we are outside his mouth (or eye), looking in. Several pages later, in Dream's "London office," the reader will be inside the Corinthian's mouth-eyes again, situated this time just over his tongues, like some kind of Jonah peering out of the mouth of a particularly perverted whale.

This spread adds two more character names—the clerk Ian Stuart and the mysterious man that the final tooth reveals is "the Corinthian" (6–7). In a Gaiman narrative, it can be hard to know who the main players will be— sometimes relatively minor characters play pivotal roles and sometimes the narrative initially focuses on a MacGuffin character while another character comes from behind and takes the reader by surprise. The text in the last tooth on this spread is read off of a printed page, which transitions to the next spread: a shot of Destiny reading his book.

Destiny's famously paradoxical book is illustrated with panels, his very own cosmic comic book, which also features *Overture*'s first appearance of Death. Williams III plays with the possibilities of real-world readers holding open a comic book while viewing an illustrated reader holding open a book that contains pictures of himself, reading a book—an Endless hall-of-mirrors. Death reveals that she is worried about Dream because she "just *took* him" (10). Her verb choice is clarified when she adds, "and when one of *us* dies, it never ends well" (10). But how can a member of the Endless end?

Before the reader gets too comfortable with this scene, Williams III whisks us off to the black-and-white dream world of portcullis-faced George Portcullis, fabulously framed on the page by a portcullis itself. Gaiman reminds the reader that, outside of this dream, Portcullis might be "a woman. Or a child. Or a butterfly" (11). Readers familiar with ancient Chinese folk tales may hear an echo of the philosopher Chuang Zhu, who one night dreamed that he was a butterfly. The dream pushed him to wonder if in fact he was a man dreaming of being a butterfly or a butterfly dreaming of being a man. When Victorian-era Dream appears, he has the same eyeslits and black and white coloring as Plant Dream, but this time, his ruby is prominently present as a cravat pin. He is the Master of this office, though Portcullis does not recognize him. As the panels progress, color slowly seeps into Portcullis's dream, a direct result of Dream's presence.

By this point in the issue, readers have become accustomed to Williams III's extravagantly detailed art, even if they are still in awe of it. Hidden within the woven-pattern frame of pages 12 and 13, carefully camouflaged in the illustrated parquet tiles, is the beginning of a message that runs across several pages, reading: "WHERE DREAMS LIVE NOW / BUT SOMETIMES / SOME DREAMS DIE" (12–17).

Readers of the original series already know that Dream died and was replaced by Daniel, but the mechanics of how a member of the Endless dies are still unclear. The issue also brings new readers up to speed: at the beginning there was the Council of the First Circle, Dream creates dreams and nightmares, he made the Corinthian to reflect the worst in humanity, and the Corinthian is crossing the boundaries between the waking and dreaming worlds.

As the men debate, Williams III puts them in shadowed profile, oddly zooming in and focusing on a seemingly insignificant, whimsical detail: a teapot in the shape of an elephant. The placement of the figures and the elegance of teapot and teacup bring to mind the advertising for "An Evening with Neil Gaiman and Amanda Palmer," a 2012 performance tour and a subsequent live recording album. Although the teapot likely has no deeper meaning, Williams III's attention to detail and use of hidden messages puts the reader on notice that no detail is too small, no moment insignificant. And in many ways, that is partly the job of this first, ambiguous narrative: without knowing where the story is going, the reader does not yet know which details or characters will prove to be pivotal.

On a first read-through, the issue is surprisingly hard to follow. This impression is magnified when the reader is completely new to the series. Some first-time readers mistake Death for Dream's wife, and while this is inaccurate, it reinforces how closely matched and complimentary the siblings are. One reader hypothesized that the Corinthian eats eyes in order to make people more like him. Many new readers are confused about whether or not Dream's motives are good. Dream's helm and ruby, well-known to fans, also inspire intriguing hypotheses from new readers. "I noticed the jewel on Sandman's tie, which is placed in close proximity to his heart," writes Nadia Eshraghi, "I began to question if this jewel is a replacement for his real heart." "Eyes appear to be a major symbol in this series," notes Tracy Ngo. "The Corinthian has mouths for eyes but can see, and Destiny is blind but can see everything—past, present, and future. This paradox reminds me of blind justice ... and made me wonder if Destiny or the Corinthian has a noble cause." Of course, *Sandman* fans know that there is nothing noble about the Corinthian, but a new reader's confusion about his motivations, as well as Destiny's, certainly fits with the ambiguous roles and motivations of several key characters. This is yet another example of, to put it candidly, Gaiman messing with his audience as he re-visions his own mythology. The issue reminds us that Dream *created* the Corinthian—and though this creation met and even exceeded Dream's expectations, Dream reserves the right to uncreate him (without a trial). The parallel is there as a reminder: Gaiman created *Sandman*, exceeding all of our expectations, but he still reserves the right to change or even uncreate his creation however he sees fit (with or without the permission of the fans).

On the verge of uncreating the Corinthian, Dream's ruby suddenly flashes—his very own ancient intergalactic pager, portkey, or TARDIS—pulling him out of the London office and dropping him onto a whole new two-page spread in a sky filled with flying manta rays circling a walled castle.

Here, Gaiman places Merv Pumpkinhead and Lucien the librarian, two more cameos for fans of the original series, another moment of familiarity in a story that is disorientingly unfamiliar. They provide levity (Merv's Freudian musings in particular), a welcome moment of comic relief in a tense, visually and mentally demanding story.

Finally, although one of the main characters has been present in different forms for several pages, his name (or one of them, rather) appears—but only hidden within the shape of the panels themselves, which in loose psychedelic shapes spell out "MORPHEUS" (20). Quorian never names him, Death calls him "Dream," George Portcullis calls him "Master," the Corinthian and Lucian call him "Lord," and now the name Morpheus appears, hidden in the panel shapes themselves. A reader new to the series may not yet connect all of these names and realize they all belong to the same entity or entities. Of course, comic readers are familiar with the idea of alternate universes and multiple iterations of a character, but this takes even that aspect two steps further.

If readers are not already disoriented by this reimagining of their beloved series, Gaiman and Williams have one final jaw-dropping surprise in store. First Dream triumphantly names himself: "I am Dream of the Endless." And then the reader opens the pages to find the big surprise: a stunning gatefold spread, where the two pages fold outwards to include four pages of a continuous scene of Morpheuses or Morphii—at least thirty other versions of Dream and the suggestion that there are even more. This *Being John Malkovich* moment, filled with both new and familiar incarnations of Dream, is what reviewer Martin Grey playfully describes as "total Morpheus porn." It is surprising in both form and content. Gatefolds are exceedingly rare in comics, requiring extra expenses in production. (It is worth noting that the physical act of opening the gatefold is one of the great arguments for the paper editions. Online, the images simply appear, no different from what came before.) As Gray notes, "Take my word for it: Williams' art makes the paper copy that much more impressive and the story becomes much more immersive when that gatefold opens, like the doors of an airplane hangar, revealing wide open spaces that invite the reader to come and explore."

Dream reassures himself that he is "prepared for whatever awaits," but clearly he is not ready for this—and neither are we. In the entire *Sandman* canon, perhaps with the exception of Daniel, no two incarnations of Dream have appeared together—much less thirty. Just as Gaiman rewrote the rules for the TARDIS when he penned his first episode of *Doctor Who*, with the first issue of *Overture* he again changes and reinvents the game. In *Overture*, Dream co-exists and even converses with versions of himself, including a Picasso Dream, an Anime Fish Dream, and a Dream with a crescent moon for a head, reminiscent of McKean's *Convergence* cover.

As Williams III states, "They're all aspects of the same person, viewed through different lenses and different dimensional perspectives, and different worlds ... they're all aspects of this entity, but they're all very distinct and they all have a time place in history ... there isn't a linear mode and pattern to all these various versions of Dream" (Bultena). By the end of the issue, it becomes apparent how Plant Dream can die while the reader still follows World War I Dream through London. They are not strictly the same entity. Except they are. "YOU: DREAM OF THE ENDLESS ARE AS/ALSO WE," announces the Robot Dream who seems to be channeling *Metropolis* (24). Dream is late to a meeting of his own selves, who want to know where he has been (although they paradoxically should know). And just as there is a murder of crows, a pride of lions, or even *A Confederacy of Dunces*, Gaiman now reveals the collective noun for Morpheuses: "a concatenation of Dreams" (28).[7] The issue bookends with the same three ringed panels that introduced the humanoids, insects, and flowers—but now they hold the helmed Dream, a surrealist melting-color Dream, and then finally Dream dressed as he was in the castle of the Dreaming, looking awfully flummoxed by all of this. The final image of Dream's dazed visage echoes the reader's own confusion. What just happened?

Gaiman has thrown down the gauntlet: *Overture* is not just filling in the story of how Dream became trapped at the start of the original series, or even how Dream was capable of dying (as a plant) at the beginning of *Overture* and (as Morpheus) at the end of *Sandman*. It is reinventing our conception of who Dream is and what he is capable of. And yes, by issue #3 we get the story of the creation of the helm and the gates of horn and ivory, along with other details readers have long wondered about, but the real takeaway from *Overture* is much more. While this *Overture* may sound like the orchestra warming up the strings for the start of *Sandman*, Gaiman is in fact warming us up to the idea that the *Sandman* we know and love can radically change, and there's still plenty of life left in this character.

Notes

1. There have been multiple spinoffs of *Sandman* stories and characters, but not all of them have directly involved Gaiman. Some of the titles written by Gaiman include *Death: The High Cost of Living* (1993), *Death: The Time of Your Life* (1996), *The Dream Hunters* (1999), and *Endless Nights* (2003). In addition to the ten trade paperbacks of the original *Sandman* series, Vertigo released the *Absolute Sandman* (2010), a collectible oversized hardcover series reproducing all of the original issues with remastered coloring as well as extras such as original scripts, notes, sketches, introductions, and an afterword by Gaiman.

2. For the purposes of this essay, the "original series" refers to the original run of Gaiman's *Sandman*, not the DC titles of the same name that preceded it.

3. Dringenberg gets a shout-out in the first issue of *Overture*. His name appears as text in the book Destiny carries, printed in very small letters on the left page that are just barely visible, one of several "Easter eggs" playfully awaiting eagle-eyed readers.

4. Some of the alternate covers include blank sketch variants (meant for fans to try out their own art or get sketches done by the artists in person); and silver, black and white, and lenticular "3D" covers. Issue #1 also had a variant cover by Jim Lee bearing the Comic Book Legal Defense Fund logo.

5. For a reader wondering which luminous hues come from the colorist and which come from the inker or artist, or which are original color and which are digitally enhanced, the special edition provides a peek behind the curtain. It also makes some of the hidden gems more obvious; for example, the panels that spell out "MORPHEUS" and the hidden message in the frame, both in issue #1, are easier to see at this stage of the coloring. There are other fun additions, such as the soundtrack Williams III listened to while drawing the issue and supplementary interviews with Williams III, allowing unprecedented behind-the-scenes access to the creation of the comic, even as the series itself is in progress.

6. Even how fans find the issues for purchase has changed dramatically from the beginning of the original series to today. Fans originally went to comic book stores (which sold individual issues and trades), then as comics became more mainstream, major bookstore chains began to devote sections specifically to comics (usually trade paperbacks only), and then when those bookstore chains went out of business, sales moved largely to Amazon.com. Therefore, the year a fan first encountered *Sandman* could really affect the format that the comic was read in (individual issues or trade paperbacks, serially or collected).

7. Issue #3 ends with the same grammatical structure as issue #1, promising "A Madness of Stars."

Works Cited

"Blastr Origin Stories: Neil Gaiman on Sandman." *Blastr*. 10 Oct. 2013. Web. 28 Aug. 2014.

Bultena, John. "Aperture for a Storyteller: An Interview with JH Williams III." *Neil Gaiman in the 21st Century*. Ed. Tara Prescott. Jefferson, NC: McFarland, 2015. Print.

Cecchini, Michael. "The Sandman: Overture #1 (DC Comics/Vertigo) Review." *Den of Geek*. 10 Oct. 2013. Web. 27 Aug. 2014.

Dickens, Donna. "Exclusive: The Cover Art for 'The Sandman: Overture #4' Is Magical." *HitFix*. 11 July 2014. Web. 27 Aug. 2014.

Eshraghi, Nadia. "Issue #1 Through a New Reader's Eyes." *Neil Gaiman in the 21st Century*. Ed. Tara Prescott. Jefferson, NC: McFarland, 2015. Print.

Evslin, Bernard. *The Adventures of Ulysses*. New York: Scholastic, 1980. Print.

Gaiman, Neil. "Seeing some people unsatisfied with Kindle/screen versions of Sandman: Overture. The paper version's special & definitely recommended by me." 30 Oct. 2013, 5:35 p.m. Tweet.

_____, with JH Williams III (a), Todd Klein (l), and Dave Stewart (c). *Sandman: Overture*. Issues #1–3. 2013–2014.

Gilmore, Mikal. "An Introduction." *The Sandman: The Wake*, Remastered ed. New York: DC Comics, 2012. Print.

Gray, Martin. "The Sandman: Overture #1 Review." *Too Dangerous for a Girl*. 30 Oct. 2013. Web. 27 Aug. 2014

Inskeep, Steve. "Recurring Dream: Morpheus Returns in Gaiman's 'Sandman' Prequel." NPR. 31 Oct. 2013. Web. Sept. 2014.

Mozzocco, J. Caleb. "Sandman: Overture #1." *Robot 6. CBR*. 1 Nov. 2013. Web. 8 Sept. 2014.

Ngo, Tracy. "Thoughts as a *Sandman* Virgin." Essay, University of California, Los Angeles, 2014. Print.

Schedeen, Jesse. "Sandman Overture #3 Review: Dream Finds Company on the Road." *IGN*. 30 July 2014. Web. 1 Aug. 2014.

Sedaris, David. "Dentists Without Borders." *Let's Explore Diabetes with Owls*. New York: Little, Brown, 2013. Print.

Issue #1 Through
a New Reader's Eyes

Nadia Eshraghi

The first issue of *The Sandman: Overture* by Neil Gaiman and JH Williams III is the most confusing, eye-catching, creepy, and just overall perplexing story that I have ever tried to follow. I read this prequel having no pre-existing knowledge about the series or Neil Gaiman, but I did know that reading comic books is definitely not my forte. Trying to comprehend this storyline was annoying and almost hopeless at points, but the images and illustrations allow one's imagination to connect the dots, or at least attempt to. I read the traditional paper copy of issue one with cover B done by Dave McKean. I will analyze this cover and the two-page spread containing the conversation between the Sandman and the Corinthian in the Sandman's office.[1] I feel as though my reaction to the cover gives a genuine representation of my visceral reaction to the comic, while my response to the two-page spread shows how my understanding developed as the plot became more intense. In *Sandman: Overture* #1, Williams III utilizes the strategy of impression management to bring life and tangibility to Gaiman's abstract text. His use of specific colors and different methods of illustration provide a separate lens for the reader to interpret a plot that cannot be understood by reading the text alone.

You cannot judge a book by its cover ... but we all do. In fact, we formulate detailed and analytical verdicts based on our first impressions. When I first held issue #1 in my hands, I looked at the cover and thought, "What the...." The first aspect of the cover that stands out is the large, red, majestic, expensive-looking chair that an extremely frail, creepy-looking human/alien/lord/male of high position is sitting on. The red chair is surrounded by a dark background, which makes it the focal point of the cover. Red instinctively reminds me of blood and malice, so the man resting on the chair is automatically affiliated with murder and death. I then noticed that right above the title, it reads, "Your very humble Servant, Sandman," which clearly categorizes the "Sandman," who I assume is the man depicted on the cover, as a subordinate. Furthermore, the word "humble" suggests that he is a modest, maybe even lowly character.

After looking more closely at the man, I noticed his human feet, fingers, ears, nose and eyes, yet I found myself hesitating to label him as entirely human. His face is shaped as an inverted triangle rather than a more normal, oval shape, and the wrinkles on his forehead accentuate the sharpness and narrowness of his facial structure, giving him a malevolent look. He is also wearing a robe, which initially reminded me of Hugh Hefner. The robe made me think of someone who is wealthy, laid-back, sexual, and powerful. It also made me question if this man is a wizard. At this point, I really did not know what to think. Is he an 87-year-old man who preys on younger women or is he a magical creature that the Disney Channel has yet to popularize?

The little spheres floating around the man's curled hands represent the planets in our solar system. There are ten planets depicted on the cover, but in reality, only eight exist.[2] This indicates a possible extraterrestrial linkage with an alternate universe, and the Sandman's curled hands imply his control over these planets because they are revolving around him. He is drawn on a much larger scale in comparison to the minute planets, which emphasizes his power and jurisdiction. In addition, the position of his hands reinforces my wizard prediction because it looks like he is about to participate in conjuring a magic spell. There is a white, cloud-like border drawn on the cover, which conveys a sense of freedom because it appears as though the Sandman is falling through the sky. Based on these observations, I assumed that the man was capable of traveling through time, and the red ladder crossing the letter "S" in the title hints at movement or an upcoming journey of sorts. To say the least, this cover gave me mixed emotions, but I felt the urge to open the book because of the confusing illustrations on the front. This cover sparked my curiosity—one of the main reasons I felt inclined to continue reading.

The two-page strip midway through the booklet showing the conversation between the Sandman and the Corinthian serves as a crucial turning point for the plot. I read the panels from left to right, the top row before the bottom row. When I looked at the spread for the first time, I noticed that the left page has horizontal panels, whereas the right page has vertical panels. As Scott McCloud explains in *Understanding Comics*, "comic panels fracture both time and space, offering a jagged, staccato rhythm of unconnected moments" (McCloud 67). The horizontal division instinctively elongates each specific scene because English dictates that one reads from left to right. Therefore, because the horizontal boxes are wider than the vertical boxes, it feels like more time passes within the span of each panel on the left page.

The first panel depicts the Sandman's hands touching fingertip to fingertip, as if he is deliberating something crucial. His skin is a dull, deathly, inhuman, bluish-gray, which supports my earlier prediction that he is extraterrestrial. The Corinthian's body is drawn in the center of the zoomed-in frame showing the Sandman's hands. His hands surround the Corinthian in a circular shape, signifying his control and supremacy. All of the Sandman's fingers are touching except for his pinkies, which indicates a slight disunity or detachment. George Portcullis, the young man in the background, stands where a black wall (in shadow) and a white wall (in light) meet, suggesting that he has yet to choose between good and evil. His face is drawn with bars and lacks all facial features. The bars reminded me of a jail cell—an inescapable place of confinement. This emphasizes Portcullis's lack of freedom.

After analyzing the second panel, my confusion escalated quite dramatically. The Corinthian removes his glasses and reveals his eyes, which are teeth. *Ew?* First thought: savage. What makes it more peculiar is that the teeth are not clenched, but rather they are drawn as though each mouth is about to chomp down on something ... something other than food. By replacing the Corinthian's eyes with teeth, Williams III symbolizes his aggressive and murderous nature and highlights his inhumane characteristics. I found it odd that the Corinthian leaves his sunglasses on in previous scenes, but decides to take them off in front of the Sandman. I assumed that this is done out of respect for his "Lord" or just because he feels comfortable, or maybe even obligated, to expose his true self in front of the Sandman. These sunglasses serve as his connection to humanity because they temporarily mask his animalistic features in public, giving him a human-like disguise.

In the third panel, I noticed the reappearance of the red chair, except it is not really red anymore. Instead, the chair is a metallic, copper color—a dramatic change from the vibrant red chair depicted on the cover. Most of this page is drawn in dark shades, but the bright green plant in the corner of the room adds a bit of liveliness to the scene. I also noticed that the Sandman's speech bubbles are black with smooth curves, whereas the Corinthian's are white with jagged edges. The Corinthian's bubbles give a robotic, non-human feel to his dialogue. The panel also shows a trail of black fog penetrating the Corinthian's ear, which not only represents his absorption of what the Sandman is saying from the black speech bubbles, but also suggests that a sense of darkness is entering his body. At this exact point, I started to question why the Corinthian is dressed in all white, giving him a god-like presence that clearly contrasts the darkness surrounding the Sandman. As I looked closer, I noticed the red jewel on the Sandman's tie, which is placed in close proximity to his heart. I began to question if the jewel is a replacement for his real heart, and so I formulated my perception of the Sandman as a callous, malicious, and literally heartless character.

The fourth panel provides more clarity to the plot by exposing new facts, which cleared some of my confusion. At first, the Sandman is shown sitting and looking downward. From his body language, one could assume that he is pondering something disappointing. He then stands up and rests his palms on the table in an attempt to establish his presence and authority. This image reminded me of a courtroom setting, when a lawyer gets up to passionately deliver her or his case. The Sandman is taller than the Corinthian, which reinforces his superiority. He reveals that he created the Corinthian and, therefore, has authority over him. In this panel, he says, "I wished only to build something that would reflect humanity." This dialogue seems to contradict the fact that the Corinthian is a demonic character with creepy mouth-eyes. Conversely, his white outfit hints at an association with innocence and goodness. He is drawn with a very straight and poised posture, which gives him a robotic and tense presence. While I was reading this section, I imagined a young child being lectured to and scolded by a parent. During this exchange, George is lurking in the background, staring at the wall. He probably feels awkward eavesdropping on the conversation, as if his confinement behind bars restricts his ability to engage in the interaction.

On the next page, the first vertical column shows the Sandman as a completely black figure towering over the Corinthian as George pours tea, servant-like, from a teapot resembling an elephant. He pours one cup of tea and since the steam from the tea blows towards the Sandman, I assumed it is poured for him. Traditionally, tea is a drink that is served to guests, so the fact that the Corinthian is not offered any is a subtle rebuke. The next column depicts the Sandman's facial profile with his bluish-grey hair and white face, distinctly inhuman characteristics. His eyebrows are tensed downward, indicating his frustration, confusion, and anger.

The Sandman states, "my subjects remain in the Dreaming," and the capitalization of the word "Dreaming" indicates that it is a proper noun describing a location. The existence of this alternate universe reinforces the supernatural theme. Although I got the sense that the Sandman is an evil character because of his visually dark representation, his dialogue challenges my initial belief. In regards to his "creations," he says, "They do NOT kill mortals for pleasure," which made me view him as a more compassionate and nonviolent character who is maybe just misunderstood and visually misrepresented. In addition, the dialogue describes the Corinthian as a malicious and murderous character, which contradicts his white, pure, and god-like appearance. This scene is one of many cases where reading just the dialogue creates a completely different interpretation than viewing the illustrations.

The next panel contains the first appearance of vibrant color on the right-hand page. Williams III uses a random burst of red color to design the Corinthian's face, along with some sporadic splotches of green and yellow. This mix of colors is similar to those used in Quorian's representation from the first pages of the comic and I pondered if there is an underlying relationship between the two since they both also have teeth in abnormal places. The dialogue confused me, but I realized that the top speech bubble is coming from his left mouth-eye, so I assumed that each one controls a specific part of the Corinthian's subconscious. The second, lower speech bubble, however, is not jagged like the others. Instead, it is drawn with smooth and circular borders. Maybe this is his human side speaking? This visual alteration to the speech bubble implies a duality to the Corinthian, making him part man and part monster.

The bottom left panel accentuates the alien-like features of the Sandman because his eyebrows and eyes are drawn very abnormally and his face is structured in a nonhuman fashion. Conversely, this is the first scene where the Corinthian actually resembles a normal man, partially because his mouth-eyes are not visible. The next image of the Corinthian, however, is honestly so scary that I became extremely uncomfortable after the first few seconds of staring at it, but I found it hard to look away. The elevated angle at which he is drawn makes it seem as though he is staring into your soul with his anomalous mouth-eyes. It also looks like he is subtly smirking in an evil, totally creepy way. The last panel on this page creates a much more solemn tone because the background is completely black, suggesting a future full of fear and the unknown. The Sandman is standing by the window with a remorseful look on his face. His entire body blends into the black background except for the bright red jewel that continues to contrast with the surrounding darkness.

My experience of reading *Sandman: Overture* #1 can be described in two words: horrifyingly addicting. I felt an urge to read on just purely because I was so confused. As a reader opening this comic for the first time, it was an absolute shock. My feelings ranged from disgust and fear to confusion and amusement. Although the artwork seems demonic and slightly overwhelming at first, studying its creativity helped me appreciate the artistic talent of Williams III and McKean and what they are able to convey through the art alone.

Without these elaborate drawings, the enigmatic plot would have been virtually impossible to follow and my experience would have transitioned from horrifyingly addicting to just plain horrifying.

Notes

1. Like most new readers, I originally did not catch the use of articles before the Sandman's and the Corinthian's names.
2. Or at most nine, for those who still include Pluto.

Works Cited

Gaiman, Neil, with JH Williams III (a), Todd Klein (l), and Dave Stewart (c). "Chapter One." *Sandman Overture* #1 (December 2013). New York: Vertigo. Print.
McCloud, Scott. *Understanding Comics*. New York: Harper, 1993. Print.

Listening to the Endless:
Music and Musicians in the
Extended *Sandman* Universe

Tom Zlabinger

"I like music. I more or less need music."—Neil Gaiman

Neil Gaiman is arguably best known for his comic book epic *Sandman* (1989–1996) and recently returned to the *Sandman* universe with the six-issue prequel *Sandman: Overture* (2013–2014) in celebration of the comic's twenty-fifth anniversary. The use of the musical term, overture, is obviously intentional, as it allows Gaiman to create a prequel to his epic. Most operatic composers employ this exact technique of writing the first piece of an opera last, as the process allows the composer to preview musical themes heard later in the work. In the spirit of Gaiman's word choice, what is the musical landscape of the *Sandman* universe? How does music tie into the Endless, the Dreaming, and beyond?

The discussion of music within silent media like comic books is challenging. How does the reader hear the music referenced? Does the music function as a soundtrack similar to a medium like film, or does music serve a different function? Surveying and examining the use of music and the placement of musicians within *Sandman* and other works by Neil Gaiman provides not only a sense of Gaiman's musical aesthetic, but also an understanding of the role of music and musicians within the extended *Sandman* universe. Sometimes the use of music is similar to film and simply helps describe or enhance a scene or moment. But Gaiman also uses music and musicians as agents of magic. More importantly, the use of music within Gaiman's *Sandman* is less about the sonic signature and more about the music's lyrical content and its contribution to the propulsion of the narrative. The inner story of the music usually drives its inclusion in Gaiman's work. Other aspects of the music (like the image or reputation of the musician who performs the song and additional associations with the particular song) may not necessarily be as important.

Music Close to Gaiman's Heart

Before examining the music and musicians found in Gaiman's work, we should contextualize Gaiman's musical background and taste prior to *Sandman* in 1987. While a teenager in late 1970s London, Gaiman fronted the punk band Chaos (later renamed the Ex-Execs), covering songs by David Bowie, the New York Dolls, the Velvet Underground, and others. The band was talented and popular enough to be offered a contract to record their original song "Victims." During this time, Gaiman started a zine called *Metro* with some friends (H. Campbell 31). This was the beginning of Gaiman's music journalism career, which would lead him to write for several magazines and later author his first book, *Duran Duran: The First Four Years of the Fab Five* (1984). Gaiman's punk rock band not only informed his musical taste, but also unexpectedly became the foundation of his writing career, including a DIY aesthetic.

Recently in an interview, Gaiman assembled a list of albums and explained why each recording inspired and informed his writing over the years (Gaiman "Peculiar Relationships"). In the original article, the albums are not arranged in any particular order. But they have been arranged in chronological order here to attempt to paint a picture of the evolution of Gaiman's musical taste over time.

One of the earliest popular musicians that Gaiman encountered at the age of twelve was Scottish singer-songwriter Al Stewart, specifically his album *Past, Present & Future* (1973) which featured "Soho (Needless to Say)," a song that reminded Gaiman of the music of the comic, light opera composers Gilbert and Sullivan, which he had heard and loved growing up. Shortly thereafter, Gaiman gravitated toward the visually stunning and provocative David Bowie and his creation of the alien rock star Ziggy Stardust. Gaiman specifically mentions Bowie's album *Diamond Dogs* (1974):

> because it was kind of *mine*. It was science fiction, it came out when I was 13-and-a-half, and it was a weird mash-up of this strange, dystopian, mutanty [version of George Orwell's] *1984*. It filled my head. I loved the imagery. I loved trying to work out what it was about ... it's overwritten, and it's stupid, but it's magic [Gaiman "Peculiar Relationships"].

Bowie's Ziggy Stardust, specifically the cover of *Aladdin Sane* (1973), was also the basis for artist Dave McKean's original version of Dream in *Sandman* (H. Campbell 100).

Most of Gaiman's fans know the author's love of the Velvet Underground and Lou Reed is deep, sustained, and nearly unconditional. Gaiman discovered the Velvet Underground via Bowie, as Bowie had produced Reed's *Transformer* (1972). Gaiman later borrowed the Velvet Underground album *Live at Max's Kansas City* (1972) from a friend, which led him to listen to *Loaded* (1970). Two additional albums Gaiman adored were Reed's post–Velvet Underground efforts *Lou Reed* (1972) and *Berlin* (1973). In 1992, Gaiman interviewed Reed and discovered that one of Reed's goals was to tell stories within a rock and roll format. Reed explained:

> There are certain kinds of songs you write that are just fun songs–the lyric really can't survive without the music. But for most of what I do, the idea behind it was to try and bring a novelist's eye to it, and, within the framework of rock and roll, to try to have that lyric there so somebody who enjoys being engaged on that level could have that and have the rock and roll too [Reed "Waiting for the Man" 20].

Other rock musicians such as Bob Dylan are known for using rock and roll songs to tell stories, but Gaiman continually returns to Reed. Stories, like the ones found in Reed's music, provided a basis for *Sandman*. Gaiman points out that

> *Sandman* celebrates the marginalized, the people out on the edges. And in grace notes that run through it, partly in the huger themes, Morpheus, Dream, the eponymous Sandman has one title that means more to me than any other. He's the Prince of Stories too, a title I stole from [the 1969 Velvet Underground song] "I'm Set Free" [Gaiman "Neil Gaiman on Lou Reed"].

Gaiman's love for Reed is nearly immeasurable. When we look at Reed's beginnings in a proto-punk band like the Velvet Underground and his evolution as a storyteller, it should not be a surprise when compared to Gaiman's similar history.

Gaiman also points to two post-punk albums: *Cast of Thousands* (1979) by The Adverts and *Imperial Bedroom* (1982) by Elvis Costello. Gaiman is fond of both albums for their more complex lyrics and melodies. Another album around this time that Gaiman loved was *Rum, Sodomy & the Lash* by the Irish band the Pogues (1985), which Gaiman called "one of my favorite albums in the early 80s" (Gaiman *What's in My Bag?*). All three of these albums are rooted in a punk rock aesthetic that was so important to Gaiman.

Gaiman's love for music and musicians is obvious, so much so that he has stated he needs music in order to write:

I like music. I more or less need music. Given the choice I want something with a faintly interesting beat, and I like songs with lyrics.... I'll use music to set the mood I want, and I'll use music to make the place I'm writing pleasant enough to get me to stay there and write [Gaiman "How Many Songs"].

Since the conclusion of the original *Sandman* series in 1996, Gaiman has been fond of recordings by contemplative and moody singer-songwriters like Thea Gilmore, Penelope Houston, Stephin Merrit of the Magnetic Fields, and Jason Webley. Gaiman also includes two recordings that are outside this singer-songwriter trend: the classical music soundtrack to *Drowning by Numbers* (1988) by Michael Nyman and the bossa nova translations of punk rock and 1980s tunes on Nouvelle Vague's self-titled album (2004).

Music and Musicians in Sandman

In the very first issue of *Sandman* entitled "Sleep of the Just" (a reference to a song of the same name on Costello's 1986 album *King of America*), the power and magic of music is used in part to capture Dream. Roderick Burgess announces, "I give you a song I stole from the dirt" (*Sandman* 1:5). This is the first of several musical allusions that appear repeatedly throughout the series. *Sandman* #3, "Dream a Little Dream of Me," references the 1931 song originally recorded by Ozzie Nelson. The most famous version is the 1968 recording by The Mamas & The Papas, which is probably what is heard on the alarm clock as John Constantine wakes up (*Sandman* 3:2). When Dream returns to the waking world for the first time after his capture, there are multiple references to songs with lyrics that refer to dreaming: "Mr. Sandman" (1954) by the Chordettes, "All I Have to Do Is Dream" (1958) by the Everly Brothers, "Dream Lover" (1959) by Bobby Darin, "In Dreams" (1963) by Roy Orbison, "Sweet Dreams" (1963) by Patsy Cline, "The Dreaming" (1982) by Kate Bush, "Sweet Dreams (Are Made of This)" (1983) by the Eurythmics, and "The Power of Love" (1984) by Frankie Goes to Hollywood. Most of these songs are heard on the radio, television, or jukebox within the comic book as part of everyday life. But when Constantine's former girlfriend Rachel is discovered barely alive and sustained only by the magic of Dream's sand, she is eerily singing the lyrics to the Everly Brothers' "All I Have to Do Is Dream" as her body rots (*Sandman* 3:20). Rachel continues to sing the lyric from Bush's "The Dreaming" as Dream and Constantine discuss her imminent death. When Dream removes the bag of sand, she will die. Dream agrees that Rachel may die peacefully, imagining she is walking with Constantine as the sun sets

(*Sandman* 3:21). The use of music in this issue firmly situates the waking world with links back to the dream world.

Songs from Broadway shows, movie musicals, and TV theme songs also appear throughout the series. Given the theme of dreams and nightmares that runs throughout the comics, references to the theme songs of television shows like *Alfred Hitchcock Presents* (1955–1965) and *The Addams Family* (1964–1966) might be expected (*Sandman* 5:1 and 6:15). Later when Urania "Ranie" Blackwell (aka Element Girl) is contemplating suicide, she refers to the television show *M*A*S*H* (1972–1983) and quotes the words from the theme song from the original 1970 film: "Suicide is painless / It brings on many changes / And I can take or leave it" (*Sandman* 20:18). References to popular culture (like the above television shows) occur frequently throughout *Sandman* alongside Greek mythology and other literary references, contesting the lines between low and high culture.

Happier songs from Broadway and movie musicals are also found throughout *Sandman*. For example, the waitress Bette casually sings the Disney classic "Zip-a-Dee-Doo-Dah" (1947) from *Song of the South* while she is working (*Sandman* 6:4). The use of such playful music before John Dee's murder spree through the diner is obviously ironic. And later in the same issue three of the people who are about to be slaughtered sing "Spread a Little Happiness" (1929), which at the time of the issue's publication was recently sung by Sting in the film *Brimstone & Treacle* (1982) (*Sandman* 6:21). In the next issue John Dee sings a fake lyric, "Death takes a holiday," referencing the 1934 film of the same name and "I Think I'm Going to Like It Here" from the musical *Annie* (1977). Though these musical moments do not mark a magical moment within the storyline, they each lend an air of eeriness to the events. The moments also contain humor, which makes the horrific scenes almost relatable. There is a certain surrealism or otherworldliness created by this tension of horror and violence with Broadway and movie musicals.

The previously-mentioned Broadway and movie musical tunes dovetail into the next issue, "The Sound of Her Wings," which introduces Dream's sister, Death. She mentions the Disney film *Mary Poppins* (1964) and the Julie Andrews classic "Supercalifragilisticexpialidocious" (*Sandman* 8:4–5). Death's use of popular culture (specifically musical references from childhood) softens her character and makes her more approachable. But the same issue also mentions one of the oldest known songs, "Dialogue of a Misanthrope with His Soul" (c. 2000 BCE) from Egypt (J. Campbell 137–139). Dream calls it the "mortal song that celebrated [Death's] gift: 'Death is before me today'" (*Sandman* 8:19). So within a short number of issues there are references to happy

Disney classics and a 4,000-year-old song praising Death. Very quickly, a vast emotional range is constructed within the *Sandman* universe through music.

The use of music from Broadway shows and movie musicals continues in *Sandman*, appropriately, within the context of the Drag Review in "The Doll's House," including mention of the Stephen Sondheim repertoire and "Hello Dolly" (1964) by Louis Armstrong (*Sandman* 11:7–13). Later, Lucifer reveals his wish to be a musician and, of all things, becomes a lounge pianist. This is not the first or last time Lucifer or another demon has aspirations to be an entertainer, as is seen in the Charlie Daniels Band's "The Devil Went Down to Georgia" (1979) and Lorne (aka "The Host") from the television show *Angel* (1999–2004). In *Sandman*, Dream asks Lucifer what he will do next after abandoning Hell. Lucifer answers, "I could lie on the beach somewhere, perhaps? Listen to music? Build a house? Learn how to dance, or to play the piano?" (*Sandman* 23:20). Later, Lucifer appears regularly at the club Lux. One night he performs the Billie Holiday classic "These Foolish Things" (1936), but refuses to play a request for "Memories" from *Cats* (1981) and opts for "Sit Down, You're Rockin' the Boat" from *Guys & Dolls* (1950) instead (*Sandman* 57:18–21). Lucifer obviously prefers classic Broadway over more modern musicals. Another night, when asked by archangel Remiel if he will ever return to running Hell again, Lucifer responds, "Been there, Remiel. Done that. Wore the tee shirt. Ate the burger. Bought the original cast album. Choreographed the legions of the damned and orchestrated the screaming" (*Sandman* 60:4). Although Lucifer has classic tastes, he is one who can ultimately tire of routine as seen later. One evening he performs a medley of fictional, risqué Cole Porter songs, but unfortunately "start[ed] to find himself bored by music; and he found himself, during the final chorus of 'She Never Went Down on the Titanic,' observing within himself the urge to move on" (*Sandman* 64:22). Though the above examples are more comical than magical, there is an almost magical mood created by the use and mention of music. The fantastic somehow becomes more relatable and familiar with Lucifer's pursuit of music and his tendency to tire of repetition.

Show tunes and other oldies are heard again when Marco Polo is wandering through the desert hallucinating at the beginning of "Soft Places" (*Sandman* 39:5). He hears in his head lyrics from such songs as "Bill Bailey, Won't You Please Come Home?" (1902) by Arthur Collins, "How 'Ya Gonna Keep 'Em Down on the Farm? (After They've Seen Paree)" (1919) by Nora Baynes, "Brother, Can You Spare a Dime?" (1932) by Bing Crosby, "I'll be Glad When You're Dead, You Rascal You" (1932) by Louis Armstrong, and, incongruously, "Coney Island Baby" (1976) by Lou Reed. Nowhere in the issue is there an explanation why the thirteenth-century Italian explorer hears the anachronistic recordings and quotes from the twentieth century. But their use creates an otherworldly atmosphere as Marco hopes to reunite with his caravan. Through these playful anachronisms, Gaiman creates a sense of disjuncture that heightens the storytelling. Instead of simply a historical tale, the air of the story is charged via music between Marco's adventure and music from the twentieth century, similar to the link created between the waking world and the Dreaming earlier via the songs about dreaming.

One of the greatest musicians in Greek mythology, Orpheus, is not only a character in *Sandman*, but is also Dream's son by the muse Calliope. *The Sandman Special* #1 tells the legend of the premature death of Orpheus' wife on their wedding day and Orpheus' subsequent journey into Hell to attempt to retrieve her through the power of his song. But Gaiman of course adds a twist to the classic story. Due to his failed attempt and grief at losing his wife a second time, Orpheus ignores his mother's warning to run from the approaching Bacchante and is subsequently torn to shreds and beheaded. Orpheus' decapitated head continues to live and reappears a few times in the comic book. Through the magic of his song, Orpheus changes the fate of the French Revolution (*Sandman* 29:21) and eases the priest Andros' pain (*Sandman* 41:4). But later at the end of "Brief Lives," Dream's decision to kill his own son, Orpheus (*Sandman* 49:5) leads to Dream's own demise. One of the oldest legends in history, the Orpheus myth and its integration into *Sandman* fits perfectly into the notion of music as magical agent.

But perhaps the most music-drenched story arc within the *Sandman* universe is the story of the folk musician Foxglove, first in "A Game of You" (*Sandman* 32–39) and later in the Death titles *The High Cost of Living* and *The Time of Your Life*. In addition to each story arc following a musician, each of the titles of the six issues in "A Game of You" is a reference to a song:

"A Game of You" Issue Title	Reference
Part One: "Slaughter on Fifth Avenue"	"Slaughter on Tenth Avenue" (1939) from the Rodgers and Hart movie musical *On Your Toes*, covered on *Slaughter on 10th Avenue* (1974) by David Bowie guitarist Mick Ronson
Part Two: "Lullabies of Broadway"	"Lullaby of Broadway" (1935) from the Busby Berkeley movie musical *Gold Diggers of 1935*
Part Three: "Bad Moon Rising"	Song from *Green River* (1969) by Creedence Clearwater Revival
Part Four: "Beginning to See the Light"	Song written by Duke Ellington (1944), but more likely a different song by the Velvet

"A Game of You" Issue Title	Reference
	Underground from *The Velvet Underground* (1969)
Part Five: "Over the Sea to Sky"	Lyric from the Scottish folk song "The Skye Boat Song" (late–19th Century)
Part Six: "I Woke Up and One of Us Was Crying"	Lyric from "I Want You" (1986) from *Blood & Chocolate* by Elvis Costello

Throughout "A Game of You" additional songs are mentioned. Barbie alludes to "Follow the Yellow Brick Road" from *The Wizard of Oz* (1939) while walking down Murphy's path with Luz and Wilkinson in the fantasy land of her dreams (*Sandman* 35:18), potentially aligning Barbie with Dorothy's journey of personal discovery. The lesser-known song "The Nightgown of the Sullen Moon" (1989) by They Might Be Giants is heard on the radio (*Sandman* 36:8), setting a more alternative and less-mainstream tone to the characters that are listening. And Wanda mentions that the gloomy, rainy evening was

> the kind of night that needs a roaring log fire, a leopard-skin rug, a bottle of fine brandy, and, mm. I dunno. Rutger Hauer, maybe. And the third Velvet Underground LP [*The Velvet Underground* (1969)] in the background [*Sandman* 36:15].

Though Wanda has set the scene for a romantic evening with a Hollywood hunk, the Velvet Underground album is conversely full of tales of longing and discontent, which sets the stage for Foxglove's struggles. *The Time of Your Life* chronicles Foxglove's rise and fall from stardom, including her relationship with her girlfriend, Hazel, and the near death of their son, Alvie. Foxglove is compared to other feminist folk singers like Melissa Etheridge, k.d. lang, Michelle Shocked, and Suzanne Vega. Both Etheridge and lang are aligned with the LGBT community, which parallels Foxglove's issues of public life and the risks she might take revealing her own sexuality. Foxglove's manager, Larry, and her bodyguard, Boris, mention several of classic rock's greatest names (like Herman's Hermits, Janis Joplin, the Kinks, the Rolling Stones, and The Who) in order to establish their rock and roll street cred. Foxglove also performs original music of her own several times within the story arc, singing the songs "Donna's Dream" (Donna is her given name), "George's Tongue" (based on the talking, decapitated head in "A Game of You"), "Tracks," and "Whole Wide World" from her fictitious albums *The Poetry Inspector* and *Slits of Love*. Later in the Foxglove storyline, Gaiman's love for Costello and the Velvet Underground resurfaces. During a tender moment while Foxglove and her girlfriend are first courting, they bond over the little-known song "Hoover Factory" (1980) by Costello (*Death: The Time of Your*

Life 71). In the epilogue of the entire story arc, Gaiman mentions the Velvet Underground founding member John Cale's "Fear Is a Man's Best Friend" (1974) stating, "Life and Death ... are just things you do when you're bored." But Gaiman immediately counters the sentiment with Costello's "London's Brilliant Parade" (1994): "I'm having the time of my life, or something quite like it" (*Death: The Time of Your Life* 94). Both lyrics beautifully illuminate the ambiguous ending of the Foxglove story arc. Foxglove says it best after she has stopped living the life of a rock star in favor of a more traditional, domestic lifestyle:

> Sometimes I lie awake at night, thinking that we're dead. That we died a couple of years ago, back when I was a rock and roll star. And that all this is Death's last joke. That we're living one last dream, before the lights go out [*Death: The Time of Your Life* 88].

Though magic does not correlate to every musical moment mentioned in the Foxglove story arc, there are several magical and dreamlike moments in "A Game of You" and the Death titles interwoven throughout Foxglove's life, from the storm and the journey to Barbie's fantasy land to the rescue of Foxglove and Hazel's son, Alvie, from Death.

Another moment in the *Sandman* universe dense with music and magic is the story of the exotic dancer and goddess Ishtar in "Brief Lives." The storyline includes several rock allusions: characters wear t-shirts referencing MTV (*Sandman* 45:3) and Madonna's 1990 Blonde Ambition tour (*Sandman* 45:7), and Ishtar dances to "I Heard It Through the Grapevine" (most likely the Creedence Clearwater Revival 1970 version, as opposed to Gladys Knight's funkier 1967 version or Marvin Gaye's 1968 version which is arguably the most famous), "Like a Virgin" (1984) by Madonna, and "Under Pressure" (1982) by Queen and Bowie. But the climax of the Ishtar story arc happens as Ishtar decides not to hold back and dances like the goddess she truly is to Iggy Pop's "Sister Midnight" (1977). She explodes, killing all the people in the Suffragette City club, a reference to the Bowie song of the same name from *The Rise and Fall of Ziggy Stardust and the Spiders from Mars* (1972). In the entire *Sandman* universe, there is only one other time MTV is mentioned (*Sandman* 38:1) and no other mention of Madonna. The Bowie references (including Pop's "Sister Midnight," which was produced by Bowie) create a tension with the more mainstream musical icons. (Though Bowie later had success on MTV with the hit singles "China Girl," "Let's Dance," and "Modern Love" from his album *Let's Dance* [1983], Gaiman uses material from Bowie's pre–MTV era.) The moment of magic and destruction takes place during Pop's song. One could argue that more mainstream cultural icons like MTV and Madonna represent the mortals who dance in the club, as magic is found in the less mainstream music of Bowie and Pop.

Some images of music and musicians are tucked into corners within *Sandman* and it is difficult to know which are Gaiman's influence and which are contributions from his collaborators. Nonetheless, the presence of these visual references of musicians shows the love of music by characters within the *Sandman* universe. For example, there are at least four posters featuring different iconic musical artwork: the cover of Frank Zappa's *Them or Us* (1984) on Rachel's bedroom wall (*Sandman* 3:1), the cover of the Scorpions' *Blackout* (1982) on Sexton Furnival's bedroom wall (*Death: The High Cost of Living* 1:8), an advertisement for *Sweeney Todd: The Demon Barber of Fleet Street* (1979) on a city street (*Sandman* 43:4), and the cover of Bowie's *Aladdin Sane* (1973) on Prez Richard's bedroom wall (*Sandman* 54:7). Also, the band Joy Division is written on the back of Judy's jacket (*Sandman* 6:2), which may be seen as a marker of gay or other counter cultures.

In addition to all the references and allusions above, one final musical dynamic cannot be ignored: Dream does not like music. His sister, Delirium, is the only musician among the seven Endless siblings. She sings several times. But none of the other members of the Endless make music. Dream is near live music a few times: for example, he listens to a woman sing a song about a dream she once had (*Sandman* 64:6) and he listens to his son Orpheus sing and even makes him musical instruments (*Sandman* 71:6). But the one time Dream hears music in his palace—Nuala sings and dances—he asks her to stop (*Sandman* 46:4). The recurring idea of Fiddler's Green (sometimes personified by the character Gilbert) may help illustrate what is happening. Fiddler's Green is an image of an afterlife sung of by sailors and other travelers where music plays continuously and dancers never tire, similar to the Greek myth of the Elysian Fields. Death reveals that Fiddler's Green was "the heart of the Dreaming" (*Sandman* 71:23) known as "[t]he paradise on Earth that some say all sailors dream of finding" (*Sandman* 39:15) where "sorrow and care are unknown" (*Sandman* 63:20). Death points out after Dream's demise that the place is no more. Though music and musicians propel the story of *Sandman* repeatedly, the idea of Fiddler's Green and the jolly character Gilbert that personifies Fiddler's Green serves as a counterbalance (and possibly antithesis) to Dream. Though Dream is the prince of stories (and thus connected to an oral/singing history), he does not sing or dance. Dream is void of music. Music surrounds Dream and permeates the *Sandman* universe, but Dream never participates in its joy. One could argue that the killing of Gilbert by The Three (*Sandman* 65:16) is a much larger disruption to the order of the *Sandman* universe than Dream's killing of his own son, Orpheus. Without a place to dream of or about, Dream has no purpose. When Dream's successor summons Gilbert from the dead, the man who personifies Fiddler's Green rejects the gift and declines to be reborn (*Sandman* 70:19–20). One could argue that there is no point for Fiddler's Green after Dream, as there is no point to dream without yearning for music.

These few observations help illuminate Gaiman's use of music and musicians within the *Sandman* universe. But to begin to understand the use of music in the context of a greater Gaiman aesthetic, we must go beyond *Sandman* and see if the use of music and musicians are unique to *Sandman* or are indicative of a greater Gaiman musical aesthetic.

Music and Musicians in Gaiman's Audiobooks and Films

Since the conclusion of the original *Sandman* series, Gaiman has been prolific in producing works within media with audio components. The music found in these non-silent works has a very different aesthetic and purpose than the music in Gaiman's audiobooks and soundtracks.

Though it may be hard to know which musical choices in television shows and movies were Gaiman's, he probably chose the music for his audiobook adaptations. Nonetheless, Gaiman's output with audio components should be viewed as a whole, since consumers usually view it as such. The BBC television series *Neverwhere* (1996) features a lush, synthesizer-driven theme by ambient music pioneer Brian Eno. Both the audiobook (2002) and the film (2009) versions of Gaiman's book *Coraline* contain very creepy music: "You Are Not My Mother and I Want to Go Home" by Stephin Merritt of the Magnetic Fields (credited as the Gothic Archies) and a spooky soundtrack featuring an imaginary language by Bruno Coulais, respectively. The original film *Mirror-Mask* (2005), a collaboration with the Jim Henson Company, features an appropriately circus-inspired soundtrack by saxophonist Iain Ballamy, with gorgeous vocals and adventurous drum and bass grooves. The film adaptation of *Stardust* (2007) features a majestic orchestral score by Ilan Eshkeri, with some Middle Eastern elements. And the audiobook version of *The Graveyard Book* (2008) appropriately features a piece that shares the title of the fifth chapter, Camille Saint-Saëns' tone poem *Danse macabre* (1874) arranged and performed by eclectic banjo player Béla Fleck as a duet with cello. The audiobook and live concert performance of *The Truth Is a Cave in the Black Mountains: A Tale of Travel and Darkness* (2014) features original music by the

FourPlay String Quartet. Finally, Gaiman's first video game *Wayward Manor* (2014) includes scary and fun original music by theBROTHERSstanton and is appropriately inspired by the game's 1920s Victorian Gothic setting. These examples could not be more different than the music and musicians found in *Sandman*. Show tunes and rock music by musicians like Bowie and Reed are notably absent. In fact, the music used is much more textured and, except for songs by They Might be Giants in *Coraline* and Burt Bacharach in *MirrorMask*, devoid of popular music.

Conclusion

While writing the afterword to *Sandman*, Gaiman looked for the perfect recording to listen to in order to help him reflect on the conclusion of the series:

> I'm not much good at good-byes.
> Some people are. I'm not. I don't think I ever got the knack.
> So I'm sitting here all alone with my real face on at the end of *Sandman* and I don't know what to say. I suspect that if I can find the right record to put on, that'll help, but every CD looks equally uncompromising, and I stare bleakly at [player-piano composer] Conlan Nancarrow and [Velvet Underground founding member] John Cale and [the all-female 1960s vocal group] the Chiffons and eventually I stick on Lou Reed's *Coney Island Baby*: comfort music, just the right blend of cynicism and sentimentality [*Sandman* 75:39].

After he mentions two unrelated, lesser-known musicians and a popular singing group, we see Gaiman returning to his beloved Reed. After the death of Reed in 2013, Gaiman wrote a lengthy article in *The Guardian* explaining the impact of the Velvet Underground and Reed on his own work, stating:

> *Sandman* would not have happened without Lou Reed.... His songs were the soundtrack to my life: a quavering New York voice with little range singing songs of alienation and despair, with flashes of impossible hope... ["Neil Gaiman on Lou Reed"].

These "flashes of impossible hope" are a common occurrence throughout *Sandman*. One could argue the magic surrounding music and musicians in *Sandman* are similar flashes. In fact, one of the most powerful moments in the series (though void of music) is when Dream beats Choronzon in a challenge in Hell to regain his helmet by simply stating: "I am hope" (*Sandman* 4:19). For Gaiman, music may be the sound of hope.

Gaiman also famously uses music as part of his writing process. He has admitted to needing music when he writes to sustain a mood and stay focused.

But looking more closely at the "flashes of impossible hope," we see that they are the moments that helped shape *Sandman*. Gaiman tells a story of titling the very first issue:

> music was always part of the writing process—different music for different stories. I remember trying and failing to come up with a title for the first episode. And then, on a train home, I noticed I was humming an Elvis Costello song from an album I'd not listened to much. It sat at the edge of my head, irritating me. I went and got the record out, put it on, and discovered that the track I was humming was called "Sleep of the Just," [1986] a perfect title for the story I had just finished. Music is the key, as a way in. Music as a way to set the mood [Gaiman *Where's Neil*].

To adopt his pun, music truly is the key to Gaiman's work. He has acknowledged its power repeatedly. And he has left markers throughout *Sandman* to remind the reader of music's power. Whether it is the use of musical terms (like titling the first *Sandman* collection *Preludes & Nocturnes* after the works of Frédéric Chopin, and the recently published *Sandman* prequel, *Sandman: Overture*), the inclusion of multiple song titles as issue titles, or magical moments surrounding music and musicians, music is a recurring, powerful element in *Sandman*. And it should be mentioned that in addition to his experience as a musician, Gaiman also has a history of collaborating with musicians, like Tori Amos, Alice Cooper, the Flash Girls, Folk UnderGround, and his wife, Amanda Palmer (formerly of the Dresden Dolls and lead singer of Amanda Palmer and the Grand Theft Orchestra).

Sandman's use of music is obviously very personal. The music he has chosen and that resurfaces again and again in *Sandman* is from a handful of musicians that are obviously among his favorites: David Bowie, Elvis Costello, and Lou Reed. All three musicians can be seen as lone outsiders singing about love, loss, and identity. Yet Gaiman loves show tunes and older jazz classics, too. Surprisingly, Gaiman's beloved music is rarely heard in his audiobooks and films. But then comic books are a much more personal and ethereal medium that must be fully assembled in the reader's mind, as opposed to the exact and literal nature of audiobooks and film. Also, the fact that you do not need to license a recording in order for it to appear in a comic book may explain the absence of Gaiman's beloved music in his audiobooks and films. Looking for a greater Gaiman aesthetic beyond *Sandman* may therefore be futile, given these differences across media. But by acknowledging the difference across media, we gain a new perspective on Gaiman and his love of certain music and music in general. Through the music found in *Sandman*, we get a window into the music that is probably deepest in Gaiman's heart, which obviously helped create the work.

Works Cited

Campbell, Hayley. *The Art of Neil Gaiman*. New York: HarperCollins, 2014. Print.

Campbell, Joseph. *The Masks of God: Oriental Mythology*. New York: Penguin, 1962. Print.

Gaiman, Neil. "Convergence." *The Sandman* #38–40 (June 1992–Aug. 1992). New York: DC. Print.

_____. *Death: The High Cost of Living*. Foreword by Tori Amos. New York: DC/Vertigo, 1994. Print.

_____. *Death: The Time of Your Life*. Introduction by Claire Danes. New York: DC/Vertigo, 1997. Print.

_____. "Dream a Little Dream of Me." *The Sandman* #3 (Mar. 1989). New York: DC. Print.

_____. "Dream Country." *The Sandman* #17–20 (July 1990–Oct. 1990). New York: DC. Print.

_____. "A Game of You." *The Sandman* #32–37 (Nov. 1991–May 1992). New York: DC. Print.

_____. "A Hope in Hell." *The Sandman* #4 (Apr. 1989). New York: DC. Print.

_____. "How Many Songs About Hearses Are There, Anyway?" *Neil Gaiman's Journal*. HarperCollins, 1 Dec. 2003. Web. 31 Aug. 2014.

_____. "The Kindly Ones." *The Sandman* #57–69 (Feb. 1994–July 1995). New York: DC/Vertigo. Print.

_____. "Neil Gaiman & Amanda Palmer." *What's in My Bag?* Episode 269. With Amanda Palmer. Amoeba Music, 28 Jan. 2013. Web. 31 Aug. 2014.

_____. "Neil Gaiman on Lou Reed: 'His songs were the soundtrack to my life.'" *The Guardian*. Guardian News and Media, 28 Oct. 2013. Web. 31 Aug. 2014.

_____. "Peculiar Relationships: Neil Gaiman's Favourite Albums." *The Quietus*. TheQuietus.com, 21 Nov. 2013. Web. 31 Aug. 2014.

_____. "Season of Mists." *The Sandman* #21–28 (Dec. 1990–July 1991). New York: DC. Print.

_____. "Sleep of the Just." *The Sandman* #1 (Jan. 1989). New York: DC. Print.

_____. "The Sound of Her Wings." *The Sandman* #8 (Aug. 1989). New York: DC. Print.

_____. "The Wake." *The Sandman* #70–75 (Aug. 1995–Mar. 1996). New York: DC/Vertigo. Print.

_____. *Where's Neil When You Need Him?* Compilation. Dancing Ferret, 2006. CD.

Reed, Lou. "Lou Reed: Waiting for the Man." Interviewed by Neil Gaiman. *REFLEX* 26 (28 July 1992): 18–20, 54. Print.

Beginnings and Endless-ings

Judd Winick

Sandman has always been an inspiration. For many reasons. Around the time I was 16, I had stopped reading comics, or at least I stopped reading them regularly. My weekly trips became semi annual. Something for me wasn't clicking anymore. I read *Watchmen*. I read *Dark Knight Returns*. I read *Maus*. I read *Why I Hate Saturn*. These books were hard to compete with. My lack of interest would continue until 1988, my freshman year of college. I wandered into the dorm room of a buddy I had made and met his roommate. I saw that there were comic book posters on the walls. "That's a George Perez *Teen Titan*s poster, right?"

"Yes," my buddy's roommate would say. It was a very knowing **yes**. A true comic geek had just walked into his room. My buddy's roommate was Brad Meltzer, and he would be one of my closest friends for the next twenty years. Among the many things he would do, Brad would go on to become a best-selling author, and host of his own TV show, *Decoded*. But right then, he was a college freshman and fanboy who met another fanboy.

I'd begin making weekly trips to the comic store with Brad not too long after that. I think on our second visit he asked, "You're reading *Sandman*, right?"

"No," I said. "What's *Sandman*?"

And I believe Brad looked at me with both sympathy and excitement.

So, by the evening's end, I was reading *Sandman*. And with that, I was reading comics again.

Jump ahead to 1995. I have graduated college, I have been a castmate on MTV's *The Real World: San Francisco*, and I was steadily employed as a cartoonist. It was a *good* time. I am in New York City visiting Brad who's attending Columbia Law School, and after consuming the largest slice of pizza I'd ever seen, we found ourselves in a comic art gallery. A place such as this was not commonplace, and the particular exhibit held special meaning. It was *Sandman* art. And it was for sale.

I was keenly aware that this may have been the first time in my life that I had "expendable" income. Simply put, I could feed myself, pay my rent, buy comics and have money left over. So, I was actually thinking of buying something. And Brad was just the guy to talk me into it. We slowly crept through the gallery, and it was like walking through the history of *Sandman*. Then, we came upon the final page of the first issue of "The Wake" storyline—the arc that would end *Sandman*—hanging on the wall. It was drawn by Mike Zulli. It was nearly a full page splash of The Endless. Brad and I stared at it...

Brad said, "This one."

"OH yeah," I said.

I won't lie and say that I was aware of how fateful this all was. I wasn't. Only in hindsight do these things become clear. But I bought that page, the beginning of the end of *Sandman*, while with my partner in crime who got me back into comics. Comics would later become a very important part of lives, our work and most importantly, our continued friendship.

That page hangs on my wall right next to my drawing table. Inspiration comes in many forms.

About the Contributors

John **Bultena** is a lecturer in the Merritt Writing Program at the University of California, Merced. He holds masters' degrees in library and information sciences as well as philosophy and literature. His academic endeavors have focused on the philosophical aspects in the works and letters of H.P. Lovecraft, information-seeking behaviors of file-sharing communities, digital comic book interfaces, and comics as pedagogical tools.

Emily **Capettini** earned a Ph.D. in English with an emphasis in creative writing from the University of Louisiana at Lafayette. Her work on *Doctor Who* was previously published in *Feminism in the Worlds of Neil Gaiman: Essays on the Comics, Poetry and Prose* (McFarland, 2012), and her fiction has appeared in places such as *Stirring: A Literary Collection*.

Renata Lucena **Dalmaso** is a Ph.D. candidate in English at the Universidade Federal de Santa Catarina, Brazil, studying graphic memoirs and disability after spending a year as a Fulbright Visiting Scholar at the University of Michigan. She has published recently in the *International Journal of Comic Art* and in the collection of essays about Neil Gaiman and feminism edited by Tara Prescott and Aaron Drucker.

Andrew **Eichel** is a Ph.D. candidate in the English Department at the University of Tennessee–Knoxville. His primary research areas are Old and Middle English literature, with special interests in translation studies, hermeneutics, and intellectual history. His dissertation is on Anglo-Saxon theories and methodologies of translation and their relation to long-lived cultural and intellectual ideologies.

Nadia **Eshraghi** is an undergraduate at the University of California, Los Angeles. She is a biology major on a premed track with the goal of becoming a cardiologist. Although science has always been a focus of hers, she has also enjoyed experimenting with creative writing. She is working on a science fiction novel that explores the topics of witchcraft and supernatural beings.

Merideth **Garcia** is a Rackham Merit Fellow at the University of Michigan where she is pursuing a doctorate in English and education. Her research interests include multimedia composition, online writing communities, and the role of narrative in promoting inclusive high school instruction practices.

Margaret Seyford **Hrezo** is a professor of political philosophy and constitutional law at Radford University. Her research interest is the intersection of political philosophy, literature, and film. She is working on a study of the Coen Brothers' *A Serious Man* and a book-length study of mythopoesis and the search for order.

Michael B. **Key** is a graduate student in English at the University of Dayton. He was raised near New Echota, the original capital of the Cherokee nation, in the Georgia Appalachians. As a child, he was captivated by local legends told by his grandparents and his community, which had a large impact on his academic interests in oral tradition and indigenous studies.

Yaeri **Kim** is a lecturer in the Faculty of Liberal Education at Seoul National University in South Korea. She received a master's degree in English literature from Rutgers University and a Ph.D. in cultural studies from Claremont Graduate University.

Courtney M. **Landis** is a graduate student pursuing an M.A. in English literature at Millersville University of Pennsylvania. Her research interests include gender and sexuality studies, twentieth-century and contemporary American and Canadian literature, and film and media studies.

Rebecca **Long** studied English literature at Trinity College in Dublin and graduated from the university's inaugural M.Phil in children's literature degree program. She is pursuing a Ph.D. in Irish children's literature. Her dissertation focuses on representations of childhood and the significance of cultural heritage in traditional narratives.

Jennifer **McStotts** is an interdisciplinary faculty member in the University of Arizona Honors College where she teaches popular culture analysis and place-based courses. She has published poetry, essays, scholarship, and critical reviews. She blogs irregularly at jennifermcstotts.com.

Monica **Miller** is a Marion L. Brittain Postdoctoral Fellow at the Georgia Institute of Technology. She received a Ph.D. from Louisiana State University, specializing in southern and American literature as well as women's and gender studies. Her recent work examines the figure of the ugly woman in the work of twentieth-century southern women writers.

Jenn Anya **Prosser** received a bachelor's degree in journalism from Dublin City University and is a post-bachelor's secondary school English education student at Metropolitan State University of Denver. She is interested in bringing graphic novels and other forms of nerdy art into the classroom.

Tara **Prescott** is a lecturer in Writing Programs and Faculty in Residence at UCLA. She has a Ph.D. in English, specializing in twentieth-century American literature, from Claremont Graduate University. She has written and edited several academic books and articles, including *Feminism in the Worlds of Neil Gaiman* (co-edited with Aaron Drucker; McFarland, 2012).

Danielle **Russell** is an assistant professor of English at Glendon College. Her areas of interest are twentieth and twenty-first-century American literature, Victorian literature, and children's literature. Her book, *Between the Angle and the Curve: Mapping Gender, Race, Space, and Identity in Cather and Morrison*, explores the intersection of identity and setting in the fiction of Willa Cather and Toni Morrison.

Laura-Marie **von Czarnowsky** holds an M.A. in English studies, German studies, and cultural anthropology from the University of Cologne, where she is an instructor. She is working on a Ph.D., analyzing the works of Neil Gaiman from a gender studies perspective. Her research interests include contemporary British drama, fantasy literature and magical realism, representations of monstrosity in literature, and detective fiction.

Judd **Winick** is an award-winning cartoonist and writer, author of *Pedro and Me,* a graphic novel chronicling his experience on MTV's *The Real World: San Francisco.* His work includes *The Adventures of Barry Ween* and *Road Trip.* He has also worked on *Batman, Exiles, Green Lantern, Green Arrow, Power Girl,* and *Justice League: Generation Lost.*

Tom **Zlabinger** is an assistant professor of music at York College/CUNY in New York City, where he directs the York College Big Band and teaches jazz history and ethnomusicology. He received a Ph.D. in ethnomusicology from the Graduate Center at the City University of New York. His scholarly interests include the pedagogy of improvisation and the use of music in film, literature, and other media.

Index